A cruising guide to Northwest England and Wales

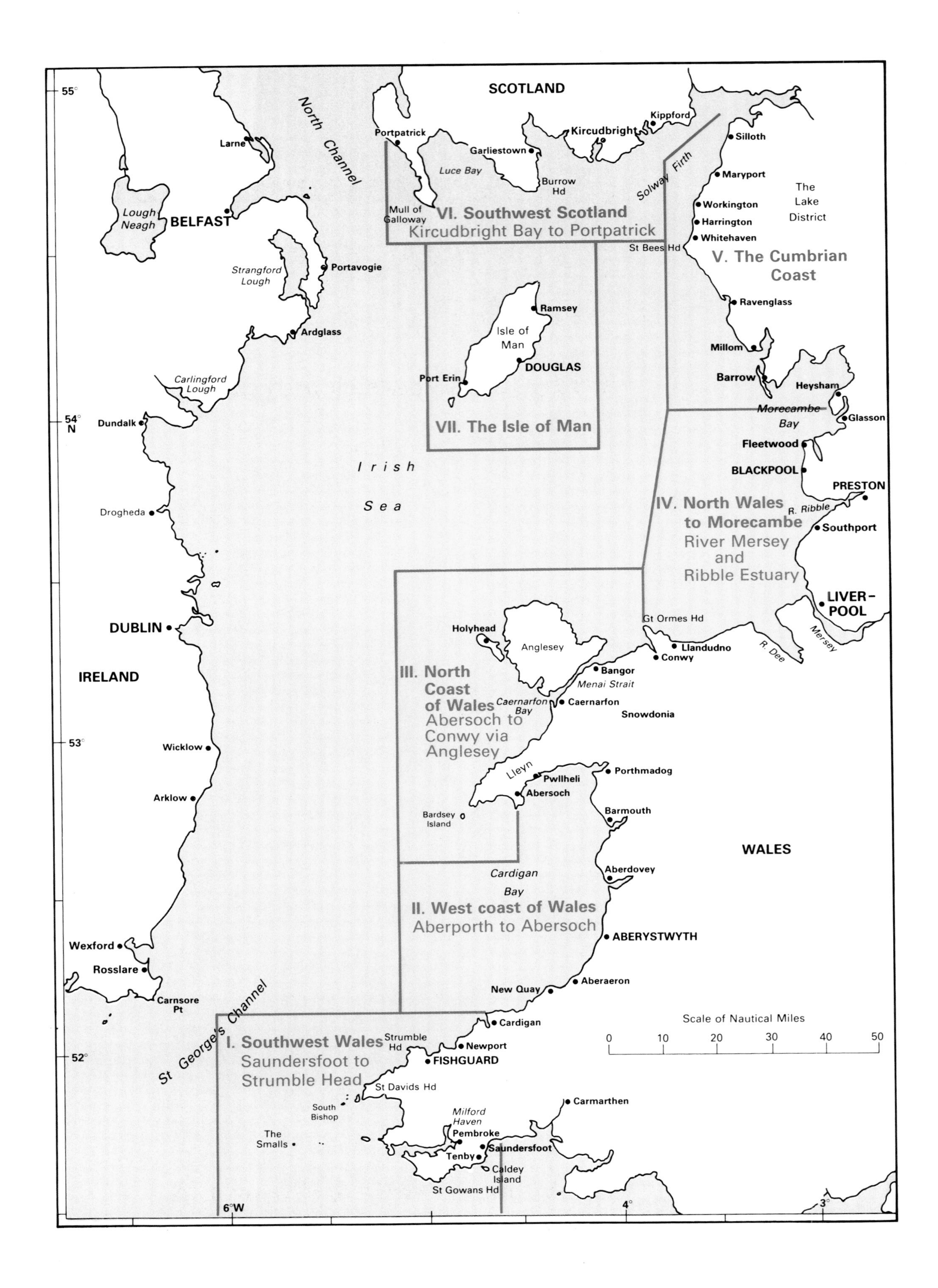

SCOTLAND
North Channel
Portpatrick
Larne
Lough Neagh
BELFAST
Garliestown
Luce Bay
Burrow Hd
Kircudbright
Kippford
Silloth
Solway Firth
Maryport
The Lake District
Mull of Galloway
VI. Southwest Scotland
Kircudbright Bay to Portpatrick
Workington
Harrington
Whitehaven
St Bees Hd
V. The Cumbrian Coast
Strangford Lough
Portavogie
Ardglass
Ramsey
Isle of Man
DOUGLAS
Port Erin
Ravenglass
Millom
Barrow
Heysham
Carlingford Lough
Morecambe Bay
Glasson
VII. The Isle of Man
Dundalk
Fleetwood
BLACKPOOL
PRESTON
Irish Sea
Drogheda
IV. North Wales to Morecambe
River Mersey and Ribble Estuary
R. Ribble
Southport
LIVER-POOL
DUBLIN
Holyhead
Anglesey
Gt Ormes Hd
Llandudno
Conwy
R. Dee
Mersey
IRELAND
III. North Coast of Wales
Abersoch to Conwy via Anglesey
Bangor
Menai Strait
Caernarfon Bay
Caernarfon
Snowdonia
Wicklow
Lleyn
Pwllheli
Abersoch
Porthmadog
Arklow
Bardsey Island
Barmouth
WALES
Cardigan Bay
Aberdovey
II. West coast of Wales
Aberporth to Abersoch
ABERYSTWYTH
Wexford
Rosslare
New Quay
Aberaeron
Carnsore Pt
St George's Channel
Cardigan
I. Southwest Wales
Saundersfoot to Strumble Head
Strumble Hd
Newport
FISHGUARD
St Davids Hd
South Bishop
Carmarthen
The Smalls
Milford Haven
Pembroke
Saundersfoot
Tenby
Caldey Island
St Gowans Hd
Scale of Nautical Miles
0 10 20 30 40 50
55°
54° N
53°
52°
6°W
4°
3°

A cruising guide to Northwest England and Wales

Tenby to Portpatrick and the Isle of Man

GEORGE GRIFFITHS

Imray Laurie Norie & Wilson Ltd
St Ives Cambridgeshire England

Published by
Imray, Laurie, Norie & Wilson Ltd
Wych House St Ives Huntingdon
Cambridgeshire PE17 4BT England
☎ (0480) 462114 *Fax* (0480) 496109
1993

British Library Cataloguing in Publication Data
A catalogue record for this book is available from the British Library.

ISBN 0 85288 190 8

This work has been corrected to July 1993.

CAUTION
While every effort has been made to ensure accuracy, neither the publishers nor the author will hold themselves responsible for errors, omissions or alterations in this publication. They will at all times be grateful to receive information which tends to the improvement of the work.
The plans are based on British Admiralty charts with the permission of the Hydrographer of the Navy.

Printed in Great Britain by The Bath Press, Avon

Contents

Preface

The west coast of England and Wales, the Isle of Man, and the snippet of southwest Scotland covered in this yachtsman's pilot provide a wide diversity of shorelines – from the high and cliffy coast of South Wales, to the fierce tides of low-lying, windblown Anglesey, and the shifting sands of Lancashire – each providing its own particular demands to test one's seamanship and navigational skills.

The freedom to be experienced in sailing these uncongested waters, and the warm welcome to be found on making landfall at the lesser-known harbours, where locals are helpful and harbour dues are easy on the pocket, will, I am sure, be like a breath of fresh air to cruising skippers, tired of the exorbitant fees, hustle, bustle and indifference often found in the saturated sailing centres of the south.

Acknowledgements

My thanks must go first and foremost to Admiral Sir John Woodward, who was instrumental in my involvement with this publication.

Alec Rollinson, who provided information on the Mersey, has been a licensed pilot on the Mersey since 1957, and is now the senior man. He is also a very keen yachtsman and a Yachtmaster Examiner, attached to Mike Lynskey's NW Area Group. With his wife, Nikki, he sails their pitch pine on oak, Peter Brett-designed yacht, *Pellegrin*. It was built locally, at Harry Allanson's yard at Freckleton (R. Ribble), in 1961.

I must also extend my gratitude to Jim Jackson and Dave Park (air pilots), for their invaluable help in obtaining the aerial photographs; to Norman Birkett, builder of my double diagonal planked Eventide 26; to my grandfather, John Griffiths, who taught me to sail from the tender age of five; to the hundreds of people I have met en route, who have made the research and groundwork such a pleasure; and lastly to Karen, my wife and first mate, and my daughter, Heather, for their encouragement.

Fair winds to one and all.

George Griffiths (RYA/DTp Yachtmaster Ocean)
Preston Marina
Lancashire
May 1993

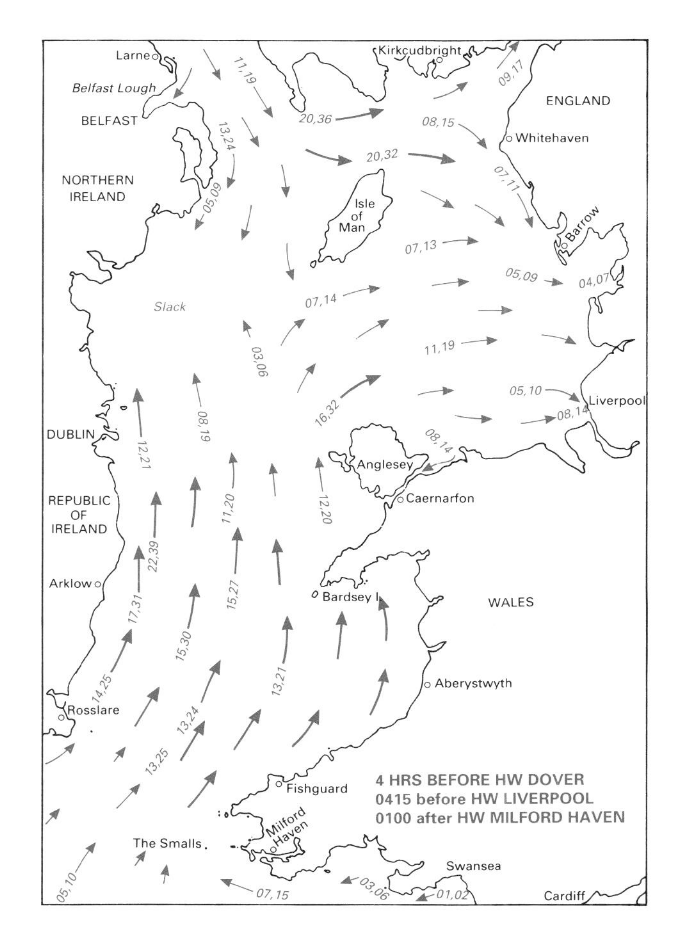
Larne
Kirkcudbright
Belfast Lough
BELFAST
ENGLAND
Whitehaven
NORTHERN
IRELAND
Isle
of
Man
Barrow
Slack
Liverpool
DUBLIN
Anglesey
Caernarfon
REPUBLIC
OF
IRELAND
Arklow
Bardsey I.
WALES
Aberystwyth
Rosslare
Fishguard
4 HRS BEFORE HW DOVER
0415 before HW LIVERPOOL
0100 after HW MILFORD HAVEN
The Smalls
Milford
Haven
Swansea
Cardiff

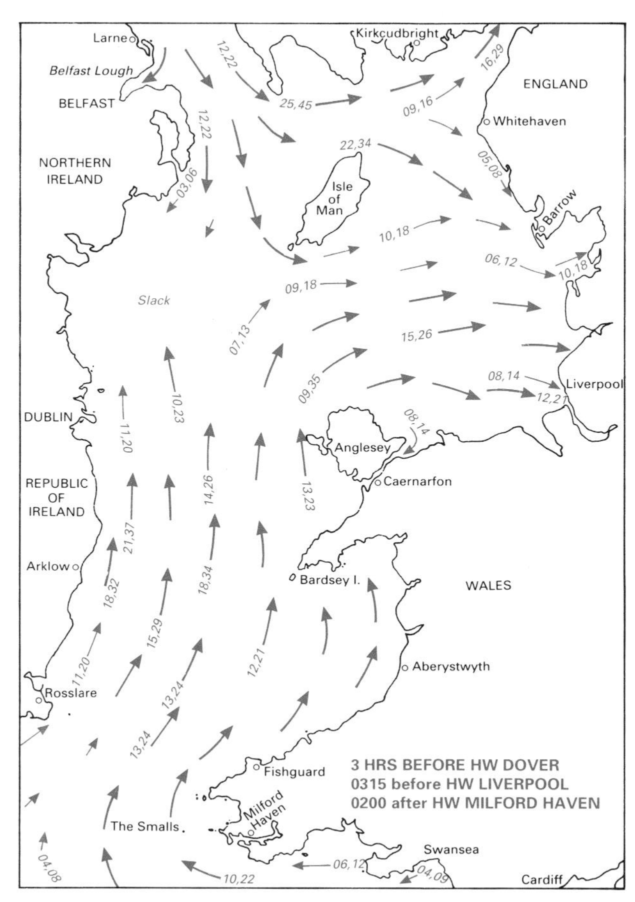
Larne
Kirkcudbright
Belfast Lough
BELFAST
ENGLAND
Whitehaven
NORTHERN
IRELAND
Isle
of
Man
Barrow
Slack
Liverpool
DUBLIN
Anglesey
Caernarfon
REPUBLIC
OF
IRELAND
Arklow
Bardsey I.
WALES
Aberystwyth
Rosslare
Fishguard
3 HRS BEFORE HW DOVER
0315 before HW LIVERPOOL
0200 after HW MILFORD HAVEN
The Smalls
Milford
Haven
Swansea
Cardiff

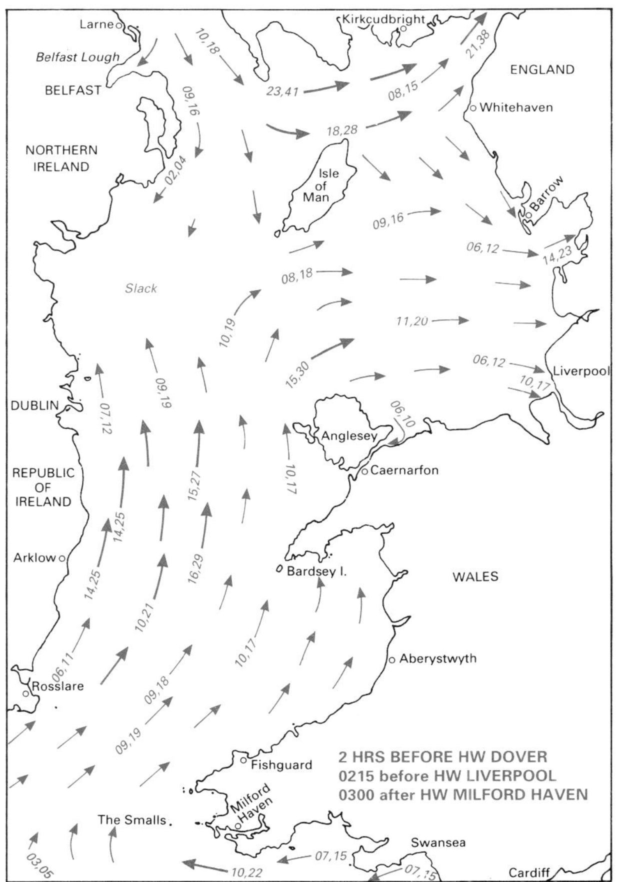
Larne
Kirkcudbright
Belfast Lough
BELFAST
ENGLAND
Whitehaven
NORTHERN
IRELAND
Isle
of
Man
Barrow
Slack
Liverpool
DUBLIN
Anglesey
Caernarfon
REPUBLIC
OF
IRELAND
Arklow
Bardsey I.
WALES
Aberystwyth
Rosslare
Fishguard
2 HRS BEFORE HW DOVER
0215 before HW LIVERPOOL
0300 after HW MILFORD HAVEN
The Smalls
Milford
Haven
Swansea
Cardiff

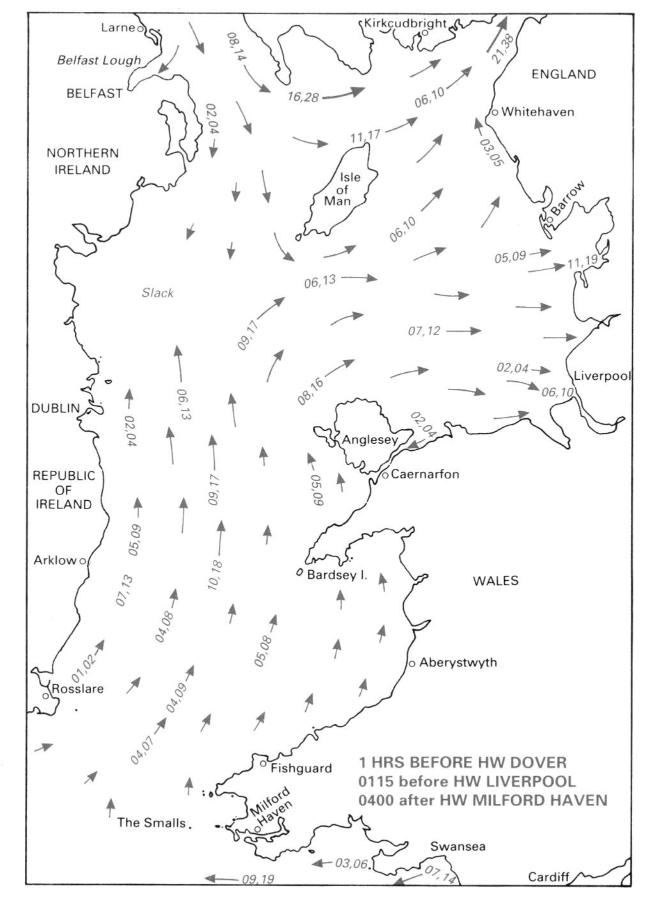
Larne
Kirkcudbright
Belfast Lough
BELFAST
ENGLAND
Whitehaven
NORTHERN
IRELAND
Isle
of
Man
Barrow
Slack
Liverpool
DUBLIN
Anglesey
Caernarfon
REPUBLIC
OF
IRELAND
Arklow
Bardsey I.
WALES
Aberystwyth
Rosslare
Fishguard
1 HRS BEFORE HW DOVER
0115 before HW LIVERPOOL
0400 after HW MILFORD HAVEN
The Smalls
Milford
Haven
Swansea
Cardiff

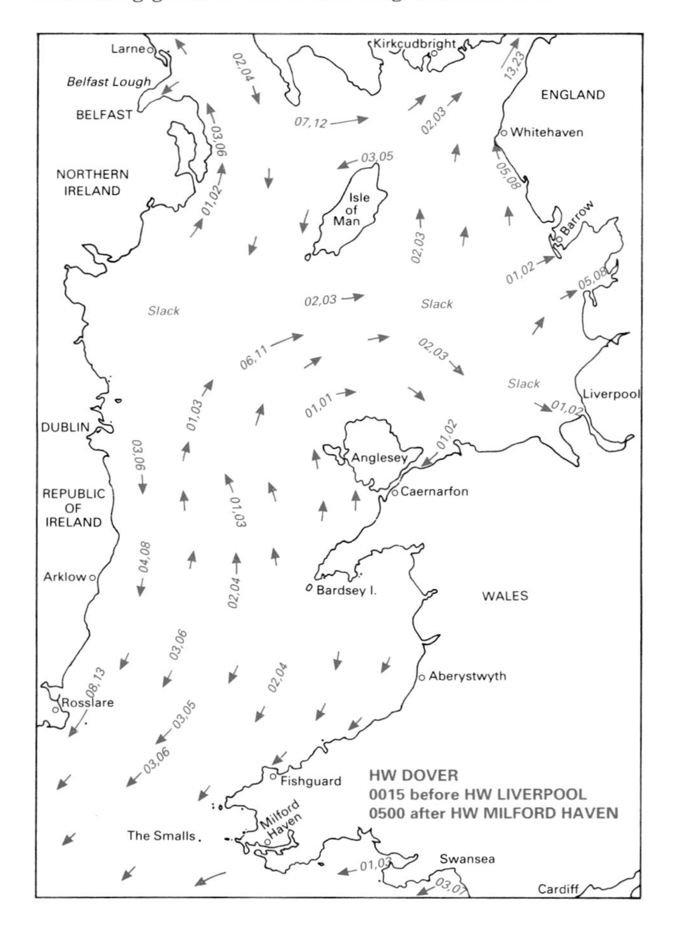
Larne
Kirkcudbright
Belfast Lough
BELFAST
ENGLAND
Whitehaven
NORTHERN
IRELAND
Isle
of
Man
Barrow
Slack
Slack
Slack
Liverpool
DUBLIN
Anglesey
Caernarfon
REPUBLIC
OF
IRELAND
Arklow
Bardsey I.
WALES
Aberystwyth
Rosslare
Fishguard
The Smalls
Milford
Haven
Swansea
Cardiff
HW DOVER
0015 before HW LIVERPOOL
0500 after HW MILFORD HAVEN

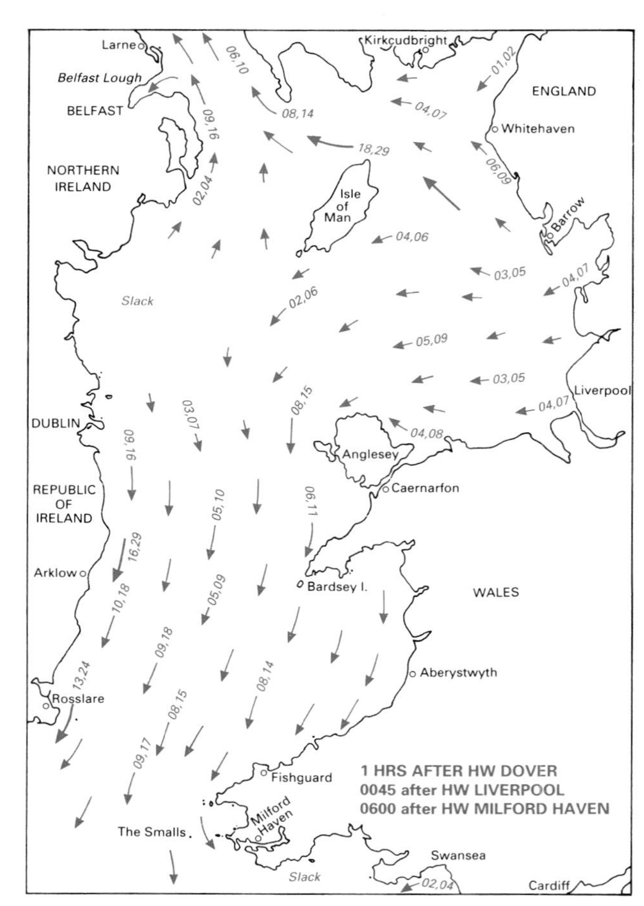
Larne
Kirkcudbright
Belfast Lough
BELFAST
ENGLAND
Whitehaven
NORTHERN
IRELAND
Isle
of
Man
Barrow
Slack
Liverpool
DUBLIN
Anglesey
Caernarfon
REPUBLIC
OF
IRELAND
Arklow
Bardsey I.
WALES
Aberystwyth
Rosslare
Fishguard
The Smalls
Milford
Haven
Slack
Swansea
Cardiff
1 HRS AFTER HW DOVER
0045 after HW LIVERPOOL
0600 after HW MILFORD HAVEN

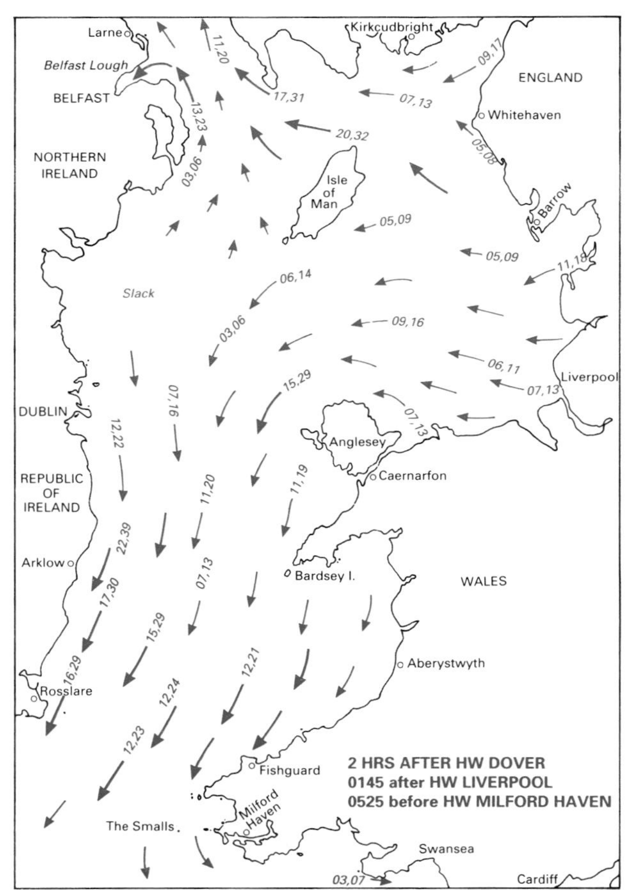
Larne
Kirkcudbright
Belfast Lough
BELFAST
ENGLAND
Whitehaven
NORTHERN
IRELAND
Isle
of
Man
Barrow
Slack
Liverpool
DUBLIN
Anglesey
Caernarfon
REPUBLIC
OF
IRELAND
Arklow
Bardsey I.
WALES
Aberystwyth
Rosslare
Fishguard
The Smalls
Milford
Haven
Swansea
Cardiff
2 HRS AFTER HW DOVER
0145 after HW LIVERPOOL
0525 before HW MILFORD HAVEN

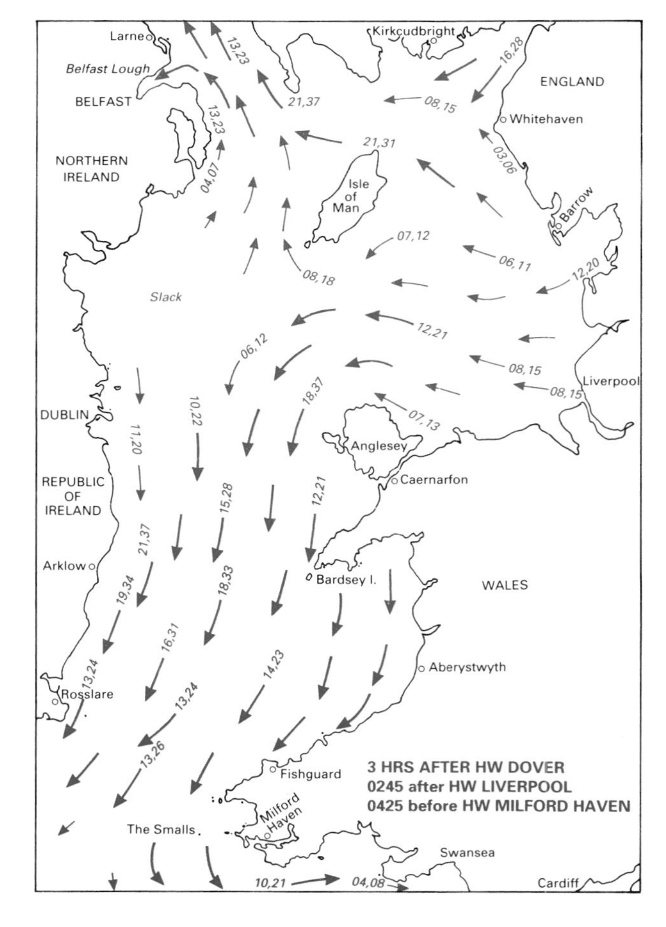
Larne
Kirkcudbright
Belfast Lough
BELFAST
ENGLAND
Whitehaven
NORTHERN
IRELAND
Isle
of
Man
Barrow
Slack
Liverpool
DUBLIN
Anglesey
Caernarfon
REPUBLIC
OF
IRELAND
Arklow
Bardsey I.
WALES
Aberystwyth
Rosslare
Fishguard
The Smalls
Milford
Haven
Swansea
Cardiff
3 HRS AFTER HW DOVER
0245 after HW LIVERPOOL
0425 before HW MILFORD HAVEN

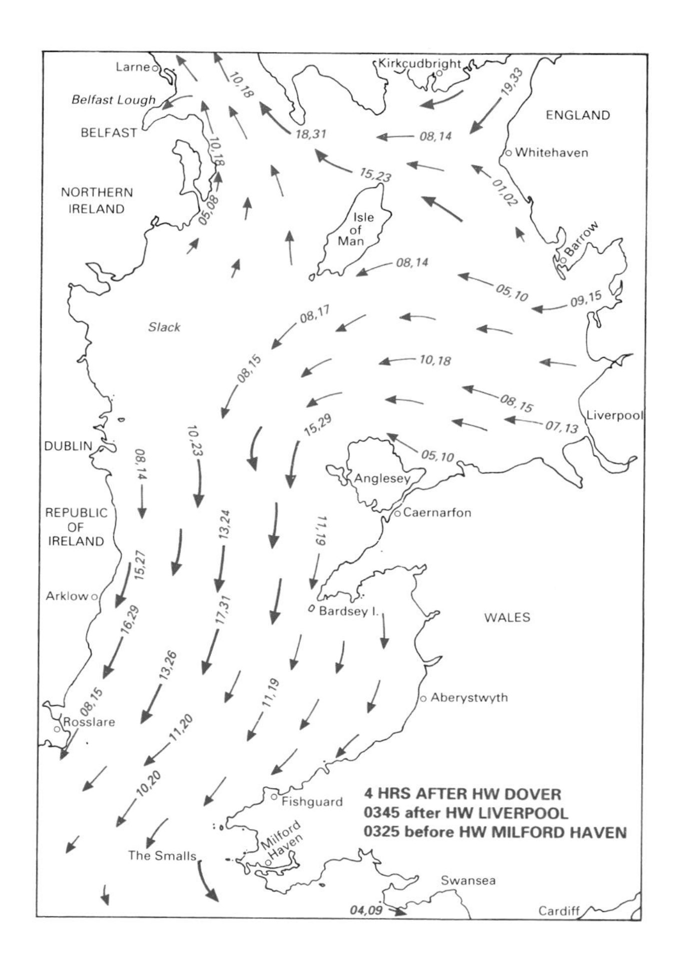

4 HRS AFTER HW DOVER
0345 after HW LIVERPOOL
0325 before HW MILFORD HAVEN

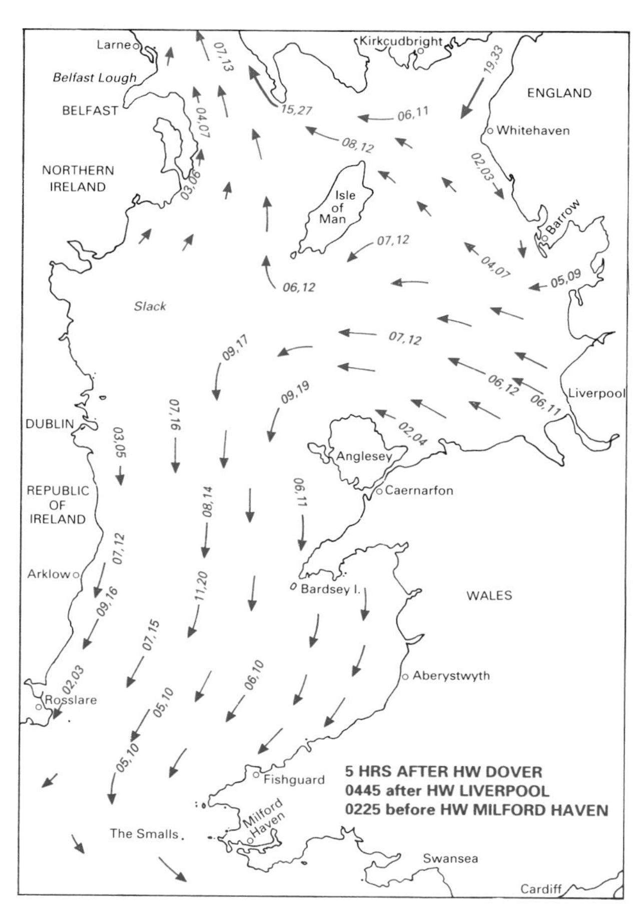

5 HRS AFTER HW DOVER
0445 after HW LIVERPOOL
0225 before HW MILFORD HAVEN

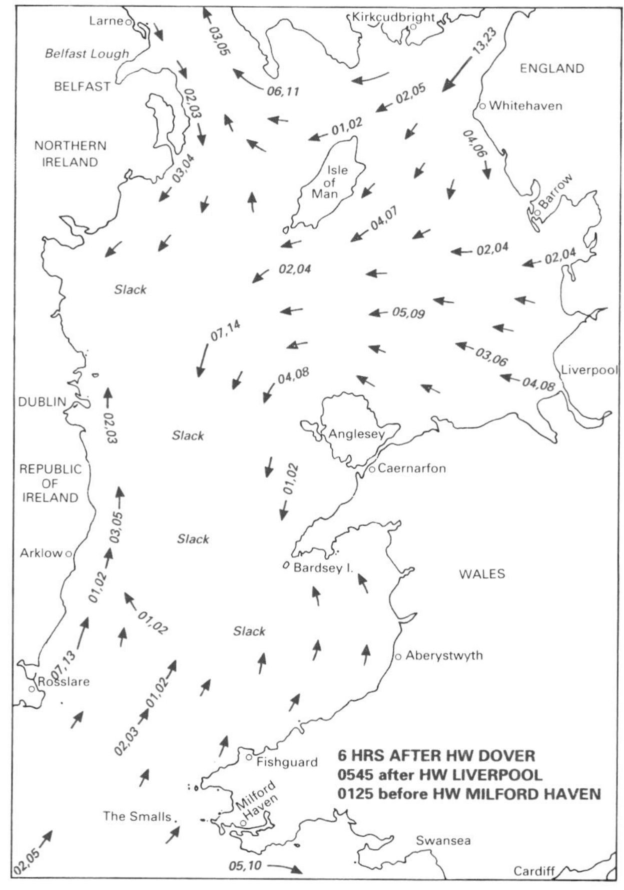

6 HRS AFTER HW DOVER
0545 after HW LIVERPOOL
0125 before HW MILFORD HAVEN

I. Southwest Wales

Saundersfoot to Cardigan

Lights

Caldey Island Fl(3)WR.20s65m14/12M White round tower 173°-R-212°-W-088°-R-102°

St Gowan HFP buoy Q(6)+LFl.15s7M Whistle Racon S cardinal, yellow above black

St Ann's Hd Fl.WR.5s48m18/14M Horn(2)60s White 8-sided tower 233°-W-247°-R-285°-R(intens)-314°-R-332°-W-124°. 129°-W-131°

The Smalls Fl(3)15s36m25M+F.R Horn(2)60s Racon White round tower, red bands (F.R 253°-vis-285° over Hats and Barrels Rock)

Skokholm Island Fl.R.10s54m17M Horn 15s White 8-sided tower Partially obscured 226°-258°

South Bishop Fl.5s44m24M Horn(3)45s RC White round tower

Strumble Hd Fl(4)15s45m26M White round tower 038°-vis-257°

The SW corner of Wales is very popular during the summer months, as many holidaymakers make for the beautiful stretches of golden sands interspersed with rocky headlands, castles, crystal-clear blue-green water, and the unspoilt villages and towns which lie along the coast. Much of the Pembroke coast is National Park land. The main refuges are Saundersfoot and Tenby.

Saundersfoot

51°42'·6N 4°41'·7W

Charts

Admiralty 1482 (1:12,500)
Imray C60 (1:128,000)

Tides

HW Dover −0510

Height in metres

MHWS	MHWN	MTL	MLWN	MLWS
8·4	6·3	4·6	3·0	0·9

Lights

Pier head Fl.R.5s6m7M Stone cupola

Radio/telephone

VHF Ch 16, 11
☎ Harbourmaster (0834) 812094

A village characteristic of this beauty is Saundersfoot, lying on the west side of Saundersfoot Bay, a wide, sweeping, sandy bay, giving good shelter from winds SW–N–NE in good holding.

It is possible to anchor anywhere in the bay to await the tide, provided that the red can buoy marking the sewer outlet running from the south of the harbour is avoided – you might also like to avoid its discharges. The small harbour dries after 4hrs ebb, and can only really be entered for 2½ hours either side of HW.

Entering the harbour, between the south pier head (Fl.R.5s7M) and the north pier, a temporary berth can usually be found directly to starboard on the inner arm of the north pier, where there is room for a couple of moderately sized yachts to dry out on even sand and mud. Alternatively, a more permanent mooring may be found by contacting the harbourmaster (☎ (0834) 812094); his office is at the NW end of the harbour, near the sailing club.

Saundersfoot was originally built for exporting coal, though no evidence of this can now be seen. The harbour is now packed with pleasure craft of all descriptions, moored fore and aft. At the top right-hand side of the slip is a fresh-water standpipe. Light chandlery and provisions can be had from the village built around the harbour, though petrol and diesel are not available. Early closing Wednesdays. Railway station.

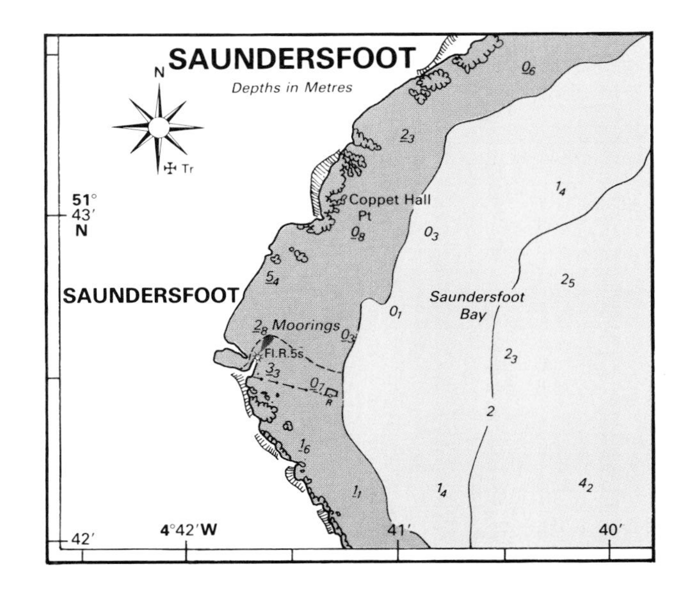

Above Entering Saundersfoot Harbour.

Below Saundersfoot Harbour – showing the slipway, centre.

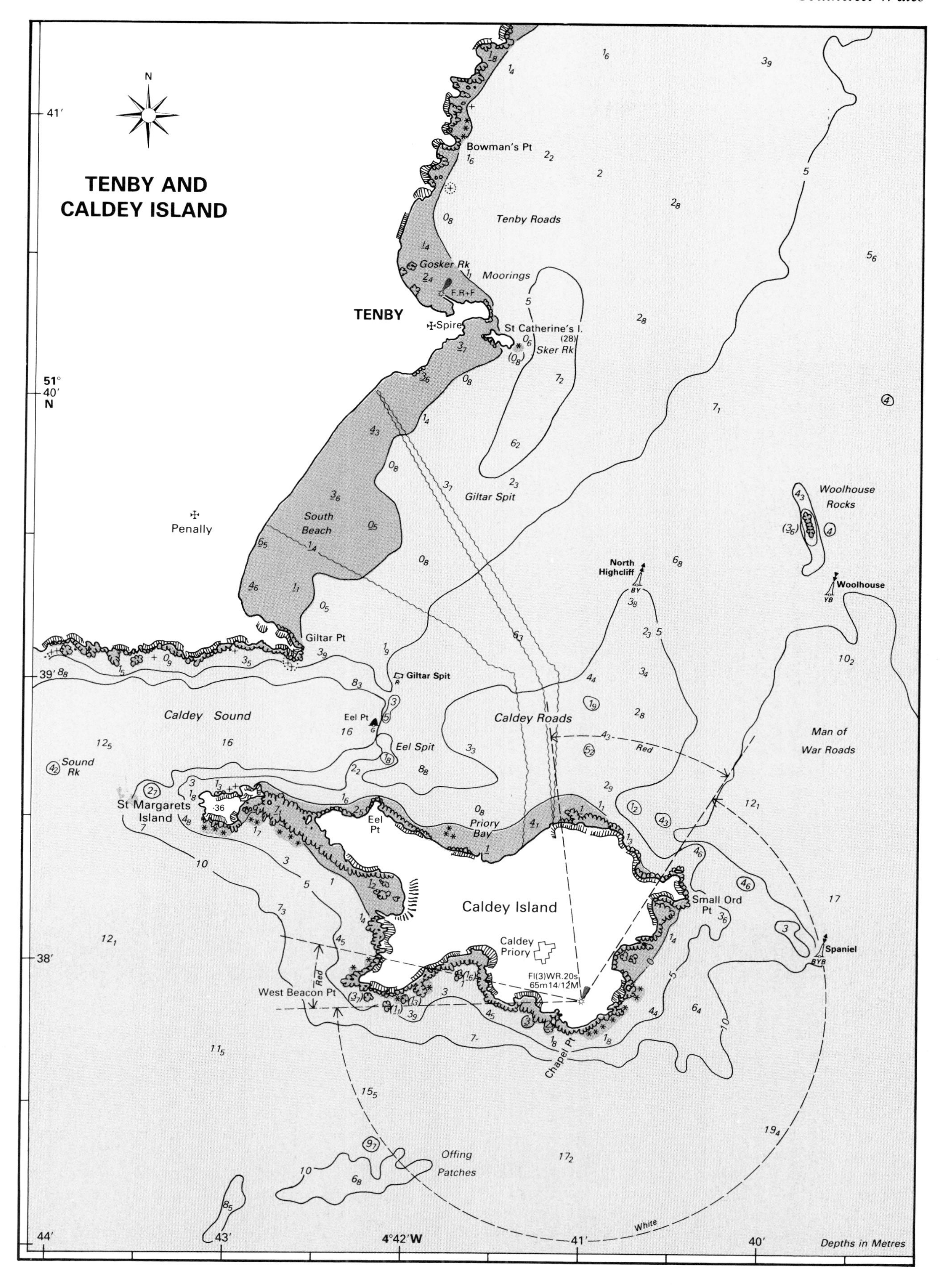
TENBY AND
CALDEY ISLAND
Bowman's Pt
Tenby Roads
Gosker Rk
Moorings
TENBY
Spire
St Catherine's I.
Sker Rk
Giltar Spit
South
Beach
Penally
Woolhouse
Rocks
North
Highcliff
Woolhouse
Giltar Pt
Giltar Spit
Caldey Sound
Eel Pt
Caldey Roads
Eel Spit
Red
Man of
War Roads
Sound
Rk
St Margarets
Island
Eel
Pt
Priory
Bay
Caldey Island
Small Ord
Pt
Caldey
Priory
Spaniel
Fl(3)WR.20s
65m14/12M
West Beacon Pt
Chapel Pt
Offing
Patches
White
Depths in Metres
44′
43′
4°42′W
41′
40′
41′
51°
40′
N
39′
38′

Tenby

51°40'·4N 4°41'·7W

Charts

Admiralty 1482 (1:12,500)
Imray C60 (1:128,000)

Tides

HW Dover −0510
Height in metres

MHWS	MHWN	MTL	MLWN	MLWS
8·4	6·3	4·6	3·0	0·9

Lights

Pier head F.R.7m7M
Harbour F.6m1M

Radio/telephone

VHF Ch 16 Office hours
☎ (0834) 842717 May to Sept

Leaving Saundersfoot and heading south, rounding Monkstone Point and Monkstone, a free-standing rock at HW, Tenby opens up on the southern edge of North Sands Bay. Many craft may be seen swinging at their moorings outside the harbour. There is plenty of room to anchor, with shelter from S–W–N in good holding, though if you are intending to use the harbour to pick up stores, contact the harbourmaster (☎ (0834) 842717); this harbour too is small and very crowded, especially during midsummer, when all the berths may be taken.

The harbour can be entered for 2 hours either side of HW, drying to sand; enter by rounding the pier (F.R and F) close to. The only major obstacle is the Gosker Rock, marked on its southern edge by an unlit beacon.

Good stores are available, and it is wise to stock up before visiting Dale in Milford Haven, if that is the next destination. Water and petrol are also available close at hand, though diesel has to be carried in containers. Early closing Wednesdays. Railway station.

The town is situated on a headland still partially constrained by the old town wall which used to surround it, ending in the old castle, which is Norman. The town was in existence much earlier than that, with records going back to the 10th century. It has a number of hotels and shops, and a vast tourist trade in the summer – not surprising, since it has two lovely sandy beaches, one on either side of the promontory. But even so the town is unspoilt, and a number of pleasurable days may be spent here, anchored in the bay.

During the season, trips run frequently from Tenby to Caldey Island, where the Cistercian monks farm and make their famous herbal perfumes. It is well worth a visit, though only men are allowed into the monastery itself. St Catherine's Island, to the south of the promontory, is also worth a visit, and one can walk out at LW to the steps which lead up the cliff side to a 19th-century fort at the summit.

Caldey Sound to Milford Haven

It is best to leave Tenby at HW, so that Caldey Sound may be taken at HW slack, and the ebb taken all the way up to Milford Haven. Upon rounding Castle Hill, St Catherine's Island and the Sker Rock, at its eastern tip, should be given a cable offing. Lay a course due south, leaving the North Highcliff N cardinal buoy well to port, until passage can be made between Giltar Spit red can buoy and Eel Point green conical buoy, leading through the sound. Then give St Margaret's Isle two cables offing until a course half a mile to seaward of Old Castle Head can be laid.

A word of warning here. Manorbier, ¾ mile inland of Old Castle Head, houses an army firing range, as I found to my consternation several years ago when, after ten minutes of cracks and bangs, a ranger came in his cutter and apologised for their firing over our heads. Apparently they had just seen us on radar and were concerned because they couldn't contact us on VHF. When I questioned him about there being no mention of it on the chart, he said, 'The army don't like to advertise it.' It would be wise to contact the coastguard for advice before rounding the head.

Castlemartin Firing Range

Firing times: Most weekdays from April to November. Range extends from St Gowan's Head to Linney Head, extending from 3 to 4 miles seaward, and possibly 12 miles. Information VHF Ch 16; call Castlemartin Range Control ☎ (0646) 661321 ext. 4336.

How close one passes to St Gowan's Head is governed by the sea state, but in fine weather St Gowan's Chapel, standing in the cove to the west of the headland, can be seen, with its path running up the steep cliff; the tiny chapel has faced the ravages of this exposed spot for seven centuries. There is a fierce tide-rip off the headland, however, and it is often wise to give it a mile or two offing, though any more than this would bring one into the turbulent seas of Gowan's Shoals, lying four miles SSW from the point.

In bad weather, the tide-rip and overfalls bridge the channel between the two with very confused seas which are impassable. The course of action then is to head back to Caldey before heading out to round the St Gowan HFP buoy, as the more direct route, rounding the HFP buoy from the east of St Gowan's Head, would lead through an area marked on the chart, unusually, 'Heavy Tide Rips'. The journey back to Caldey will, in any case, leave open the option of taking shelter at Tenby if the weather should deteriorate further.

From St Gowan's Head, the course is set to give a wider berth to Linney Head and its associated offlying rocks (Crow Rock drying to 5·5m), which also takes us around the worst of the tide-rips.

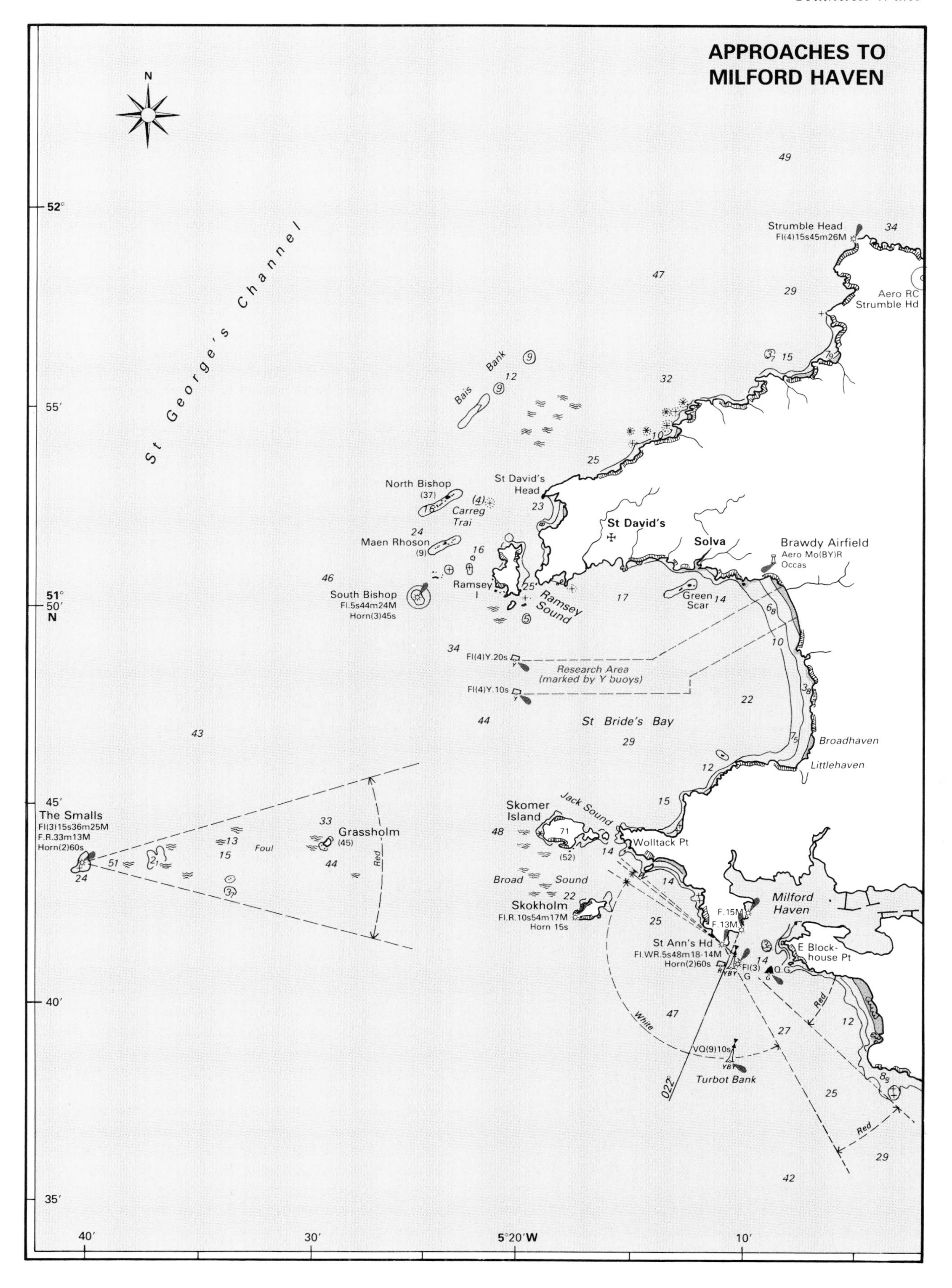
APPROACHES TO MILFORD HAVEN
N
St George's Channel
Strumble Head
Fl(4)15s45m26M
Aero RC
Strumble Hd
Bais Bank
North Bishop
Carreg Trai
St David's Head
Maen Rhoson
South Bishop
Fl.5s44m24M
Horn(3)45s
Ramsey I
Ramsey Sound
St David's
Solva
Brawdy Airfield
Aero Mo(BY)R
Occas
Green Scar
Fl(4)Y.20s
Research Area
(marked by Y buoys)
Fl(4)Y.10s
St Bride's Bay
Broadhaven
Littlehaven
Skomer Island
Jack Sound
Wolltack Pt
The Smalls
Fl(3)15s36m25M
F.R.33m13M
Horn(2)60s
Grassholm
Foul
Red
Broad Sound
Skokholm
Fl.R.10s54m17M
Horn 15s
F.15M
F.13M
Milford Haven
St Ann's Hd
Fl.WR.5s48m18-14M
Horn(2)60s
Fl(3) G
Q.G
E Blockhouse Pt
White
VQ(9)10s
Turbot Bank
022°
52°
55′
51° 50′ N
45′
40′
35′
40′
30′
5°20′W
10′

Rounding Linney Head, Freshwater West Beach opens up behind it, when a course may be laid of approximately 330°, leaving Turbot Bank to port and Sheep Island to starboard, to enter the haven. Alternatively, or at night, a course may be laid onto St Ann's Head light (Fl.WR.5s48m18/14M), keeping on the red sector to avoid Turbot Bank, until the West Channel buoys are picked up. There are few navigational hazards in the haven for small craft. Chapel Rocks have 3·5m over them at chart datum, and there is no need to use the channels; indeed, right of way must be given to the tankers.

Milford Haven

51°42'N 5°01'W

Charts

Admiralty 2878 (1:25,000), 3274 (1:12,500), 3275 (1:12,500)
Imray C60 (1:128,000)

Tides

HW Dover −0454

Height in metres

MHWS	MHWN	MTL	MLWN	MLWS
7·0	5·2	3·8	2·5	0·7

Lights

St Ann's Head Fl.WR.5s48m18/14M Horn(2)60s White 8-sided tower 233°-W-247°-R-285°-R(intens)-314°-R-332°-W-124° 129°-W-131°
Middle Channel rocks Fl(3)G.7s18m8M Black round metal tower, aluminium lantern
West Blockhouse Point Ldg Lts 022·5° Front F.54m 13M Black vertical topmark, white stripe, on white concrete tower 004·5°-vis-040·5° *By day* range 10M On request through Milford Haven port radio
Lts in line 021·33° Auxiliary *Front* 20m 112° F.R.53m 12M Black ◆ topmark on white concrete tower 014°-vis-031° Mark E side of channel *By day* range 5M 017°-vis-028° On request through Milford Haven port radio
Lts in line 023·73° Auxiliary *Front* 20m 292° F.R.53m 12M Black ◆ topmark on white concrete tower 014°-vis-031° Mark west side of channel *By day* range 5M 017°-vis-028° On request through Milford Haven port radio
Watwick Point *Rear* 0·5M from front F.80m15M Black vertical topmark, white strip 013·5°-vis-031·5° Common rear *By day* range 10M On request through Milford Haven port radio
Great Castle Head F.WRG.27m5-3M 243°-R-281°-G-299°-W-029° White square tower, black stripe
Ldg Lts 039·75° *Front* Oc.4s27m15M Same structure 031·2°-vis-048·2° *By day* range 10M 032·2°-vis-047·2° On request through Milford Haven port radio
Little Castle Head *Rear* 890m from front Oc.8s53m 15M White vertical topmark, black stripe, on white round concrete tower 031·2°-vis-048·2° *By day* range 10M 032·2°-vis-047·2° On request through Milford Haven port radio
Castlebeach Bay Mussel farm 2F.R(vert)4m
West Blockhouse Point Q.WR.21m9/7M Red lantern on white base 220°-W-250°-R-020°-W-036°-R-049°
Dale Fort Fl(2)WR.5s20m5/3M 222°-R-276°-W-019°

Marinas

Westfield Marina access HW +3½hrs
Milford Marina access HW−2 to HW
Pembroke Dock Lower basin 24hr access. Upper basin HW +3½hrs

Radio/telephone

Milford Haven Radio VHF Ch 11, 12, 14, 16 (24hrs); 09, 10, 11, 12, 14, 16, 67 – Shipping movements VHF Ch 12
Milford Haven Marina VHF Ch M, M2+80
Westfield Marina Ch 80M
Lawrenny Yacht station Ch M
☎ Harbourmaster (0646) 692342
☎ Milford Marina (0646) 692271

Weather forecasts

Milford Haven Radio VHF Ch 12, 14 at 0300, 0900, 1500, 2100 UT. Gale warnings on receipt.

It is approximately 23 miles to Dale, a large, sheltered bay on the northern edge of Milford Haven, but although the haven may be entered in any state of weather, passage through Caldey Sound, past St Gowan's Head and Linney Head, where there are fierce tide-rips, should only be taken in the most favourable conditions. With anything of Force 5 or above, take the much longer route rounding Caldey Island and the St Gowan's HFP light buoy, Q(6)+LFl.15s7M; the latter marks the southern edge of St Gowan's Shoals, where white breaking water can always be seen. Alter course when past the HFP buoy to leave Turbot Bank W cardinal to starboard before altering course into Milford Haven.

Tankers at Milford Haven. *Peter Cumberlidge*

Milford Haven authorities

Milford Haven is under the jurisdiction of Milford Haven Conservancy Board, based at Hubberston Point. It is therefore prudent to maintain a dual listening watch on VHF Chs 16 and 12, to keep abreast of any unusual shipping movements.

All unauthorised vessels are required to keep a nominal 100m safety distance from oil terminals and tankers whilst navigating within the haven. Failure to do so will result in the swift attention of one of the port authority launches, which are unmistakable with their green hulls and white upper marks. They will also be flying either code flag 'HOTEL' (pilot) or a blue flag with 'HARBOURMASTER' in white letters.

Any instruction from port authority vessels must be obeyed immediately, without question.

Dale

51°42'·4N 5°09'·2W

Charts

Admiralty 3274 (1:12,500)

Tides

HW Dover −0454

Height in metres

MHWS	MHWN	MTL	MLWN	MLWS
7·0	5·2	3·8	2·5	0·6

Lights

Dale Fort Fl(2)WR.5s20m5/3M Metal column 222°-R-276°-W-019°

Telephone

Dale Sailing Co. ☎ (0646) 636 349

Dale Point (Fl(2)WR.5s20m5/3M) is the fourth headland on the western side of the haven, and can be rounded close to, thereby avoiding the restricted areas marked by two yellow buoys, one (Fl.Y.2s) four cables to SE of Dale Point, and the other (Fl.Y.5s) four cables to the NE.

The moorings at Dale, a useful passage anchorage near Milford Haven entrance. *Peter Cumberlidge*

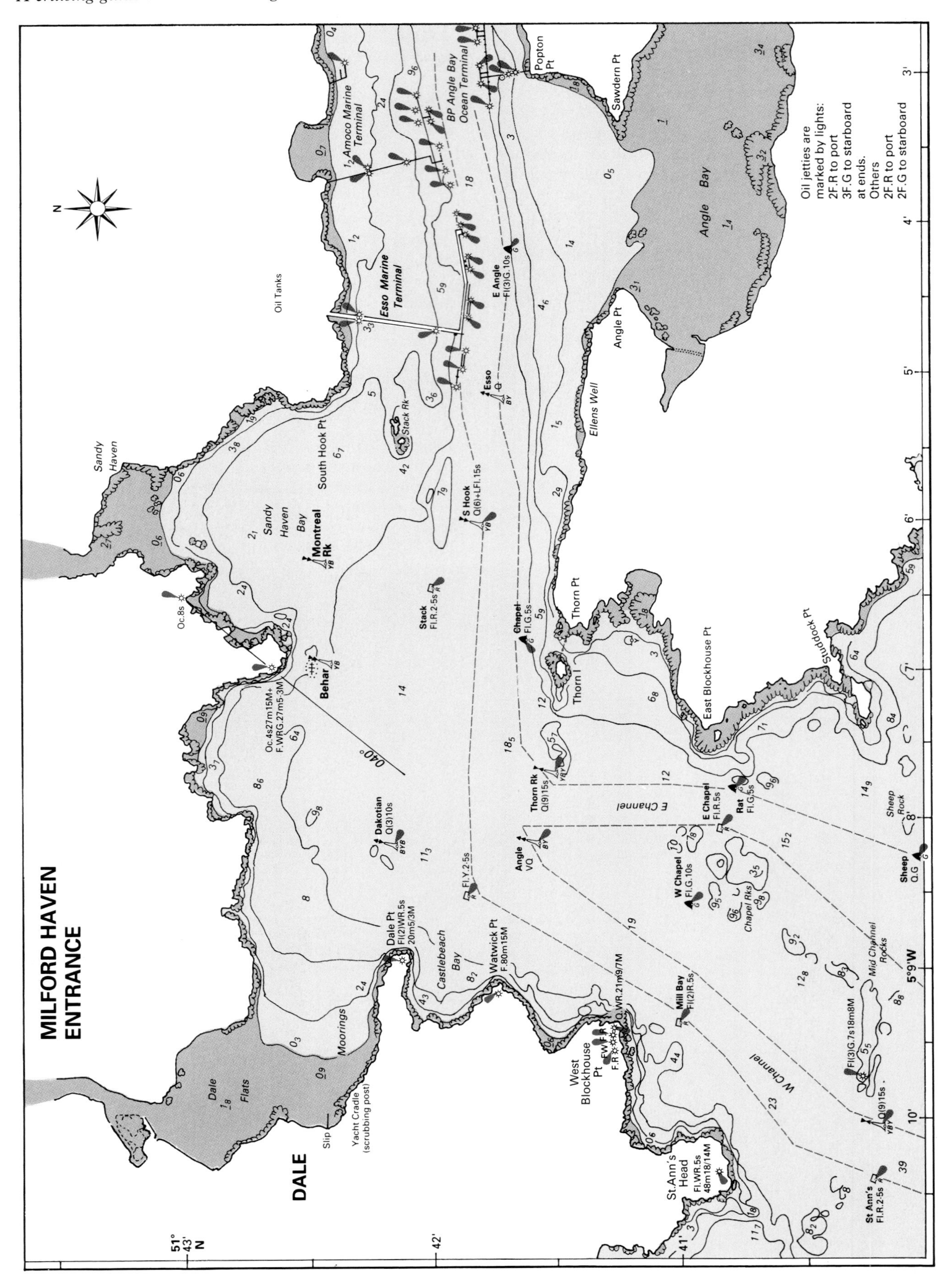

MILFORD HAVEN
ENTRANCE
DALE
Dale Flats
Moorings
Slip
Yacht Cradle (scrubbing post)
Dale Pt
Fl(2)WR.5s 20m5/3M
Castlebeach Bay
Watwick Pt
F.80m15M
West Blockhouse Pt
Q.WR.21m9/7M
Mill Bay
Fl(2)R.5s
St.Ann's Head
Fl.WR.5s 48m18/14M
St Ann's
Fl.R.2·5s
Q(9)15s
Fl(3)G.7s18m8M
Mid Channel Rocks
W Channel
Chapel Rks
W Chapel
Fl.G.10s
Sheep
Q.G
Sheep Rock
Angle
VQ
E Chapel
Fl.R.5s
Rat
Fl.G.5s
E Channel
Thorn Rk
Q(9)15s
Dakotian
Q(3)10s
Fl.Y.2·5s
Oc.4s27m15M+
F.WRG.27m5-3M
040°
Behar
Montreal Rk
Sandy Haven Bay
Sandy Haven
Oc.8s
Stack
Fl.R.2·5s
Chapel
Fl.G.5s
Thorn I
Thorn Pt
East Blockhouse Pt
Studdock Pt
S Hook
Q(6)+LFl.15s
South Hook Pt
Stack Rk
Esso
Q
Esso Marine Terminal
Oil Tanks
E Angle
Fl(3)G.10s
Ellens Well
Angle Pt
Angle Bay
Amoco Marine Terminal
BP Angle Bay Ocean Terminal
Popton Pt
Sawdern Pt
N
Oil jetties are marked by lights:
2F.R to port
3F.G to starboard at ends.
Others
2F.R to port
2F.G to starboard
51° 43' N
42'
41'
5°9'W
10'
8'
7'
6'
5'
4'
3'

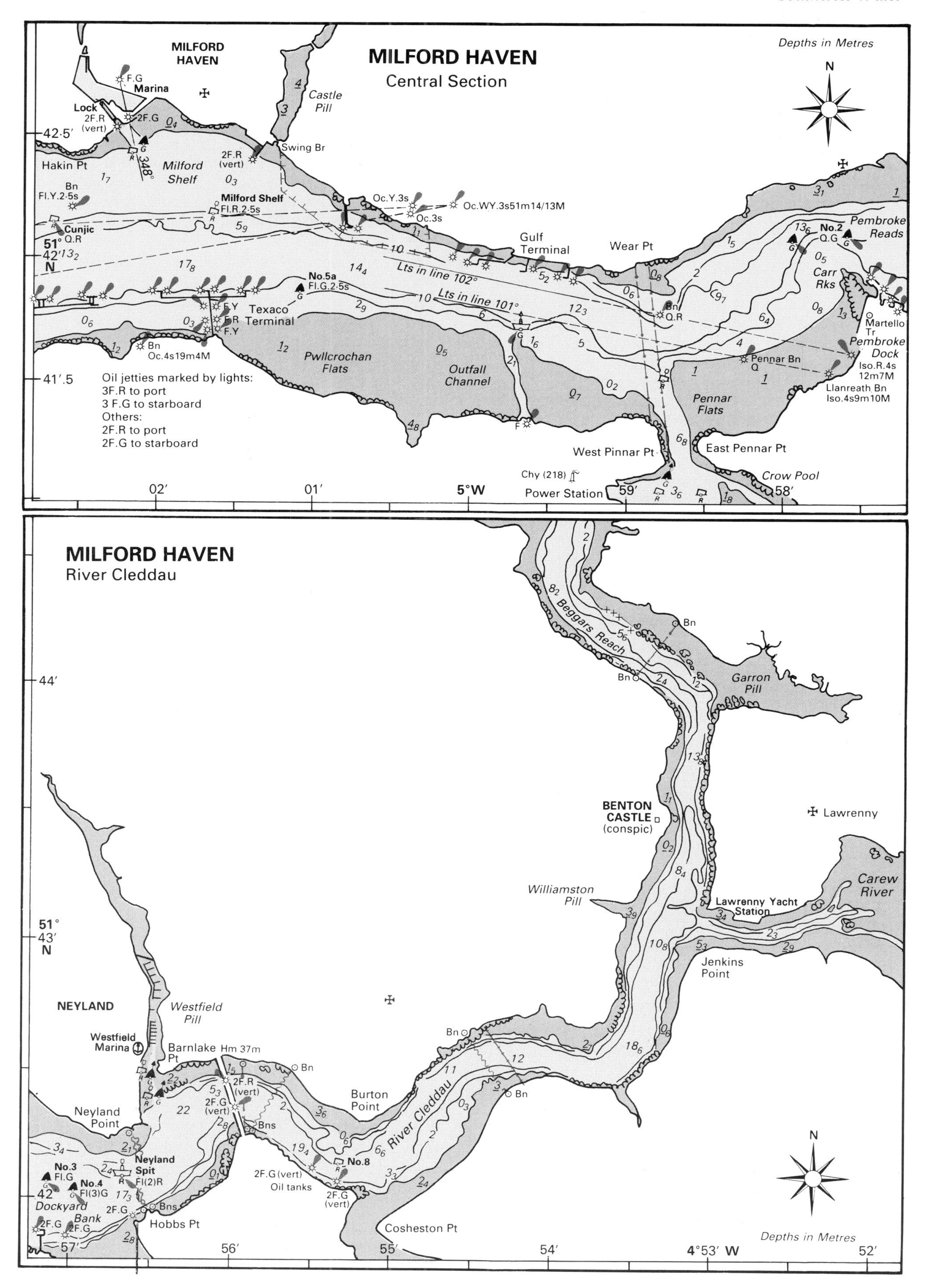
MILFORD HAVEN
Central Section
Depths in Metres
MILFORD HAVEN
Marina
Lock
Hakin Pt
Milford Shelf
Castle Pill
Swing Br
Cunjic
Milford Shelf Fl.R.2·5s
Oc.Y.3s
Oc.3s
Oc.WY.3s51m14/13M
Gulf Terminal
Wear Pt
No.2 Q.G
Pembroke Reads
Carr Rks
Martello Tr
Pembroke Dock
Iso.R.4s 12m7M
Llanreath Bn Iso.4s9m10M
No.5a Fl.G.2·5s
Lts in line 102°
Lts in line 101°
Texaco Terminal
Bn Oc.4s19m4M
Pwllcrochan Flats
Outfall Channel
Pennar Bn
Pennar Flats
West Pinnar Pt
East Pennar Pt
Crow Pool
Chy (218)
Power Station
Oil jetties marked by lights:
3F.R to port
3 F.G to starboard
Others:
2F.R to port
2F.G to starboard
5°W
MILFORD HAVEN
River Cleddau
Beggars Reach
Garron Pill
BENTON CASTLE (conspic)
Lawrenny
Williamston Pill
Lawrenny Yacht Station
Carew River
Jenkins Point
NEYLAND
Westfield Pill
Westfield Marina
Barnlake Pt
Hm 37m
Burton Point
Neyland Point
Neyland Spit Fl(2)R
No.3 Fl.G
No.4 Fl(3)G
Dockyard Bank
Hobbs Pt
No.8
Oil tanks
River Cleddau
Cosheston Pt
Depths in Metres
4°53′ W

The bay opens up to reveal a concave sand and shingle beach, backed by the little village of Dale, off which there are many small craft moorings. There is ample room to drop anchor in good holding, the only open aspect being to the east, where there is a fetch of three miles across the haven. In the days of sail, many ships would anchor here to be loaded by smaller craft from Haverfordwest, further up the haven, and large tankers still anchor here, though further out, awaiting instructions.

It is here at night that one of the most startling contrasts I have ever seen appears. Looking west, the rural little village of Dale can be seen nestling on the shore with the wavelets lapping on its beach. It is a scene that has changed little in a hundred years. To the east, however, the glaring lights of Milford Haven Oil Refinery make it look like a gigantic space ship ready for takeoff.

Ashore, Dale is a popular sailing village, with an extensive chandlery and a sailboard and dinghy school, though this doesn't detract from its peacefulness. General stores are available, there is a local hostelry, and petrol can be obtained from 'Sid the milkman', who opens a petrol pump for an hour or so after his milk round (approximately 1130 hours).

Milford Haven

A number of days can pleasurably be spent exploring Milford Haven.

SANDY HAVEN

The inner reaches dry to sand, providing good holding, though beware Bull Rock on approach and the foul eastern shore of the bay.

It is possible to take the ground here; otherwise anchor in 3m further out. The area is quite exposed to the SW, however; more shelter from this direction can be found on the south shore of the haven, off Angle Point, in 1–2m.

GELLISWICK BAY

The residence of Pembrokeshire Yacht Club, on the north shore, it also provides anchoring in good holding, though this site can be uncomfortable in a southerly blow.

MILFORD DOCKS MARINA

VHF M, M2, 80; has room for 151 craft, and may be entered HW −2 to HW by a narrow channel with 2·4m at MHWS; leading lights 349°.

On entering the dock, the marina lies to starboard; it has the usual marina facilities, and a chandlery.

Entering further into the haven (it should now be more correctly named the River Cleddau, for it takes on the appearance of a river), keeping clear of the foul southern shore of Pwllcrochan Flats, the entrance of Westfield Pill on the north shore can be seen just before Cleddau Bridge. It gives access to Westfield Marina, at Neyland – VHF 80, with berthing for 380 resident craft and 40 visitors. There is access to the lower basin at all states of tide by following the buoyed channel, dredged to 2m. Access to the upper basin is viable HW ±3½ hours, when there is a least depth over the sill of 1·5m.

Westfield Marina offers full marina facilities, a 15-ton lift, and diesel and petrol from a fuel raft. The nearby Dale Sailing Co. specialises in engine repair and GRP work, while Copp Sails have a large sail loft where urgent repairs can be undertaken at short notice.

Full supplies are available at Neyland. Early closing Wednesdays.

Due south from Neyland Point lies Hobbs Point, on the opposite bank, where many local craft swing to their moorings. Visitors' moorings are usually available; apply to Kelpie Boatyard ashore, though the tide runs quite fast here and care is needed when going ashore by tender.

There are a number of anchorages beyond Cleddau Bridge (with 37m clearance under the main arch, marked by F.R and G lights), the most popular being off Williamston Pill, opposite Lawrenny, or off Lawrenny itself, at the entrance to Carew River, where one can either pick up a vacant visitors' mooring or temporarily secure alongside the floating pontoon (maximum stay 15 minutes) whilst enquiries are made for a more permanent berth. Fuel is available here, and there are also a chandlery and a boatyard.

CASTLE REACH

Castle Reach anchorage, just to the north of the conspicuous Benton Castle on the west shore, is another popular anchorage.

St Bride's Bay

Tides at Littlehaven

HW Dover −0444

Height in metres

MHWS	MHWN	MTL	MLWN	MLWS
5·9	4·4	3·3	2·3	0·7

From Dale, part of the Pembrokeshire Coastal Path leads around St Ann's Head, passing the West Blockhouse Battery, built in 1857 to guard the entrance to the haven. It then runs north along the coast, passing Gateholm Island, accessible by foot at LW, and crowned by a now overgrown monastic settlement, until at Wooltack Point a grand view appears to Jack Sound. This is at its most spectacular during a SW gale and a spring tide, when the race runs at 7 knots through the narrow opening. South-going stream begins at HW Dover −0300, north-going at HW Dover +0300. Passage should be made at slack water; there is considerable turbulence when the wind is against the stream.

Just around the headland lies Martin's Haven, a small, deep cove, sheltered from the arc W–S–E, from which craft organised by the West Wales Naturalist Trust leave for Skomer Island (weather permitting), where wildlife and rare seabirds abound. (This is also the case with Skokholm Island, to the south, but this island is reserved for Naturalist Trust members only.)

Leaving Milford Haven, departure must be timed to arrive at Solva in daylight, as it is impossible to enter at night. If possible the tides should be used, for although the tide runs very weakly in St Bride's Bay itself, there are tide-rips and a very strong flow off the western coasts of Skokholm and Skomer Islands which can be taken advantage of to hurry us on our way.

Broad Sound

This is the route to take if intending a landing on Skomer Island, which is run by the Naturalist Trust – a landing charge is payable to the warden. Care must be taken, particularly during the nesting season, not to disturb the wildlife.

Provided that there is no south in the wind, a good anchorage can be had in South Haven, a secluded bay sheltered W–N–E, at the southeast of the island. A group of drying rocks guards the entry into the bay from the east, requiring a course to be set to overshoot the bay. Mew Stone (52m) is a prominent landmark; head for it until entry can be made into the bay from the SSW, anchor in 8m, and land on the main island by tender.

Around Skokholm and Skomer, good progress can be made on the tide which runs due north at 4 knots at springs. Bearings on Skokholm light (Fl.R.10s54m17M) will show the effect of the tide.

Over to the west, Grassholm Island, which is surrounded by overfalls, can be seen six miles distant, the home of thousands of gannets and seals, and looking very green, as its name implies. Rounding Skomer Island, the free-standing Garland Stone (29m) marks the northern tip of the island. The expanse of St Bride's Bay, where the tidal streams are quite weak, then opens up to the NE, with its magnificent coastal scenery. Its rocky cliffs, rising up to 90m, are deeply indented with many inlets, which with offshore winds may provide a good night's anchorage.

Broadhaven

51°46'·5N 5°07'W

Broadhaven, at the SE corner of the bay, is the most popular anchorage, with good holding in sand and shelter from NE–S–SW. It is, however, wide open to the west when a large surf enters, and very uncomfortable from N–NW. There is also shelter to be found in North Haven, on Skomer, where visitors' moorings are laid. This is an ideal place to await favourable tidal conditions for Jack Sound – though be careful of the reef which fans the eastern side of the entrance. The only anchorage providing all-round shelter in St Bride's Bay is Solva, midway along the northern side of the bay.

Solva

51°52'N 5°12'W

Charts

Admiralty 1478 (1:75,000)
Imray C60 (1:128,000)

Tides

HW Dover −0450

Height in metres

MHWS	MHWN	MTL	MLWN	MLWS
5·5	4·2	3·2	2·3	0·7

Radio/telephone

☎ Harbourmaster (0437) 721373

Solva harbour lies 20M to the north of Dale, and leaving Dale 2 hours before HW enables the now weak northbound flood to be taken for the first stages. Rounding St Ann's Head, we have the choice of two courses:

- Through Broad Sound, between Skokholm and Skomer Islands, passing to the north of Wild Goose Race, renowned for being a particularly nasty stretch of sea, especially around spring tides with a contrary wind.
- Passing outside the islands, with an offing of at least 2 M to keep us well outside the Wild Goose Race.

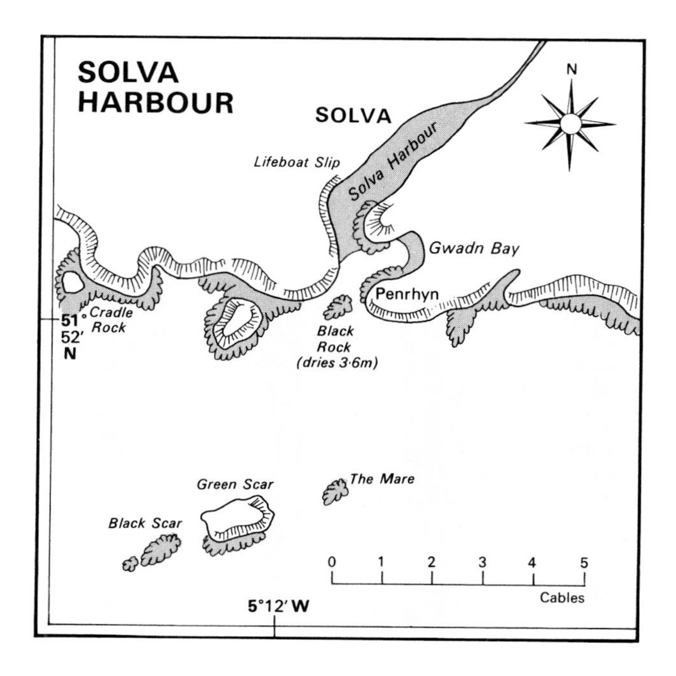

Either route is satisfactory in moderate conditions, though the course outside both islands is wiser if conditions are deteriorating; give the islands a wide offing if the sea becomes too confused.

There is yet a third option: going through 'Jack Sound'. This is only 3 cables wide, and runs between Skomer and the mainland. It has the advantage of cutting a number of miles off the journey, but is little used because of its 7-knot race at springs, coupled with the numerous drying rocks which make it a testing passage. British Admiralty Chart 1482 is essential, and local knowledge is an added advantage.

Jack Sound

Tidal streams

South-going starts HW Dover −0300
(HW Milford Haven +0200)
North-going starts HW Dover +0300
(HW Milford Haven −0425)

From the south, it is vital to identify the Blackstones (1·5m) and Tusker Rock (2m) before entering the sound. Leaving the Blackstones close to port, pilotage is a matter of heading directly for Tusker Rock (there is hardly any time to use clearing bearings) until the Garland Stone (29m), to the north of Skomer, opens off Midland Isle, when a course can be laid out of the sound.

From the north, once again Tusker Rock and the Blackstones must be identified prior to entering. Passing Tusker Rock to port, the Blackstones are then brought into transit with the western cliffs of Skokholm Island, and this course is held until the Blackstones are passed close to starboard.

Approach and entry to Solva

A course may be laid directly across the bay, crossing the research area marked by yellow buoys. The harbour approach is guarded by three large rocks (islets), 5 cables to the south of the harbour entrance. The largest is Green Scar (33m), lying centrally, with Black Scar, 1 cable long, to the west of it, and the Mare, a pillar rock, standing a cable to the east. But although these may seem to be good landmarks on the chart, in practice when you are approaching from the south they merge with the background, and may not be identified until you are within a mile or so.

Leaving Black Scar 3 cables to starboard, to avoid the off-lying rocky patches to the SW with 2·8m clearance, and rounding up between Green Scar and the mainland, it may take a moment to identify Solva entrance, which is approximately half a cable wide, with Black Rock (dries 3·6m) at its centre. Entry can be made on either side of Black Rock, though the channel runs on the western side.

Mooring

Craft unable to take the ground can anchor just behind Black Rock in 3m, or go further into Gwadn Bay to await the tide in 1·8m. At half tide, craft able to take the ground may anchor closer in, near the permanent moorings, leaving the channel (running along the western side) clear. The harbour itself is strongly reminiscent of a miniature fjord, and provides a very secure anchorage (almost a hurricane hole), being cliffy and steep on all sides. Land

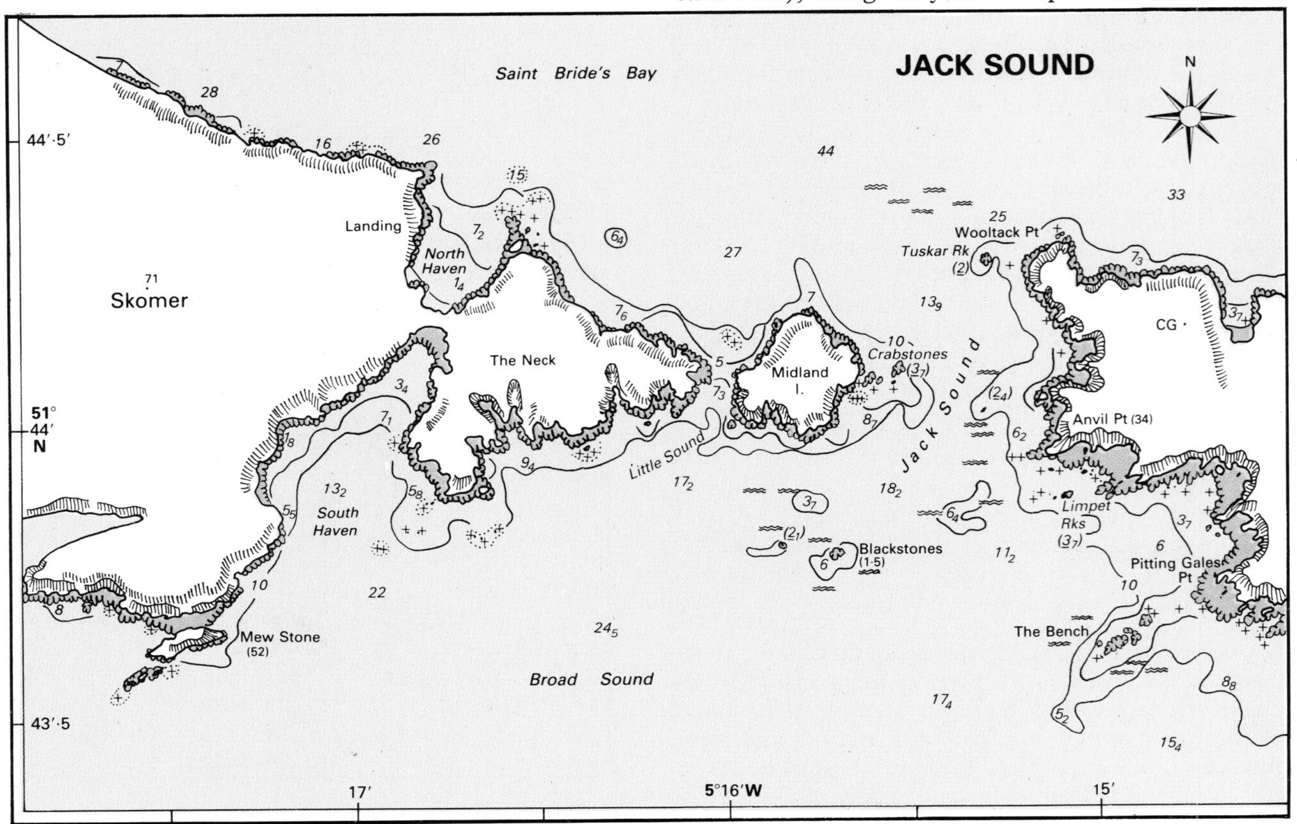

by tender on the old lifeboat slip; the harbour-master's office is next door.

The village itself is beautifully kept and quiet, sporting two hostelries. Supplies are limited, and the nearest place to buy petrol or diesel is St David's, 3 miles away – well worth a visit, via the scenic route, the Pembrokeshire Coastal Path.

St David's is in fact a city, though it is very small for one, with a population of just over 2,000. Its cathedral, dating from the 13th century, looks its age, with its leaning walls and sloping floor, and seems as if only a sustained act of faith kept it up. This may well be the case, for it was given international religious standing by the Pope, and two visits to St David's are equal to one visit to St Peter's in Rome.

The coastal path also leads past St Noon's Chapel, overlooking the sea to the south of St David's.

Fishguard

Charts

Admiralty 1482 (1:12,500)
Imray C60 (1:128,000)

Note Target buoys are to be found in the southern part of Cardigan Bay; they are frequently moved.

The route chosen for rounding St David's Head to Fishguard will fix the state of tide for departing Solva. There are two routes:

- Through Ramsey Sound
- Around the Bishops and Clerks (the only option for a night passage).

Through Ramsey Sound

Tidal streams

South-going starts HW Dover −0200
(HW Milford Haven +0300)
North-going starts HW Dover +0400
(HW Milford Haven −0325)

Note The stream in Ramsey Sound can run at 6 knots at springs, with back eddies being set up, and although rounding the Bishops is about 15 miles longer than rounding St David's Head, it may still be preferable to using the sound during springs or rising wind. You can expect a very confused sea off the Bishops, thanks to its 5-knot stream.

Allowing an average speed of 4 knots, departure from Solva should be taken 4 hours before local HW (HW Solva = Dover −4¾ hours), so that the southern end of the sound is arrived at just as the northbound stream starts to flow.

When you are clear of the harbour, a course of 250° will leave Porth-Clais Rock (dries 1·5m) to starboard, until the rocky peninsula of Carreg-Fran (15m) bears due north. Then come into 290°, leaving Shoe Rock (dries 3m), off Pen-Dal-Aderyn, well to starboard. This course is held until St David's Head, not to be confused with Point St John, opens off Pen-Dal-Aderyn. A course between the east end of the Bitches and Penmaenmelyn can then be laid (approximately 355°), leaving Horse Rock to starboard, and passing between Gwahan (dries 3m) to port and Carreg Gafeiliog (dries 3m) to starboard at the upper reaches of the sound.

Leaving Ramsey Island, the reputed burial place of thousands of saints, behind, the course leads around St David's Head. A course is laid off on Strumble Head (Fl(4)15s45m26M) in the distance, the coastline continuing in an unbroken chain of jagged cliffs interspersed with sandy bays all the way to Fishguard.

From the north
On rounding St David's Head close to, Carreg Gafeiliog should be left half a cable to port. The course is then set to lead midway between the Bitches and Pen-Dal-Aderyn, edging more towards the Ramsey side of the channel to ensure that Horse Rock (dries 0·9m) is left comfortably to port. The course can then be altered to close slightly with Pen-Dal-Aderyn, which is steep-to, in order to clear the Bitches. From here, a heading of due south, keeping St David's Head open astern, clears Shoe Rock (dries 3·0m).

Timing should be arranged so that you arrive at the entrance to the sound with the beginnings of the southbound stream, which commences at HW Dover −2 hours (2 hours after local HW at Fishguard).

Around the Bishops and Clerks

As has been mentioned, the stream around the Bishops can run at up to 5 knots at springs, running northbound from 2 hours before HW Milford Haven until 5 hours after, when it turns southbound from 5 hours after HW Milford Haven until 2 hours before HW.

Rounding the Bishops is quite straightforward, if a little uncomfortable, in clear weather. The only navigational problem, at the south tip of Ramsey Island, is Sylvia Rock, with 5m over it (not that this is a danger to most yachts, but it is unnerving to see the flat area of sea which it sometimes causes when the rest of the sea is very lumpy). The Meini Duon Rocks strike 3 cables or so SW from Ynys Berry.

South Bishop lighthouse is open for most of the journey, standing at 44m. This affords ample opportunity to take bearings and find out exactly what the tide is doing. An offing of one mile leads outside the worst of the overfalls. After rounding South Bishop, a course of due north leaves an armada of rocks (Daufraich, Carreg Rhoson, and Maen Rhosen, to name but three) to starboard. The course runs with the northbound stream, enabling cracking progress to be made until North Bishop (37m) bears due E. Then come directly onto Strumble Head (Fl(4)15s45m26M). This course is

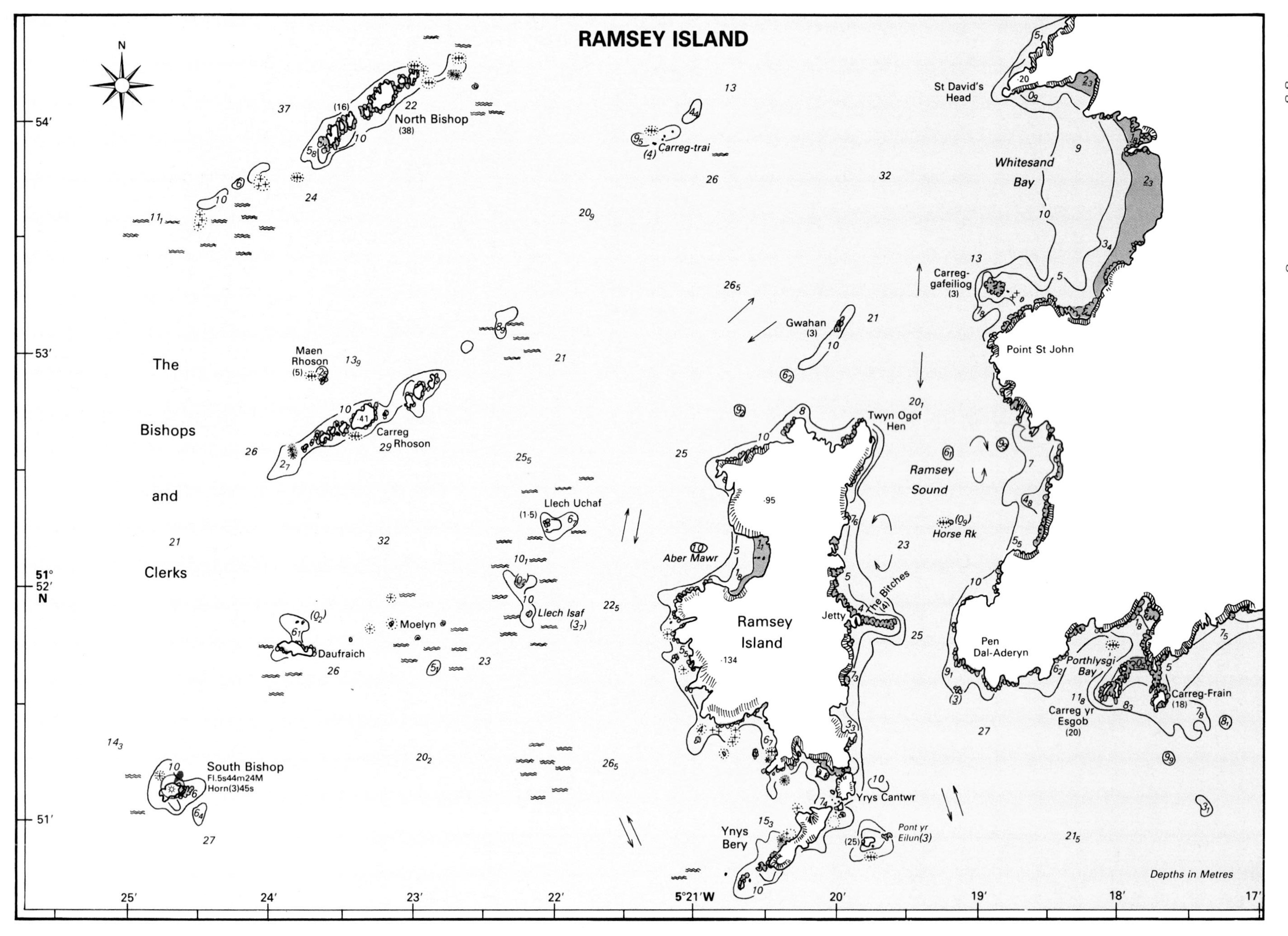
RAMSEY ISLAND
St David's Head
Whitesand Bay
Point St John
Carreg-gafeiliog (3)
Twyn Ogof Hen
Ramsey Sound
Horse Rk
The Bitches
Jetty
Ramsey Island
Aber Mawr
Pen Dal-Aderyn
Porthlysgi Bay
Carreg-Frain (18)
Carreg yr Esgob (20)
Yrys Cantwr
Pont yr Eilun(3)
Ynys Bery
Gwahan (3)
Carreg-trai
North Bishop (38)
Carreg Rhoson
Maen Rhoson (5)
Llech Uchaf
Llech Isaf
Moelyn
Daufraich
South Bishop
Fl.5s44m24M
Horn(3)45s
The Bishops and Clerks
Depths in Metres
5°21'W
51° 52' N
54'
53'
51'
17'
18'
19'
20'
22'
23'
24'
25'

the most direct, and leaves the foaming seas of Bais Bank to port, though it does lead through a tidy rip; this can be avoided in uncomfortable weather by plotting a course further inshore.

Note During thick weather, in a rising sea, or against a foul tide, a course leading well outside the Bishops, where there are weaker tidal streams (2–3 knots), would be advisable.

Fishguard

52°00'·5N 4°58'·5W

Charts

Admiralty 1484 (1:15,000), 1973 (1:75,000)
Imray C60 (1:128,000)

Tides

HW Dover −0347

Height in metres

MHWS	MHWN	MTL	MLWN	MLWS
4·8	3·5	2·8	2·1	0·8

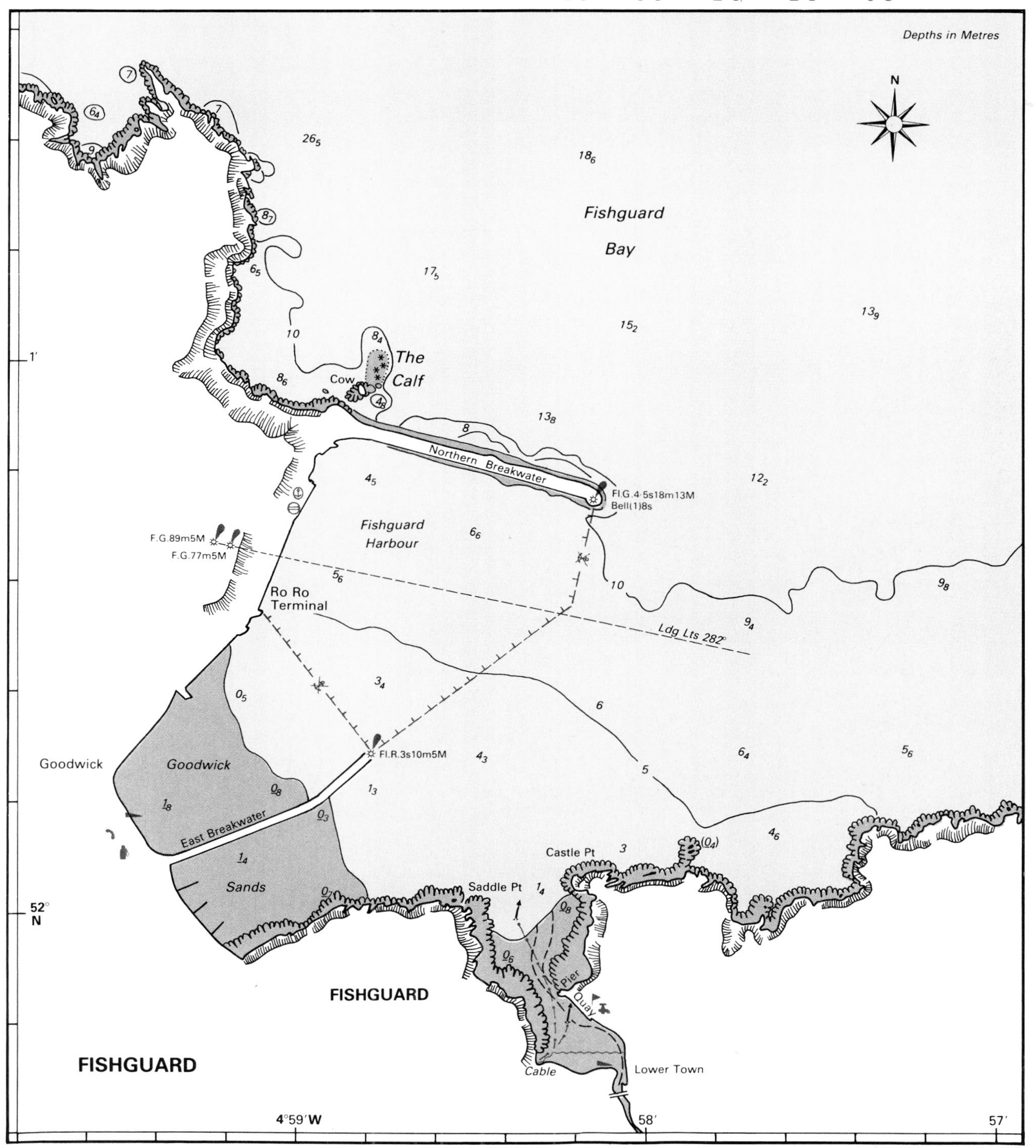

The northern breakwater of Fishguard Harbour.

Fishguard Old Harbour – drying to sand.

Lights

N breakwater head Fl.G.4·5s18m13M Bell(1)8s 8-sided concrete tower
E breakwater head Fl.R.3s10m5M Metal framework tower
Lts in line 282° *Front* F.G.77m5M *Rear* 46m from front F.G.89m5M White ◆ on white mast

Radio/telephone

Goodwick Marine Ch M (occas)
☎ Harbourmaster (0348) 872881
☎ Harbourmaster Lower Harbour (0348) 5203
☎ Goodwick Marine (0348) 874950

Approach

After rounding the black cliffs of Strumble Head and negotiating Strumble Bank overfalls, the northern breakwater opens in Fishguard Bay (Fl.G.4·5s 18m13M Bell(1)8s). Leave the tip of the breakwater to starboard, keeping well clear of Calf and Cow

Fishguard Old Harbour provides good shelter. Full supplies are available from the town.

Next, a course can be laid off for a line between the east breakwater and Saddle Point, where it is possible for craft drawing up to 1·5m to anchor in good holding; deeper-draught vessels can anchor a little further out. Bilge keelers may take the ground, if desired, by entering a little further into the bay, the anchorage being sheltered in all but NE winds.

The Old Harbour (Lower Harbour), once a fishing port but now a busy small boat sailing centre, lies between Saddle Point and Castle Point. It provides good shelter, drying to sand, and a berth may be found by contacting the harbourmaster. Full supplies are available from the town.

The large Fishguard Harbour (Goodwick Harbour would have been a better name), across the bay, was originally built for transatlantic liners in 1906, and is now the major port for ferry traffic to and from Rosslare, in Ireland (arrivals 1200 and 0100, sailings 1500 and 0315). Take care when entering or leaving not to encounter one head-on.

Cardigan

52°06'N 4°41'W

Charts

Admiralty 1484 (1:37,500)
Imray C60 (1:128,000), C61 (1:270,000)

Tides

HW Dover −0350
MTL 2·7m Barhas, 2·5m at MHWS

Lights

Beacon Fl(2) 5s

Radio/telephone

☎ Harbourmaster (0545) 612084

Cardigan is 12 miles to the NE of Fishguard. As there is a large bar guarding its entrance, with only 1·5m at MHWN, departure from Fishguard should be timed so as to arrive at Cardigan at around high water.

Round Dinas Head, the headland at the eastern end of Fishguard Bay, giving it at least half a mile offing to clear off-lying rocks. The sandy shores of Newport Bay open to the east, with the town of Newport, lying on the banks of the Afon Nevern estuary.

This bay provides good shelter in winds NE–E–SW, in good holding, with stores available from the town. As an added bonus, Carningli Mountain (345m), to the south of Newport, has an old hill fort with stone circles dating from the Iron Age, and is well worth the climb on a fine day.

Crossing Newport Bay, the Carregedrywy Rocks, striking 3 cables NW at the northern end of the bay, should be given a good offing. A course may then be laid along the coast, keeping half a mile offing for comfort, until, after rounding Cemaes Head, Port Cardigan opens to the SE.

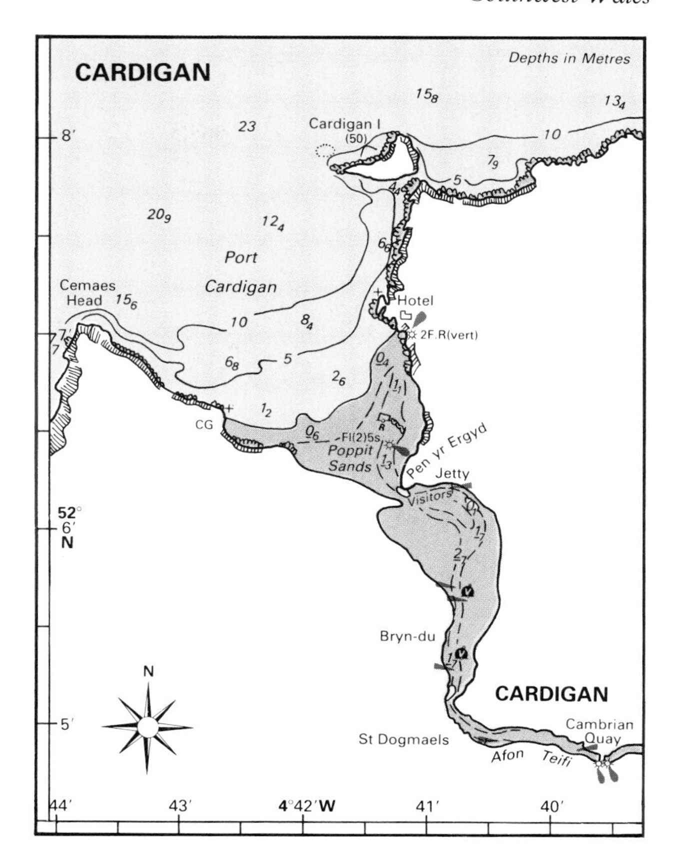

Approach

The conspicuous Cliff Hotel, on the eastern side of the estuary, at Craig-Y-Gwbert, marks the approach, on a bearing of approximately 100°.

On closing with the promontory, four recently established white spar daylight markers, with retro-reflective tape, can be distinguished along the shore, and the channel can be found within 50m of the cliffs. It can then be followed by using the depth sounder, typical soundings being around 2–3m. Entrance is difficult and dangerous in strong N–NW winds.

With the last spar day marker abeam, the course is altered onto the lit isolated danger mark (Fl(2)15s) indicating the centre of the channel, leaving it to starboard, and then onto Pen-Yr-Ergyd Point, at the edge of the caravan site; round this close to port to avoid the shoal area to starboard.

Ashore, the Teifi Boat Club welcomes visitors. The latest information on pilotage can be obtained from the harbourmaster for Cardigan; ☎ (0545) 612084.

Before attempting the shifting channel leading to Cardigan, it is wise to seek local advice, or to await LW, when the channel can be inspected. Shoal-draught craft should have little difficulty in entering at HW and anchoring between St Dogmael's and Cardigan in mud, well sheltered from all directions.

Full stores are available at Cardigan; early closing Wednesdays, landing by tender.

Cardigan was once one of Wales' principal ports, but is now used almost exclusively by pleasure craft. It has a market and an old ruined castle, and is connected to St Dogmael's, a smaller town on the southern bank of the Afon Teifi, by an old 18th-century six-arch road bridge.

II. West coast of Wales

Aberporth to Abersoch

This stretch of coast follows the concave shore of Cardigan Bay from New Quay to Aberystwyth, Aberdovey and Barmouth. It is a fine-weather coast only, as all of these harbours are untenable in strong westerly winds. The nearest safe havens are at Pwllheli Harbour, at anchor off Llanbedrog Beach, or at St Tudwal's Roads, on the SE coast of Lleyn Peninsula, to the north.

Main coastal lights

St Tudwal's Island Fl.WR.20s46m15/13M White round tower 349°-W-169°-R-221°-W-243°-R-259°-W-293°-R-349° Obscured by East Island 211°-231°
Strumble Head Fl(4)15s45m26M White round tower 038°-vis-257°

New Quay

52°13'N 4°21'W

Charts

Admiralty 1484 (1:12,500)
Imray C60 (1:128,000), C61 (1:270,000)

Tides

HW Dover −0335
MTL 2·6m Harbour dries

Lights

Pier head Fl.WRG.3s12m8/5M Green triangle 135°W-252°-G-295°-R-shore
Breakwater Q.WR

Radio/telephone

☎ Harbourmaster (0545) 560368

New Quay Harbour lies 15 miles to the NE of Cardigan; as it dries, departure from Cardigan should ideally be taken 3 hours before HW. This may mean anchoring off in the bay, or setting off earlier and anchoring off New Quay Bay, avoiding the foul eastern side (Carreg Ina), marked by a N cardinal buoy.

The harbour lies behind New Quay Head. The pier head is visible to the southeast when you are round the head. The harbour lies behind this, though a groyne, running SSE from the end of the pier and marked by a beacon with yellow topmark, must be left to starboard before steering into the harbour. Craft may lie head-to anchor, stern-to pier; the southernmost point of the harbour is marked by the breakwater (Q.WR) near the lifeboat slip. The harbour itself is very small, and with a strong northerly wind a dangerous and sick-making swell rolls in, though good shelter is provided from

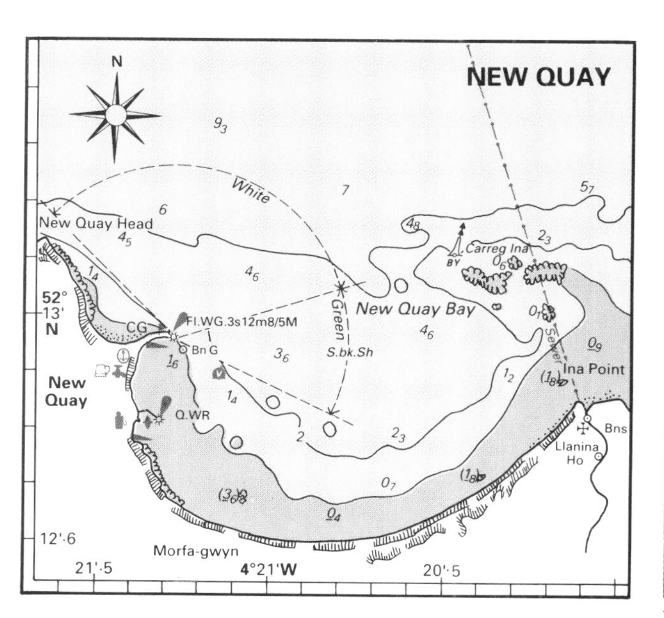

New Quay entrance. *Peter Cumberlidge*

New Quay.

W–S–E. A more permanent berth may be found by contacting the harbourmaster (☎ (0545) 560368), though vacant berths are quite a rarity. Ashore, New Quay is a small fishing and sailing town linked together by very steep and narrow winding lanes – just the place to exercise one's legs after a few days aboard. Supplies are a little limited, though petrol and diesel are available.

New Quay pier head.

Aberystwyth

52°24'·4N 4°05'·3W

Charts

Admiralty 1484 (1:18,000)
Imray C61 (1:270,000)

Tides

HW Dover −0510

Height in metres

MHWS	MHWN	MTL	MLWN	MLWS
4·8	3·7	2·7	1·8	0·5

Lights

S breakwater head Fl(2)WG.10s.12m10M Black metal column 030°-G-053°-W-210° 4F.R(vert) on radio tower 2·8M S

Ldg Lts 138° *Front* F.R.4m5M White lantern *Rear* F.R.7m6M White post

Timber jetty head Q.WR.9m4M Metal column 244°-W-141°-R-175°

Radio/telephone

Harbourmaster VHF Ch 16, 14 ☎ (0970) 611433

Above Aberystwyth Harbour looking seaward.
Left Aberystwyth Harbour looking upstream. *Peter Cumberlidge*

Above Aberystwyth inner harbour and slipway.

Below Aberystwyth outer harbour.

The natural harbour of Aberystwyth, formed where the Afon Ystwyth and Afon Rheidol combine.

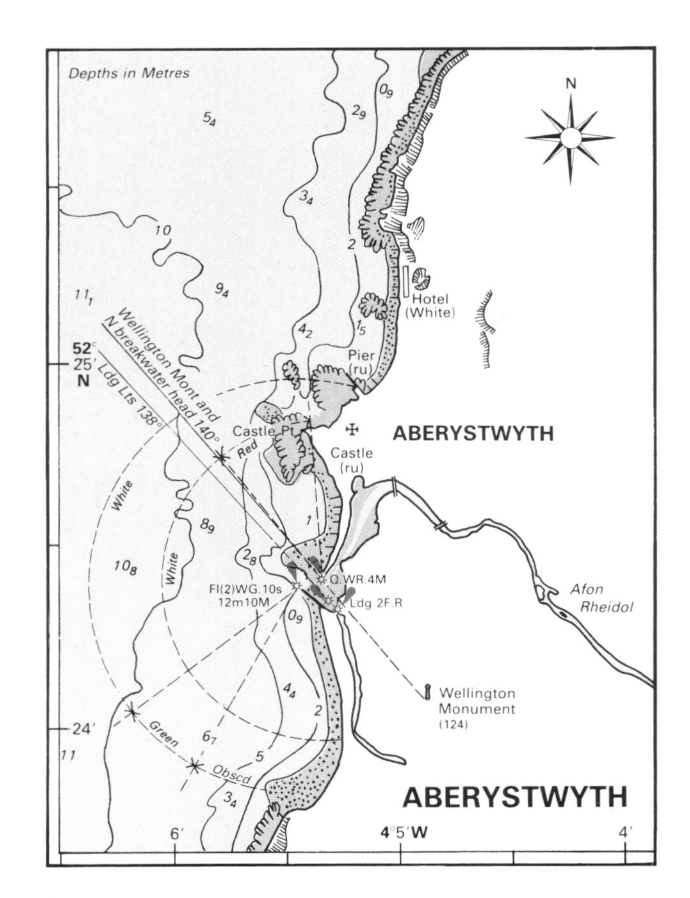

Aberystwyth is a natural harbour formed where the Afon Ystwyth and Afon Rheidol combine; it lies 15 miles NNE of New Quay. Like New Quay, it dries, but it differs from New Quay in that anchoring off Aberystwyth to await the tide leaves you very exposed from N–W–S; arrival should therefore be planned to coincide with HW. Pendinas, a hump-backed hill (124m) which rises steeply out of the sea, crowned at its peak by a 19th-century cannon-like monument, is a good landmark, just to the south of the harbour. Entry into the harbour is achieved by rounding the south pier (Fl(2)WG.10s 12m10M). The course then leads 120° between North Pier (Q.WR) and South Pier, before turning sharply to port to lead into the harbour; here a berth may be found alongside the quays. Water is available at the quays, while chandlery, petrol, diesel, and full supplies are available from the town. The harbourmaster's office (☎ (0970) 611433) is located at the inner end of the Town Quay, and should be contacted shortly after arrival.

Aberystwyth is the largest town on Cardigan Bay, and is very Victorian in appearance. It is characteristic of many towns along this coastline, having its own ruined castle, Bastide Castle, to the north of the harbour.

Aberdovey

52°32'·5N 4°02'·5W

Charts

Admiralty 1484 (1:25,000)
Imray C61 (1:270,000)

Tides

HW Dover −0320

Height in metres

MHWS	MHWN	MTL	MLWN	MLWS
4·8	3·7	2·7	1·8	0·5

Radio/telephone

Aberdovey Harbour VHF Ch 12, 16
☎ Harbourmaster (065472) 767626

Aberdovey (Aberdifi) lies 9 miles north of Aberystwyth; sailing from one to the other entails crossing the Patches, a shoal area of only 1·5m clearance at chart datum, where turbulent water can be seen in moderate to fresh conditions. How difficult it is to cross this area depends on the state of tide and the draught of the vessel; it is necessary to use the unmarked main channel. The other option is to round Patches W cardinal, 6 miles to seaward, which increases the journey to 17 miles.

It is important to time departure from Aberystwyth so that arrival at Aberdovey is not more than 3 hours either side of HW, although craft may enter up to 4 hours either side in favourable conditions, when there will be approximately 2·5m over the bar. The sea here breaks in moderate to fresh onshore weather, making entry impossible.

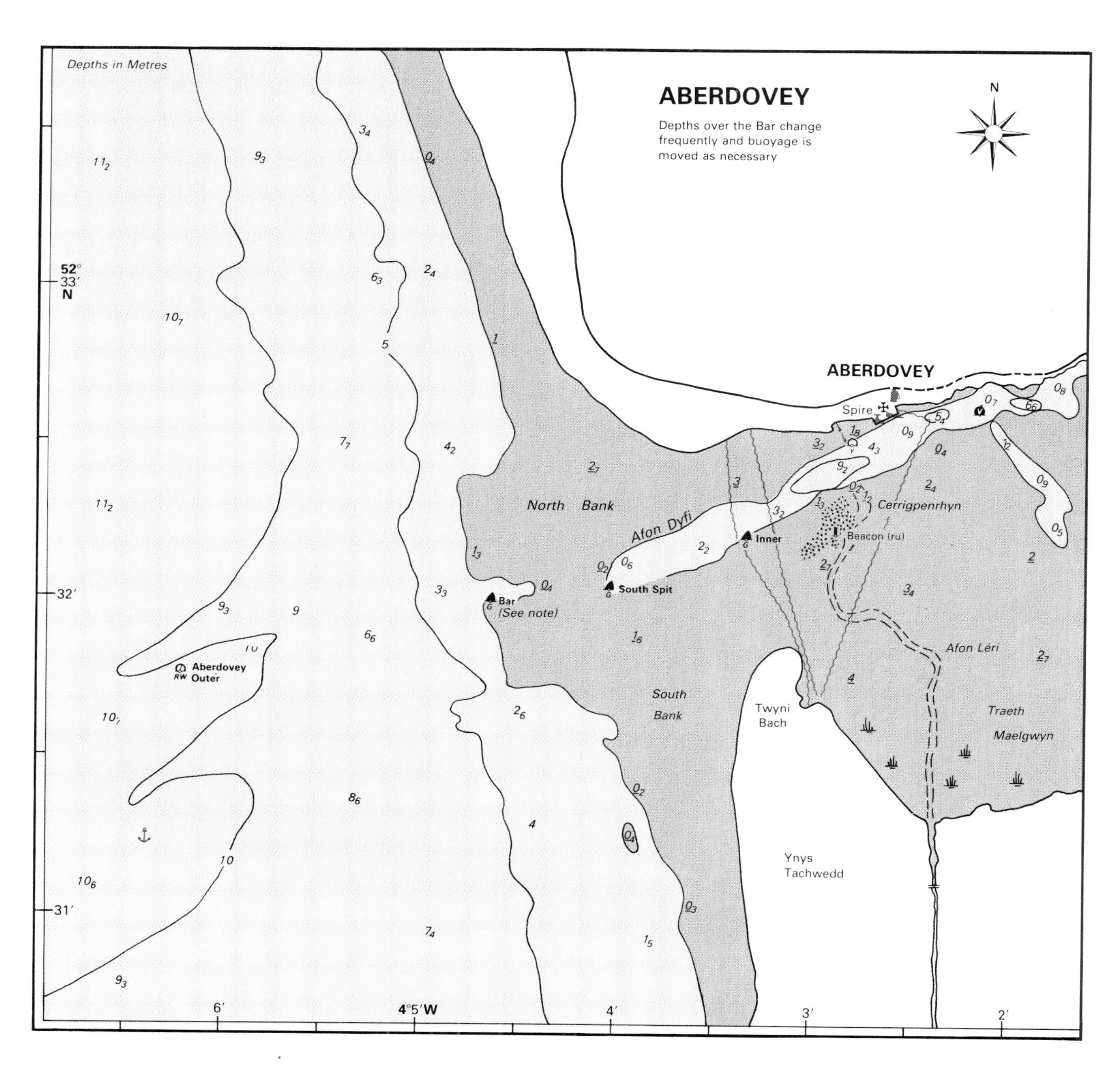

Aberdovey Harbour. There is now a visitors' mooring to the east of the jetty in 0·8m.
Opposite Aberdovey Harbour.

As at Aberystwyth, anchoring off awaiting the tide when there is any west in the wind leaves you very exposed, and entering at night should not be attempted without local knowledge, as there are few lights. After locating Aberdovey Outer RWVS buoy, a course may be laid onto the lit (Fl.G.10s) Bar G conical buoy to the east, 1 mile distant. From here, navigation is from buoy to buoy, all being G conical and left to starboard (they are moved frequently as the channel shifts), until a course can be steered for the wooden jetty to port, where one can berth alongside. Anchoring inside the harbour needs careful forethought, as there are two submarine cables, marked at their shore ends by beacons, crossing the harbour; local advice should be sought. Fortunately, there is now a visitors' mooring, to the east of the jetty in 0·8m. The harbourmaster can be contacted by telephoning (065472) 767626 (VHF Ch 12), should advice or a more permanent berth be sought.

Water is available at the jetty, while petrol, diesel, chandlery and stores are available from the town. The Dovey Yacht Club, at the west end of the quay, welcomes visiting yachtsmen/women. Early closing Wednesdays.

Barmouth

52°42'·8N 4°03'W

Charts

Admiralty 1484 (1:25,000)
Imray C61 (1:270,000)

Tides

HW Dover −0250
Height in metres

MHWS	MHWN	MTL	MLWN	MLWS
4·9	3·9	2·8	1·7	0·6

Lights

North bank Y perch Q.R.4m5M Red framework tower
Ynys y Brawd breakwater SE end Fl.R.5s5M
Bridge NW end 2F.R(hor)

Radio/telephone

VHF Barmouth Harbour Ch 12, 16
(Apr–Sept 0900–1200; Oct–Mar 0900–1600)
Harbourmaster ☎ (0341) 280671

Above Barmouth Harbour, showing the railway bridge, which spans the estuary, bottom right.

Below The entrance to Barmouth Harbour between the north breakwater and Penrhyn Point.

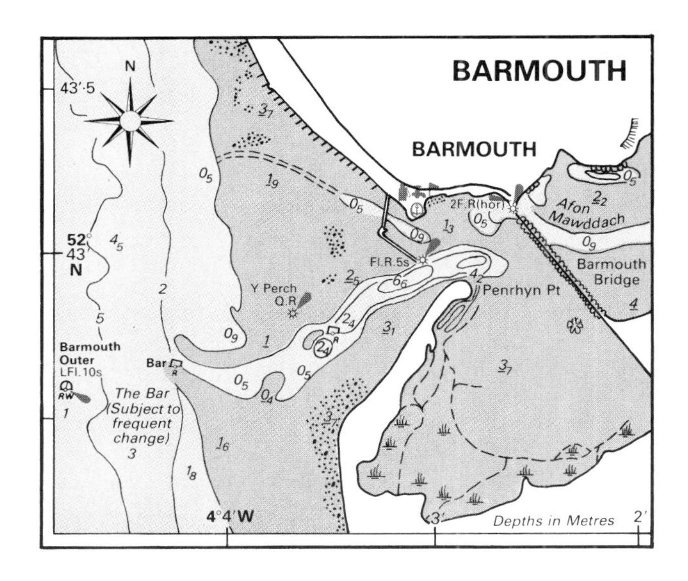

Barmouth, the next landfall, lies 14 miles up the coast from Aberdovey, or 19 miles, if Bwch W cardinal buoy is rounded; the choice of route depends upon tide, wind and draught. There is 1·6m midway between the point and the buoy, increasing to 4·3m a little further out.

Barmouth Harbour is not viable during strong S–W winds, as an ugly sea forms over the bar, which extends 1 mile to the west, and has only 0·5m over it. With an ebb stream running at up to 4 knots, dangerous seas quickly develop. It is best to enter on the last two hours of the flood; again, anchoring off to await the tide leaves you very exposed if there is any west in the wind.

On reaching Barmouth Outer RWVS light buoy, the Bar R can buoy, 3 cables to the east, should be left to port, as should the Inner R can buoy. Perch Rock, a cable to the northwest of the Inner R can, is indicated by light Q.R.4m5M. The course then leads into the estuary, leaving the North Breakwater (Fl.R.5s) to port. It is possible to anchor near the railway bridge, taking care not to foul the cables crossing the estuary, which are indicated by shore marks. Buoying the anchor may be prudent.

General supplies and water are available from the town, although landing at the quay, which is small and usually quite busy, may be difficult due to lack of space.

The estuary is especially beautiful, and a grand view can be had from the footbridge which runs alongside the railway bridge crossing the estuary. (Harbourmaster ☎ (0341) 280671.)

The quayside at Barmouth.

Tremadoc Bay

The north coast of Tremadoc Bay provides two very secure harbours and two secure anchorages, all within a distance of 15 miles, between Porthmadog to the east and Abersoch (St Tudwal's Roads) to the west.

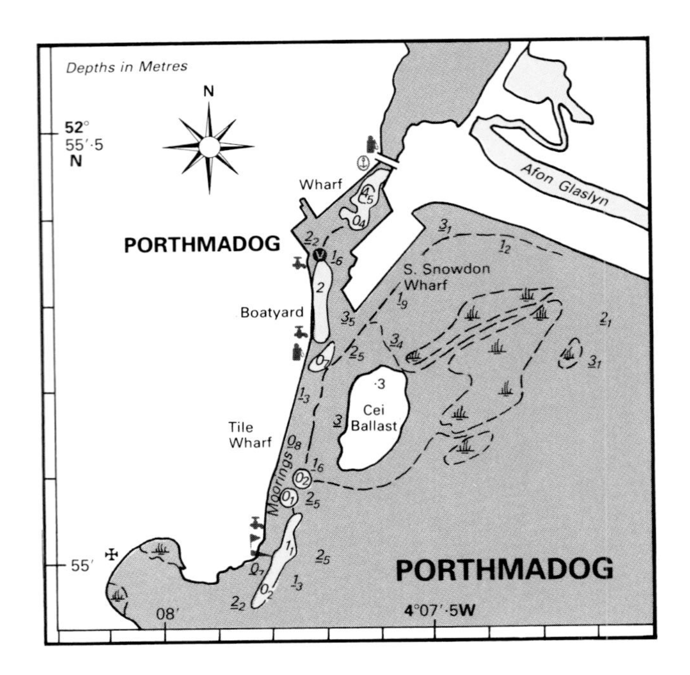

Porthmadog

52°55'·4N 4°07'·7W

Charts

Admiralty 1512 (1:7,500), 1971 (1:75,000)
Imray C52 (1:140,700), C61 (1:270,000)

Tides

HW Dover −0232

Height in metres

MHWS	MHWN	MTL	MLWN	MLWS
5·1	4·0	2·8	1·6	0·7

Porthmadog Harbour. There may be a vacant berth alongside the north wall of the inner harbour, or a vacant mooring could be used.

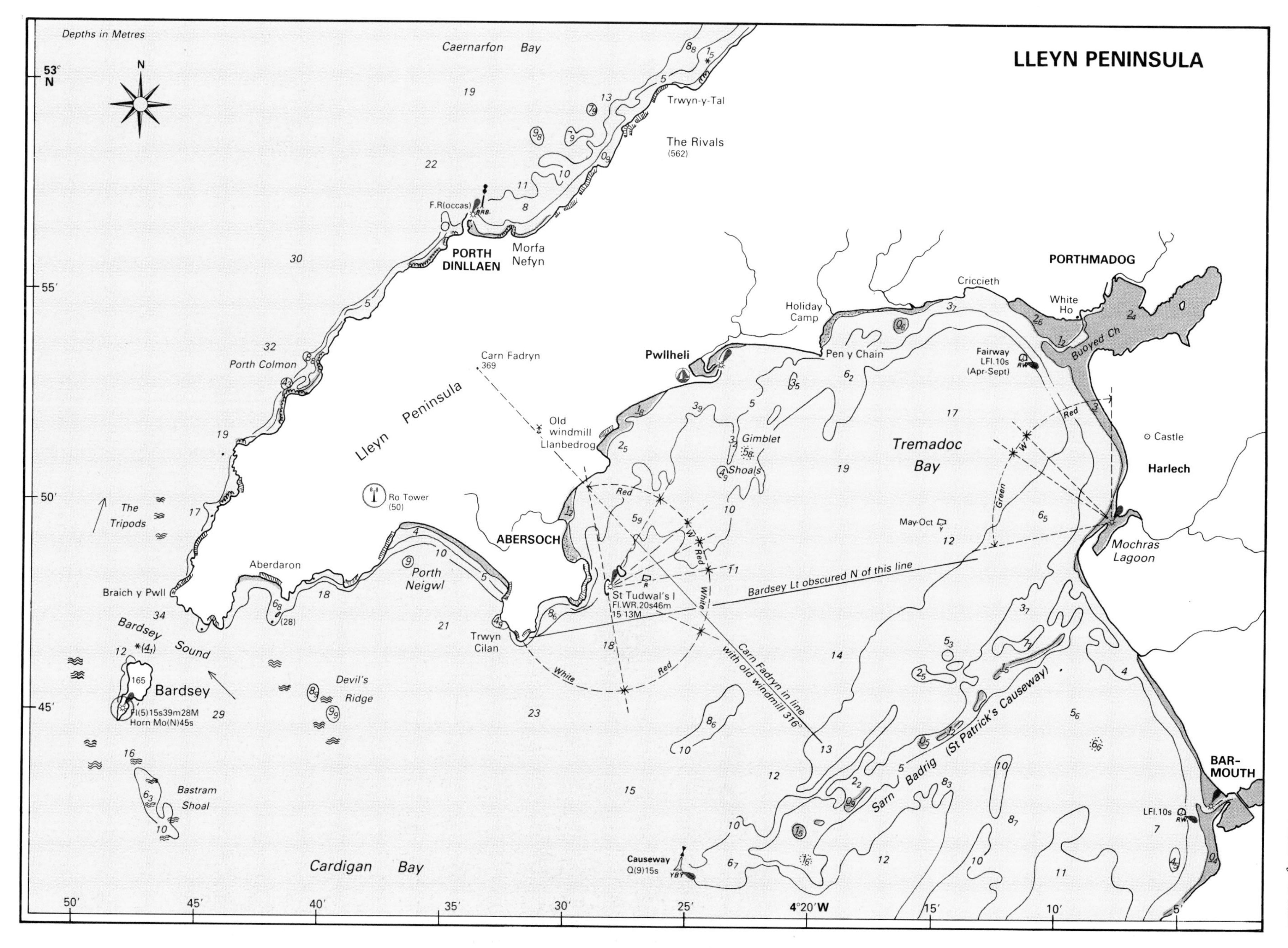

LLEYN PENINSULA
Depths in Metres
Caernarfon Bay
Trwyn-y-Tal
The Rivals (562)
F.R(occas)
PORTH DINLLAEN
Morfa Nefyn
Porth Colmon
Carn Fadryn 369
Lleyn Peninsula
Old windmill Llanbedrog
Pwllheli
Holiday Camp
Criccieth
PORTHMADOG
White Ho
Buoyed Ch
Fairway LFl.10s (Apr-Sept)
Pen y Chain
Gimblet Shoals
Tremadoc Bay
Castle
Harlech
Mochras Lagoon
May-Oct
Ro Tower (50)
The Tripods
ABERSOCH
Aberdaron
Porth Neigwl
Braich y Pwll
Bardsey Sound
St Tudwal's I Fl.WR.20s46m 15 13M
Bardsey Lt obscured N of this line
Trwyn Cilan
Carn Fadryn in line with old windmill 316°
Bardsey
Fl(5)15s39m28M Horn Mo(N)45s
Devil's Ridge
Sarn Badrig (St Patrick's Causeway)
BAR-MOUTH
LFl.10s
Bastram Shoal
Causeway Q(9)15s
Cardigan Bay
Red
White
Green
53° N
55'
50'
45'
40'
35'
30'
25'
4°20'W
15'
10'
5'

Radio/telephone

Madoc YC VHF Ch 16, 80M
Harbourmaster VHF Ch 16, 14, 12 ☎ (0766) 512927

Pilotage note

St Patrick's Causeway is composed of large, loose rocks. At its inner end, 4 cables offshore, there is a channel which can be attempted for 3 hours either side of HW in favourable conditions.

Approach

On rounding Causeway buoy (Q(9)15s Bell), marking the westernmost tip of St Patrick's Causeway, which strikes 10 miles SW from Mochras Point and dries 1·5m, a course may be laid directly to make the Porthmadog Fairway buoy RWVS (LFl.10s). From there, entry into the harbour is made by following the chain of lateral buoys (16 in total), with reflective topmarks, which is removed from November to April.

Entry should be made between 2 hours either side of HW in the case of moderate-draught vessels. There may be a vacant berth alongside the N wall of the inner harbour, near the harbourmaster's hut, or a vacant mooring could be used. Alternatively, anchor and take the ground near the bridge. The harbourmaster should then be contacted for payment of dues.

Ashore, full provisions are available, and as it is a very popular yachting centre, major refits can be organised; early closing Wednesdays. From the harbour, the Festiniog Narrow Gauge Railway runs to the slate workings of Festiniog, while Harlech Castle, made famous by the song 'Men of Harlech' (about a particularly long and bloody siege in its history), is a short trip to the south. It was built by Edward I of England, in 1290, to quell the Welsh. It is quite fantastic to imagine that the sea lashed at the foot of the castle when it was constructed; now, a mere 700 years later, fertile green pastures lie where the sea once was.

(It was also a Lancastrian stronghold during the Wars of the Roses, and was the last fortress to fall to the Yorkists – being a Wiganer, I had to mention this Lancashire version of the Alamo.)

Pwllheli

52°53'N 4°24'W

Charts

Admiralty 1512 (1:7,500), 1971 (1:75,000)
Imray C52 (1:140,700), C61 (1:270,000)

Tides

HW Dover −0300

Height in metres

MHWS	MHWN	MTL	MLWN	MLWS
4·9	3·7	2·7	1·5	0·6

Lights

Crib groyne Q.R.3m3M
Training Arm head Q.G.3m3M
Channel N side Fl.G.2·5s3M, Fl.G.5s3M, Fl.G.10s3M
Marina SE end 2F.G(vert)
SW end 2F.G(vert)

Radio/telephone

VHF Ch 16(occas) 80M
☎ Harbourmaster (0758) 613131
☎ Marina (0758) 701219

Pwllheli lies 10 miles due west from Porthmadog, and can now be entered at virtually all states of tide, thanks to the extensive dredging operations which accompanied the building of the new deep-water marina in the inner harbour.

Leaving Porthmadog, Criccieth Castle, the main feature of the coastline, can be seen perched on a large rock to the north. Built in the early 13th century, it was largely destroyed by Glendower in 1404, and has remained that way ever since. Continuing west and passing Pen Ychain (or 'Butlin's Point', as I call it, because of the holiday camp it houses), the main feature of Pwllheli, Gimblet Rock – a conical rock 30m high – comes into view. The approach to the harbour is to the north of this, the entrance being indicated by light beacons Q.G and Q.R, after which the channel is well marked by lateral beacons and buoys (leave the pile moorings to port) all the way to the marina.

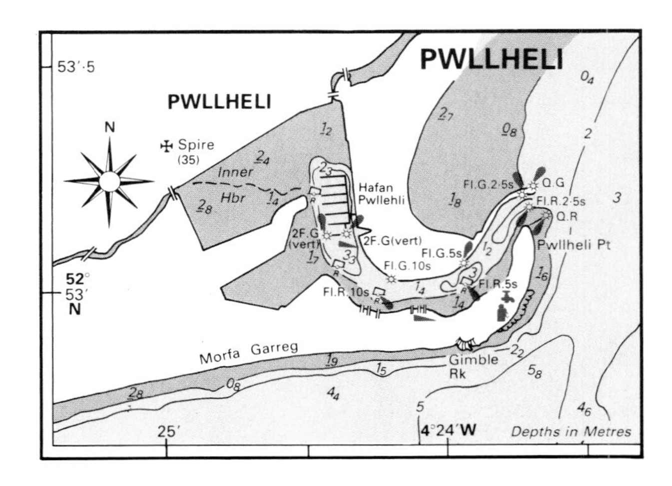

The new layout at Pwllheli Harbour, showing the pile moorings and the new marina complex.

The marina, as I have mentioned, has been built in the old inner harbour. The site is quite large, having originally been developed in the late 18th century for the busy shipbuilding industry and the transportation of farm produce and slate, and affords ample opportunity for further marina development in the future.

The marina currently boasts 120 pontoon berths, is manned 24 hours a day, and maintains a listening watch on VHF Ch 80M. Visitors are very welcome, and are issued with a security card so that they can pass through the bridge gate and gain access to the toilets and showers. There is a night patrol on duty 1900 to 0700, seven days a week (☎ (0758) 701219).

Pwllheli harbour is well equipped, with chandlery, two boatyards, a hoist, and drying-out posts. Petrol and diesel are both available from the harbour side. A berth can be arranged in the harbour by contacting the harbourmaster (☎ (0758) 613131), while Pwllheli Yacht Club, at Gimblet Rock, provides toilet and shower facilities for visitors by sea.

Stores are available from the town, ½ mile distant; it is the district's market town (market day Wednesday), and the centre of communication of Lleyn peninsula. Early closing Thursdays.

Llanbedrog

Charts

Admiralty 1512 (1:12,500), 1971 (1:75,000)
Imray C52 (1:140,700)

Four miles to the SW of Pwllheli lies a favourite anchorage of mine, at Llanbedrog Beach, which provides shelter from winds N–W–S in good holding. Land by tender, near the boathouse (landing on the beach can make you very wet).

On approach, the beach is unmistakable, with its long line of multicoloured bathing huts; these are seen well in advance of the local yachts, which lie to their moorings, sheltering behind the large, rugged headland. Provided that the local craft are given a good berth, as they tend to swing in a wide arc, one can anchor anywhere, with no fees to pay.

Ashore, the inner man can be satisfied at the local hostelry, at the top of the hill (note – the pubs on Lleyn are not allowed to open on Sundays), while petrol and diesel are available ½ mile away, on the road to Pwllheli. If exercise is the order of the day, the 132m scramble to the top of Llanbedrog Crag is worth the effort; a 'tin man' marks the summit, which affords a fine view of Tremadoc Bay.

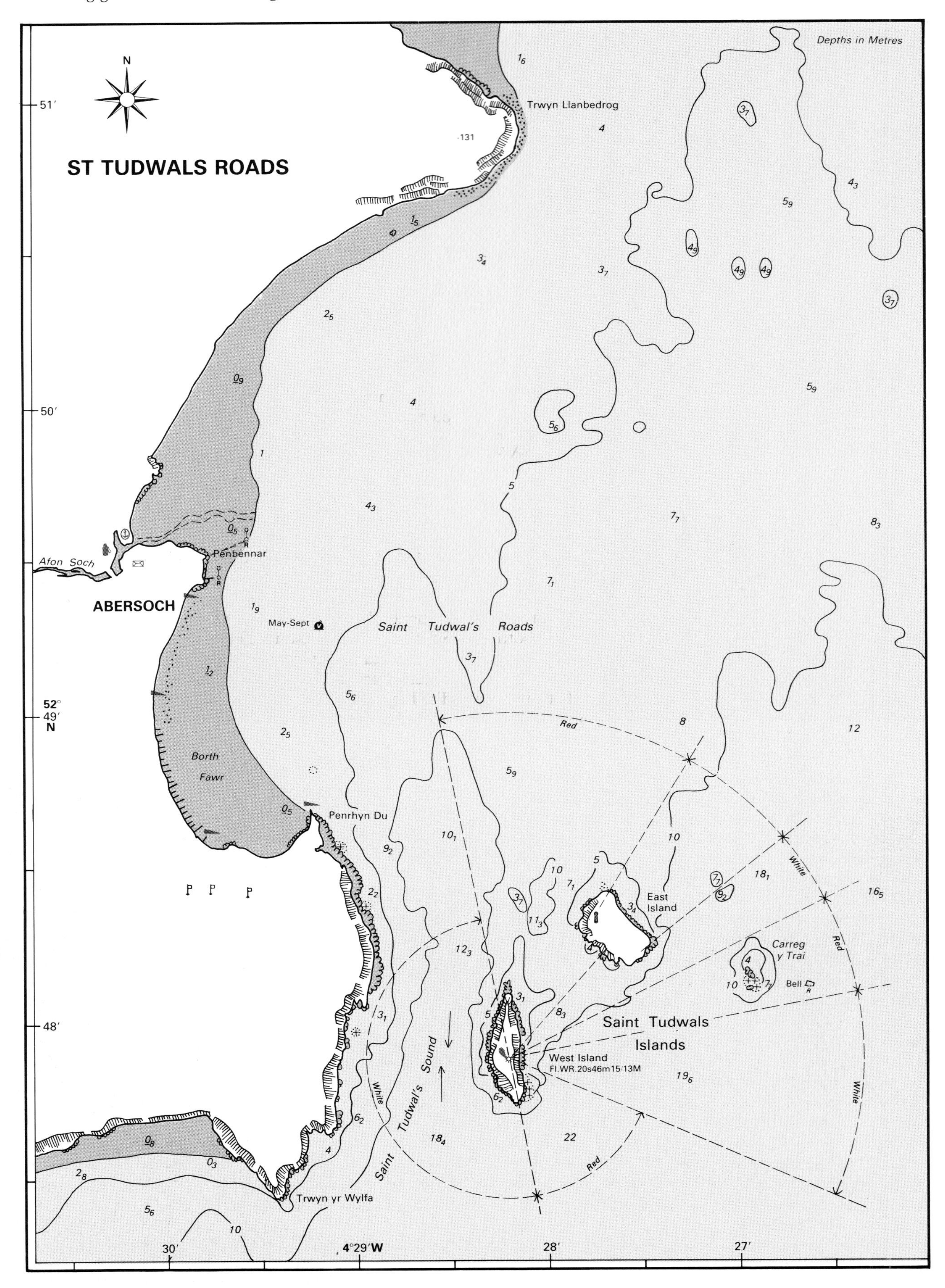

ST TUDWALS ROADS
Depths in Metres
N
Trwyn Llanbedrog
Afon Soch
Penbennar
ABERSOCH
May-Sept
Saint Tudwal's Roads
Borth Fawr
Penrhyn Du
East Island
Carreg y Trai
Bell
Saint Tudwals Islands
West Island
Fl.WR.20s46m15/13M
Saint Tudwal's Sound
Trwyn yr Wylfa
Red
White
51′
50′
52° 49′ N
48′
30′
4°29′W
28′
27′

Caution Strong easterly winds have a fetch right across Tremadoc Bay, some 15 miles, so one's ground tackle should be up to the job.

Abersoch

52°49'·5N 4°30'·2W

Charts

Admiralty 1512 (1:12,500), 1971 (1:75,000)
Imray C52 (1:140,700), C61 (1:270,000)

Tides

HW Dover −0315
Height in metres

MHWS	MHWN	MTL	MLWN	MLWS
4·7	3·6	2·5	1·3	0·6

Lights

St Tudwal's W Island Fl.WR.20s46m15/13M White round tower 349°-W-169°-R-221°-W-243°-R-259°-W-293°-R-349° Obscured by East Island 211°-231°

Radio/telephone

S Caernarfon YC VHF Ch 80M
☎ Harbourmaster (0758) 812684

Abersoch is a very popular yachting centre which lies 2 miles to the south of Llanbedrog, unmistakable with its armada of moored-off craft. Both inner and outer harbours are very small and tatty, however, with no room for visiting yachts.

Since it is a yacht centre, I try to avoid it at all costs; it tends to get overcrowded and noisy during the summer months, though the town itself is pleasant enough, and is more in keeping with the Mediterranean than with the North Wales coast, having sparkling green sea and 3 miles of golden sandy beach on either side of it.

Anchoring in St Tudwal's Roads, but outside the armada, you are sheltered from N–W–S, though several years ago many craft came to grief on Abersoch Beach when they were hit by a severe southeasterly storm. If such a blow is expected, Pwllheli, 6 miles to the NE, is the nearest haven.

Visitors' moorings are available, owned by the South Caernarfonshire Yacht Club, which operates a water taxi service to the club's jetty. The wide beach has access points suitable for launching dinghies, provided that there is no E–S in the wind. Chandlery at Abersoch Land and Sea.

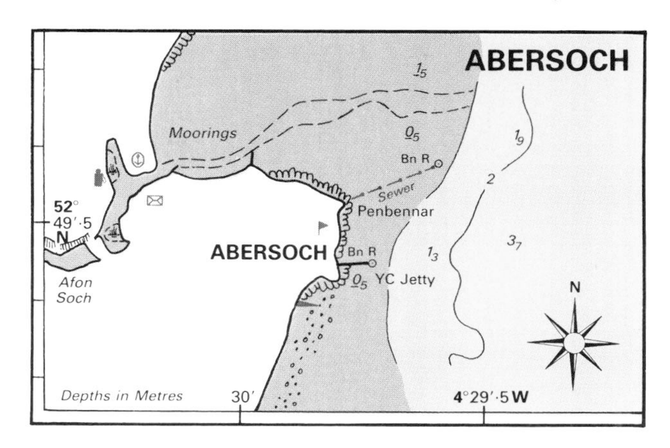

The shallow entrance to Abersoch inlet. *Peter Cumberlidge*

III. North coast of Wales

Abersoch to Conwy via Anglesey

Main coastal lights

Bardsey Island Fl(5)15s39m26M Horn Mo(N)45s White square tower, red bands Obscured by Bardsey Island 198°-250° and in Tremadoc Bay when bearing less than 260°

South Stack Fl.10s60m23M Horn 30s White round tower

Holyhead Fl(3)15s21m14M Siren 20s White square stone tower, black band F.R on chimney 2M SSE

The Skerries Fl(2)10s36m22M+F.R.26m16M Horn(2) 20s White round tower, red band (F.R 231°-vis-254°)

Point Lynas Oc.10s39m20M Horn 45s White castellated tower 109°-vis-315°

Trwyn-Du Fl.5·5s19m15M Bell(1)30s White round castellated tower, black bands 101°-vis-023° F.R on radio mast 2M SW R Lt on radio mast 3·3M W

Submarine exercise areas

A good look out must be kept at all times for submarines when navigating in north Irish Sea areas.

There are two routes open for the passage around the westernmost tip of the Lleyn Peninsula – marked by Bardsey Island – to landfall at Porth Dinllaen:

- Round Bardsey Island
- Through Bardsey Sound

Bardsey Island lies like a humpback whale 2 miles off the headland, marked by the square white lighthouse with two red hoops (Fl(5)15s39m26M) at its southern tip. This remote place has been the retreat of holy men since the 6th century, and is reputed to be the burial place of 22,000 saints – it seems that Wales has a near-monopoly on saints.

Its early Celtic monastery was demolished long ago, and only the remains of the 13th-century tower of St Mary's can now be seen, at the north of the island.

Bardsey Island

52°45'N 4°47'·9W

Charts

Admiralty 1971 (1:75,000)
Imray C52 (1:140,700)

Rounding Bardsey Island

As may be deduced from its position, heavy overfalls and tide-rips can be encountered almost everywhere around this area, and these are further propagated by the off-lying Devil's Ridge and Bastram Shoal. These should be given a good offing and left to the north, while leaving the Devil's Tail to the south. Maintain a respectable distance until you have completely rounded Bardsey. A course can then be laid up the coast, keeping a 2-mile offing in fresh conditions, to Porth Dinllaen. The overall distance is approximately 40 miles.

Through Bardsey Sound

Bardsey Sound has an evil reputation, earned by its particularly vicious tide-rip, which has caused many a ship to come to grief in past centuries. Horror stories aside, however, the route through the sound is viable when conditions of tide and wind are at their best (it saves 10 miles on the passage to Porth Dinllaen), though the more conditions degenerate from this ideal, the worse the passage becomes – a Force 8 against a spring tide makes the water in the sound look like hell itself! Departure from Abersoch should ideally be timed so that arrival at Bardsey Sound is at 4 hours before local HW, when there is comparative slack in the sound, and the beginnings of the northbound flood may be taken, once through the sound, along the coast to Porth Dinllaen.

Leaving Abersoch, a course may be laid along the coast, during fine weather, between St Tudwal's Islands and the mainland. (In a rising wind, a course outside the R can bell buoy of Carreg-Y-Trai (dries 3·3m), ½ mile to the east of St Tudwal's, where seals can often be seen basking on the rocks, is wise). The course then leads around Trwyn Cilan, giving ½ mile offing because of the tide-rip – if things seem too hectic here, the course around Bardsey should be taken. Heading from north to south, either slack water period (0·5 hours before

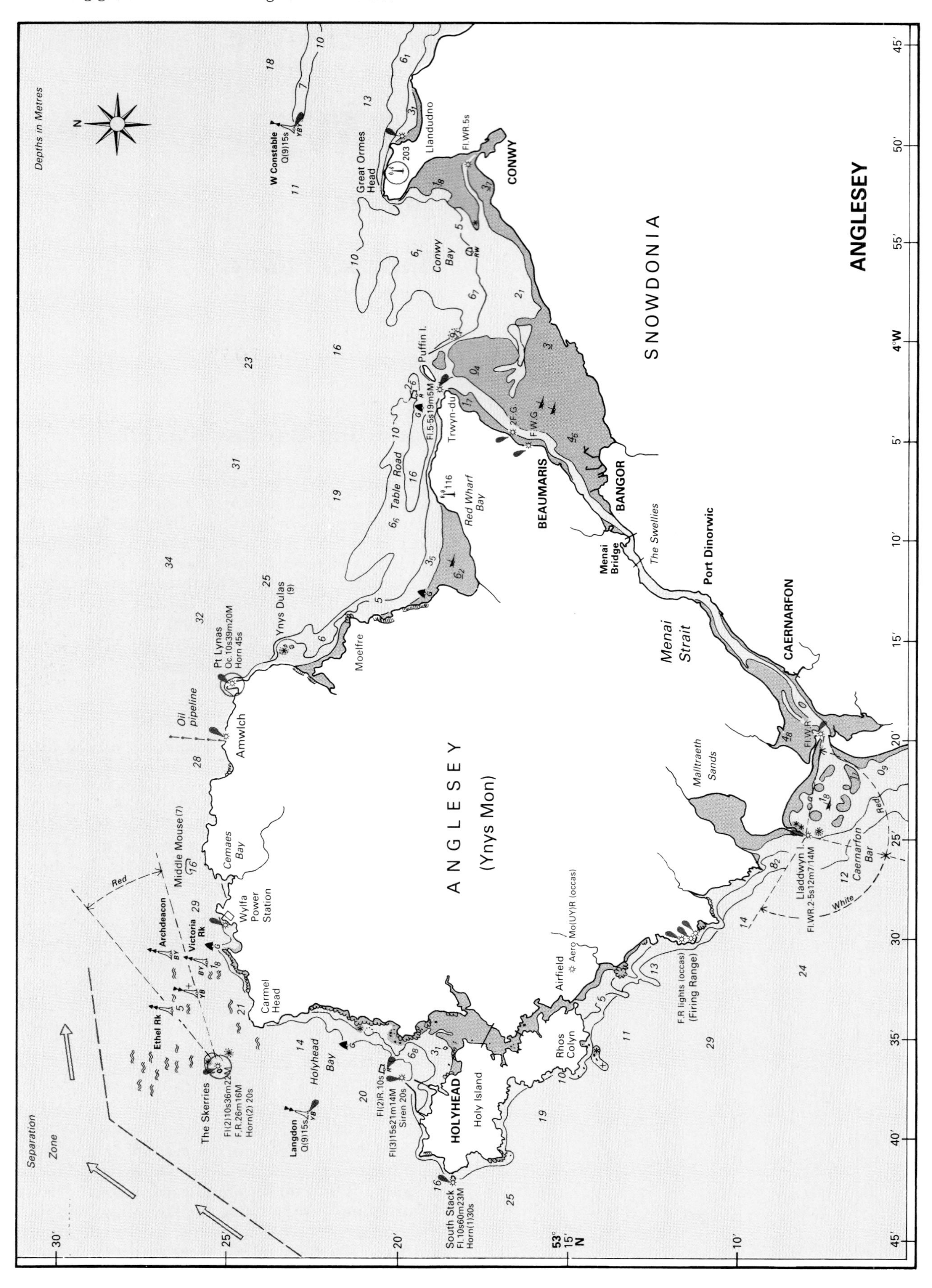

Depths in Metres
ANGLESEY
(Ynys Mon)
SNOWDONIA
ANGLESEY
Great Ormes Head
Llandudno
CONWY
Conwy Bay
Puffin I.
Trwyn-du
Red Wharf Bay
Table Road
BEAUMARIS
BANGOR
Menai Bridge
The Swellies
Port Dinorwic
CAERNARFON
Menai Strait
Malltraeth Sands
Llanddwyn I.
Caernarfon Bar
Moelfre
Ynys Dulas
Pt Lynas
Oc.10s39m20M
Horn 45s
Oil pipeline
Amlwch
Middle Mouse
Cemaes Bay
Wylfa Power Station
Archdeacon
Victoria Rk
Ethel Rk
Carmel Head
The Skerries
Fl(2)10s36m22M
F.R.26m16M
Horn(2) 20s
Holyhead Bay
Langdon
Q(9)15s
HOLYHEAD
Holy Island
South Stack
Fl.10s60m23M
Horn(1)30s
Rhos Colyn
Airfield
Aero Mo(U)Y R (occas)
F.R lights (occas)
(Firing Range)
W Constable
Q(9)15s
Separation Zone
Red
White

either HW or LW Holyhead) can be used, depending upon final choice of landfall.

Rounding Trwyn Cilan, the wide-stretching bay of Hell's Mouth (Porth Neigwl) opens to the north, where heavy surf can usually be heard pounding. Wide open to SW gales, it was a death-trap in the days of square riggers, which, once inside, were unable to beat out. A course of due west can now be set, and this can be held until well into Bardsey Sound, leading just to the north of the turbulent waters of Devil's Ridge. Six miles on, the rocky islets of Ynys Gwylan-Bach and Ynys Gwylan-Fawr (28m), marking the eastern edge of Aberdaron Bay, are left to starboard. The pretty fishing village of Aberdaron then opens up, with whitewashed cottages nestling centrally on its sand and shingle beach, where one can find good holding, and shelter from the arc W–N–NE.

The village is small, and usually packed with tourists during the summer months. Good food supplies are available, and it is a convenient place to await slack water at Bardsey Sound – provided that there is no south in the wind. The old 12th-century church makes an interesting visit. It has suffered from the ravages of the sea, losing some of its churchyard in the process. The remainder is now secured by a sea wall.

Continuing due west, the course sets straight for Maen Bugail, a drying rock (4·1m) 3 cables to the north of Bardsey, and leaves Carreg Ddu to starboard. From midway between Bardsey and the mainland, a northwesterly course then leads straight through the sound.

Rounding Braich y Pwll, the most westerly point of the mainland, and giving it a wide berth because of a number of rocks and the tide-rip, the course sets in a northeasterly direction along the mountainous northern coast of Lleyn, over the underwater rock formation of the Tripods, where overfalls may be encountered. There is little in the way of shelter to be found until landfall at Porth Dinllaen.

Porth Dinllaen

52°56'·6N 4°33'·6W

Charts

Admiralty 1512 (1:18,000)
Imray C52 (1:140,700)

Tides

HW Dover −0240

Height in metres

MHWS	MHWN	MTL	MLWN	MLWS
4·6	3·4	2·6	1·7	0·6

Radio/telephone

☎ Harbourmaster (0758) 720295

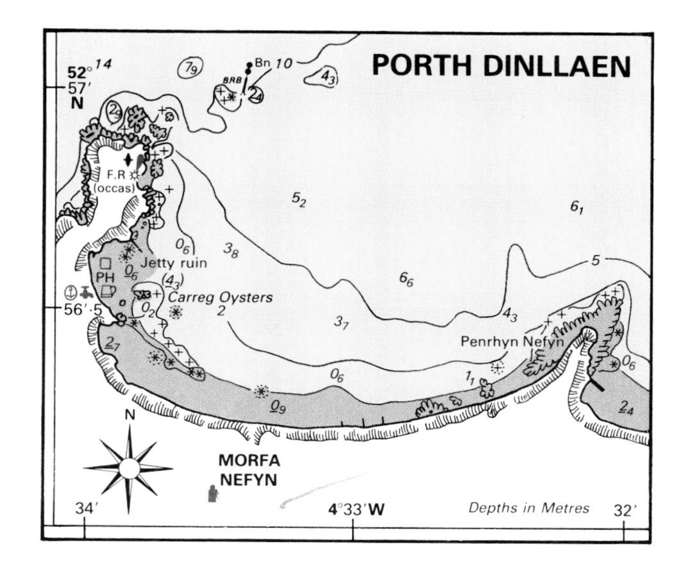

Approaching from the southwest, Carreg Y Chad, a rock lying 7 cables to the west of Porth Dinllaen Point, must be left well to starboard, as must the off-lying rocks marked by a beacon 2 cables to ENE of the point. From here, the sheltered crescent bay of Porth Dinllaen opens up – a natural harbour, protected from the west by the rocky headland. It shelters the tiny hamlet by the water, which boasts an inn, on the beach, and a row of cottages. Anchor, in good holding, a cable or so to the south of the Lifeboat House, in 2–3m, just outside the permanent moorings; keep well to the north of the rocks which guard the southern edge of the bay. If supplies are needed, a 2-mile walk up the coast to Morfa Nefyn (early closing Wednesdays) will provide most food supplies, petrol and diesel.

From Porth Dinllaen, two routes are open as we continue north:

- Via the Menai Strait
- Rounding Anglesey.

The tiny hamlet of Porth Dinllaen. An excellent natural harbour, providing shelter from the prevailing westerlies.

Porth Dinllaen to Conwy via Menai Strait

Charts

Admiralty 1464 (1:25,000) Menai Strait
Imray C52 (1:140,799)

Tides

Beaumaris HW Dover −0025
Caernarfon HW Dover −0105

Menai Strait tidal information

Based on timings at Holyhead (standard port)

The tide is approximately 1 hour later, with a spring range of 2·5m or more, at the NE entrance of the strait than at the SW end.
The basic patterns of the streams are as follows:

HW −0040 to HW +0420. Stream runs SW between Garth Point (Bangor) and Abermenai Point (SW end of strait).

HW +0420 to HW +0545. Stream runs outwards from the Swellies, NE towards Garth Point, and SW towards Abermenai Point.

HW +0545 to HW −0040. Stream runs NE between Abermenai Point and Garth Point.

These timings can differ according to meteorological conditions.

A general spring rate of 3 knots is to be expected, though this increases substantially at constrictions such as the Swellies (up to 8 knots) and at Abermenai Point (6 knots).

Lights

Trwyn-Du Fl.5·5s19m15M Bell(1)30s White round castellated tower, black bands 101°-vis-023° F.R on radio mast 2M SW R Lt on radio mast 3·3M W

Beaumaris pier F.WG.5m6M Mast 212°-G-286°-W-014°-G-071°

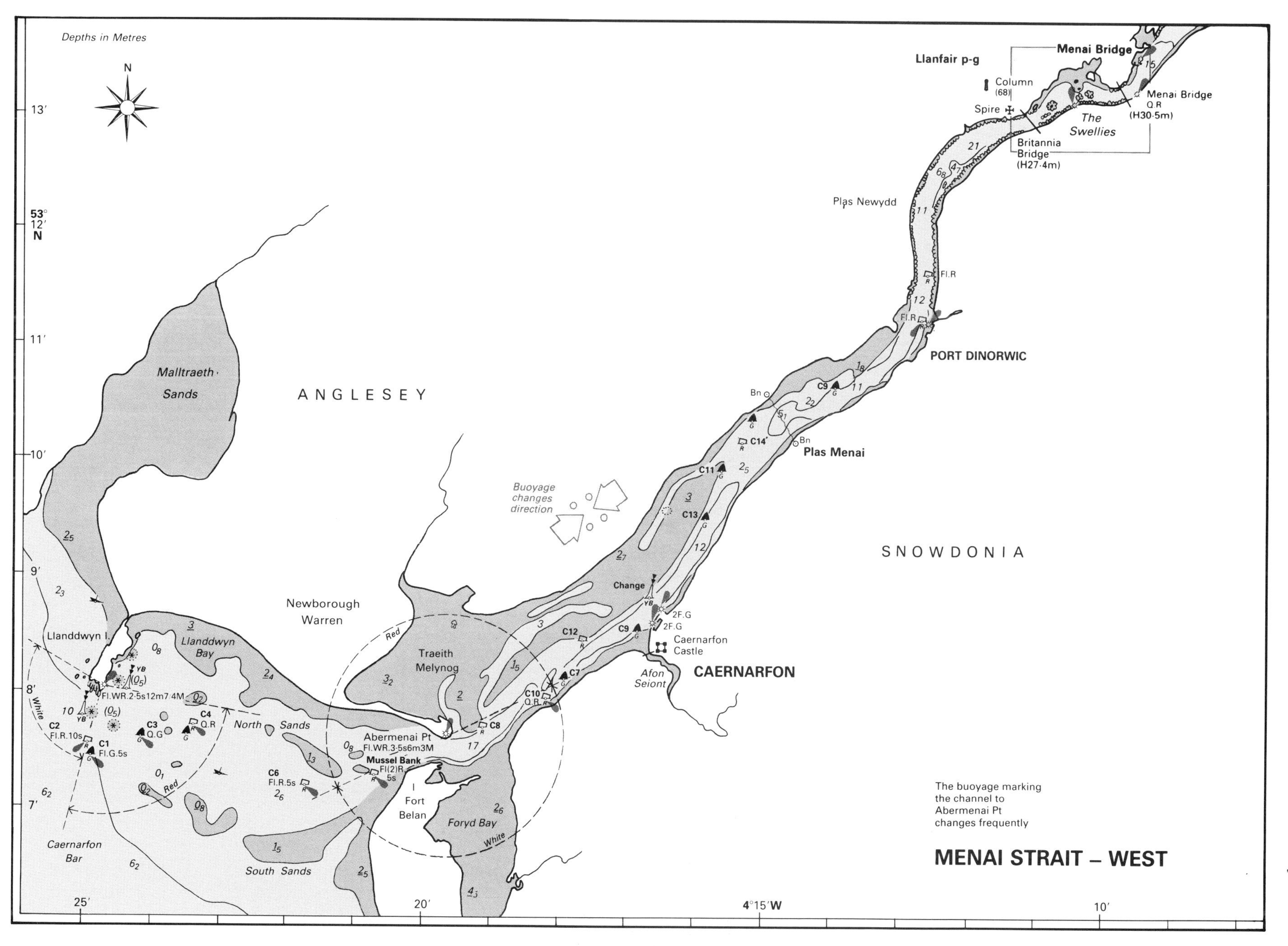
MENAI STRAIT – WEST
The buoyage marking the channel to Abermenai Pt changes frequently
Depths in Metres
N
ANGLESEY
SNOWDONIA
CAERNARFON
Caernarfon Castle
Afon Seiont
PORT DINORWIC
Plas Menai
Plas Newydd
Llanfair p-g
Menai Bridge
Menai Bridge Q.R (H30·5m)
The Swellies
Britannia Bridge (H27·4m)
Column (68)
Spire
Buoyage changes direction
Change
2F.G
Traeith Melynog
Abermenai Pt Fl.WR.3·5s6m3M
Mussel Bank Fl(2)R 5s
Fort Belan
Foryd Bay
Newborough Warren
North Sands
South Sands
Llanddwyn Bay
Llanddwyn I.
Malltraeth Sands
Caernarfon Bar
C6 Fl.R.5s
C4 Q.R
C3 Q.G
C2 Fl.R.10s
C1 Fl.G.5s
C8
C10 Q.R
C7
C12
C9
C11
C13
C14
Fl.WR.2·5s12m7·4M
Fl.R
Bn
Red
White
25'
20'
4°15'W
10'
13'
53° 12' N
11'
10'
9'
8'
7'

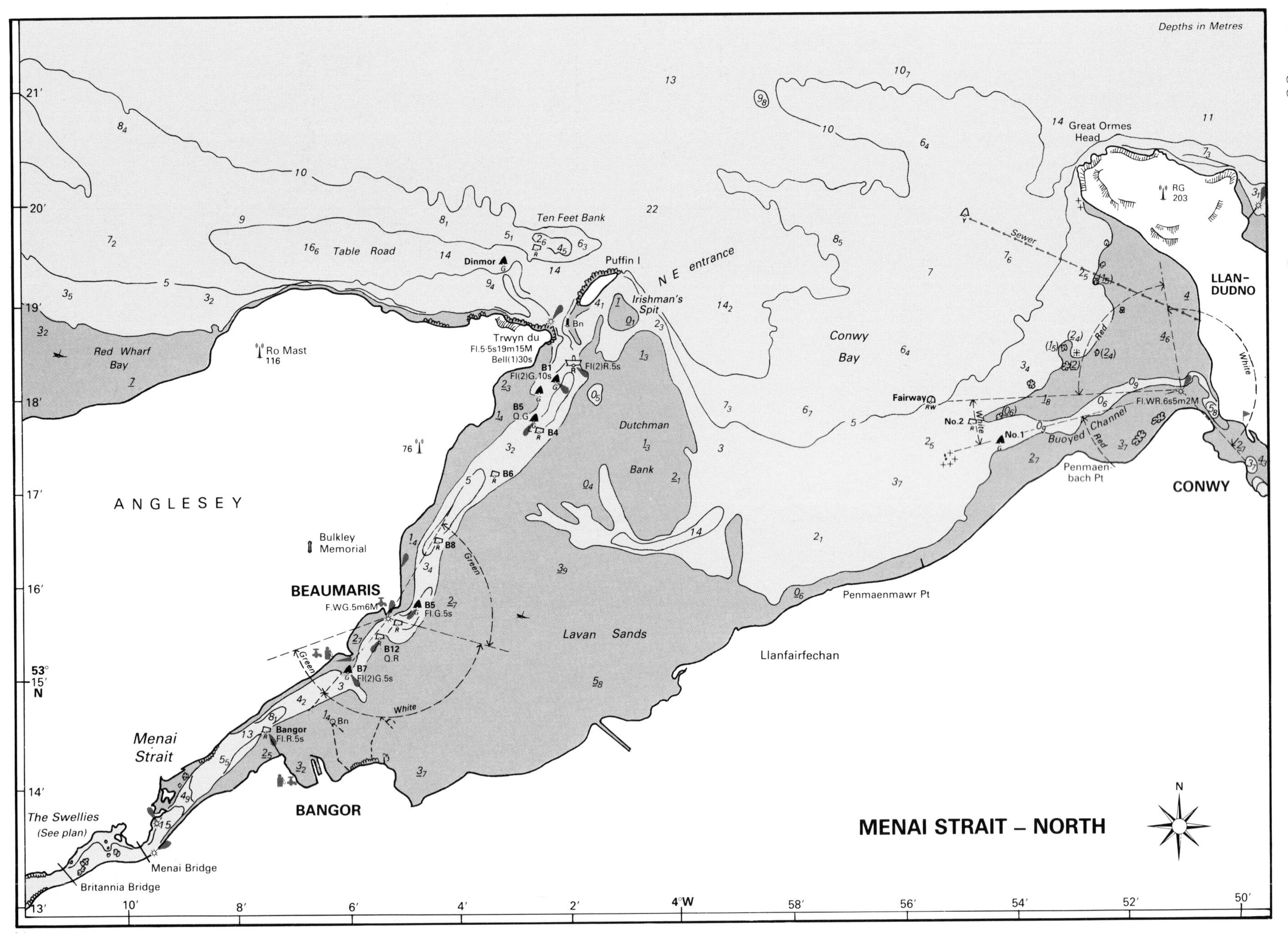
Depths in Metres
Great Ormes Head
LLAN-DUDNO
CONWY
Penmaen-bach Pt
Buoyed Channel
Fl.WR.6s5m2M
Fairway
No.1
No.2
Sewer
Conwy Bay
Penmaenmawr Pt
Llanfairfechan
Puffin I
Irishman's Spit
N E entrance
Dutchman Bank
Lavan Sands
Ten Feet Bank
Table Road
Dinmor
Trwyn du
Fl.5·5s19m15M
Bell(1)30s
Fl(2)G.10s
Fl(2)R.5s
Red Wharf Bay
Ro Mast
116
ANGLESEY
Bulkley Memorial
BEAUMARIS
F.WG.5m6M
Fl.G.5s
Q.R
Fl(2)G.5s
Bangor
Fl.R.5s
BANGOR
Menai Strait
The Swellies
(See plan)
Menai Bridge
Britannia Bridge
MENAI STRAIT – NORTH

Saint George's pier Fl.G.10s Mast
E side of channel Q.R.4m Red metal mast 064°-vis-222°
Price's Point Fl.WR.2s5m3M White beacon 059°-R-239°-W-259°
Britannia Tubular bridge S channel Ldg Lts 231° E side *Front* F Metal framework tower
W side *Rear* 45m from front F Metal framework tower
Centre Iso.5s27m3M Centre of span On either side of bridge
S end F.R.21.3M On either side of bridge
N side F.G.21m3M On either side of bridge
Llanddwyn Island Fl.WR.2·5s12m7/4M White tower 280°-R-015°-W-120°
Albermenai Pt Fl.WR.3·5s6m3M 065°-R-245°-W-065° F.R lights on radio mast 6·8M SSE

Buoys

Llanddwyn S cardinal
C1 green Fl.G.5s, C2 red can Fl.R.10s, C3 green can Q.G, C4 red can Q.R, C5 green conical, C6 red can Fl.R.5s, Mussel Bank red can Fl(2)R.5s, C7 green conical unlit G, C8 red can unlit R, C10 red can Q.R

SW entry into the Menai Strait can be a very hazardous task in onshore winds of Force 5 or over, particularly if there is a strong swell running. It is some 13 miles west from Porth Dinllaen; departure from the latter should be calculated so that you arrive at the Menai Strait between 3 hours flood and HW, when the NE-bound flood sets to Port Dinorwic. Leaving Porth Dinllaen, a course may be laid 025° onto Llanddwyn Island (Fl.WR.2·5s12m 7/4M), 13 miles distant. Keep in the white sector when closing, until the lit lateral buoys are picked up before reaching Llanddwyn S cardinal buoy.

Note The North Sands channel, shown in many publications, now dries. The new channel, opened up by a storm three years ago, is now used in preference to it, and the buoys have been moved accordingly. Contact Caernarfon harbourmaster for latest details, as the channel continues to shift.

The channel across the bar is well buoyed; leave green to starboard and red to port. Leave Mussel Bank (dries 2m) to port before entering the Menai Straits by leaving Abermenai Point to port, and the 18th-century Belan Fort (built to protect the western approaches of the strait from the French) to starboard. Once inside, the channel runs on the mainland side until the E cardinal buoy, marking the channel into Caernarfon, is seen ahead.

Caernarfon

53°08'·5N 4°16'·7W

Charts

Admiralty 1464 (1:25,000)
Imray C52 (1:140,700)

Tides

Beaumaris HW Dover −0025
Caernarfon HW Dover −0105
Height in metres

MHWS	MHWN	MTL	MLWN	MLWS
5·3	4·1	2·9	1·9	0·6

Radio/telephone

VHF Ch 16, 12, 14 (daytime only)
☎ Harbourmaster (0286) 672118

Lights

S pier head 2F.G(vert)5m2M Stone column
Pile pier head 2F.G(vert)5m2M White tower, black stripes
Inner harbour E side 2F.R(vert) Ruined pier
W side 2F.R(vert) Ruined pier

Entry into Caernarfon Harbour, which dries to mud, is gained by signalling for the swing bridge to be opened (one long and three short blasts), after which the harbourmaster (☎ (0286) 672118) must be contacted for allocation of a temporary berth in

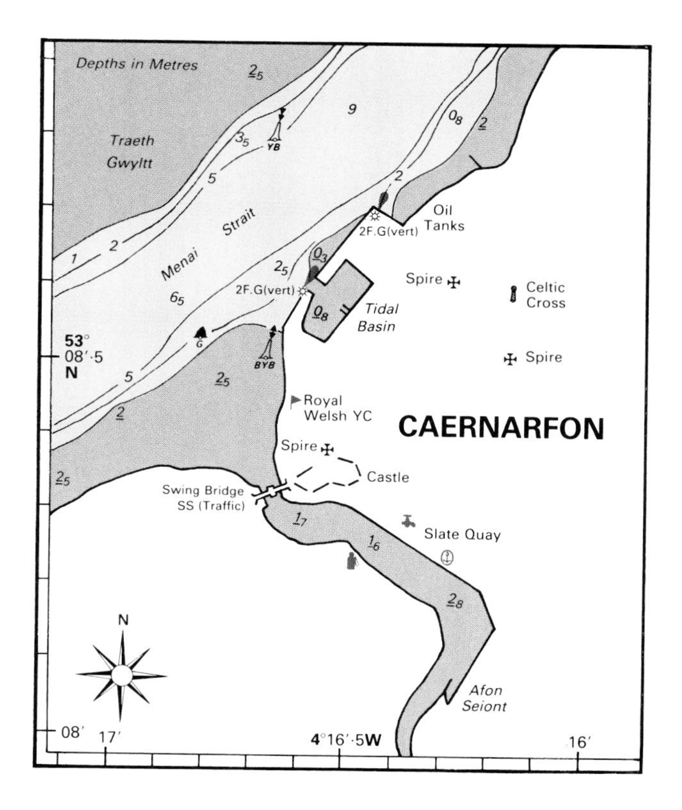

Approaching Caernarfon – showing the swing bridge, centre.

The magnificent Caernarfon Castle, overlooking the harbour.

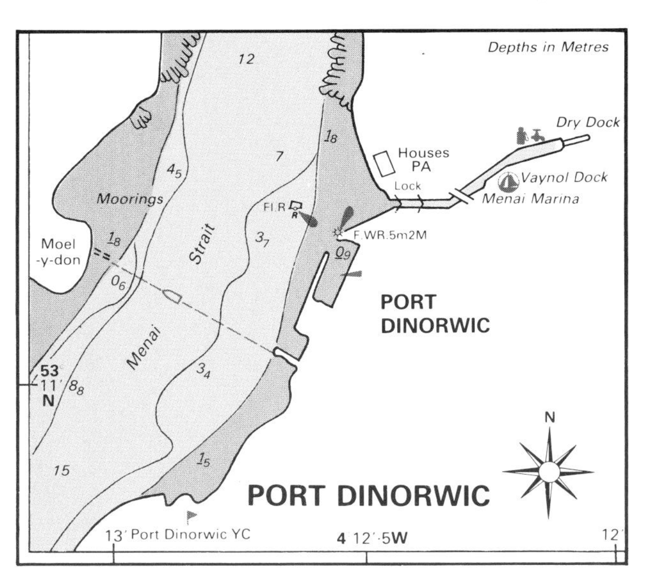

this ancient port. Caernarfon was an established port long before Edward I built the magnificent 14th-century castle here, which, incidentally, is one of the most beautiful I've seen, even though it has had a very functional past.

Full supplies are available from the town, which is very clean and smart, having grown outside the confines of the castle wall; there is a comprehensive bus service. Saturday is market day; early closing Thursdays.

Port Dinorwic

53°11'·2N 4°12'·6W

Charts

Admiralty 1464 (1:25,000)
Imray C52 (1:140,700)

Tides

Beaumaris HW Dover −0025
Caernarfon HW Dover −0105

Height in metres

MHWS	MHWN	MTL	MLWN	MLWS
5·7	4·5	3·9	2·0	0·8

Radio/telephone

Port Dinorwic Marina VHF Ch 80M (office hours)
☎ Harbourmaster (0248) 670441
Plas Menai VHF Ch 80, 37
☎ (0248) 670964

Continuing past Caernarfon E cardinal, the S cardinal marking the head of navigation is left to port, from where the lateral buoyage changes and all G conical buoys are left to port. The Plas Menai (Welsh National Sailing School Centre) is passed on the mainland side before the town of Port Dinorwic opens to starboard. It is a pretty sight, with its many moored-off craft, near which one can anchor in good holding in 4m, always remembering to buoy the anchor, as the bottom of the whole of the Menai Strait is very foul. Full supplies are available from the town, and there is a frequent bus service to Bangor and Caernarfon. For a longer stay, Port Dinorwic Marina, where there are full facilities, can be entered by a lock HW ±2. VHF Ch 80.

Leaving Port Dinorwic, the course leaves two R can light buoys to starboard, and continues mid-channel to the Britannia Bridge. However, between Britannia Bridge and the Menai Bridge, each with over 27m clearance, lies an area of jagged rocks known as the Swellies – the greatest danger to navigation in the Menai Strait.

The Swellies

Charts

Admiralty 1464 (1:10,000)
Imray C52 (1:140,700)

Lights

Britannia tubular bridge S channel
Ldg Lts 231° E side *Front* F Metal framework tower
W side *Rear* 45m from front F Metal framework tower
Centre Iso.W.5s27m3M Centre span On either side
S end F.R.21m3M On either side
N side F.G.21.3M On either side

The tide runs very swiftly here, running NE on the flood and SW on the ebb at up to 6 knots, except for a short period of slack 2 hours before HW, and 2 hours before LW Liverpool.

The exact timing of slack water is important, and as the tide tables tend to be inaccurate, the best guide is to watch local craft swinging on their moorings.

View of the Menai Strait, from Britannia Bridge. The Swellies are still covered, though the tide race can easily be seen.

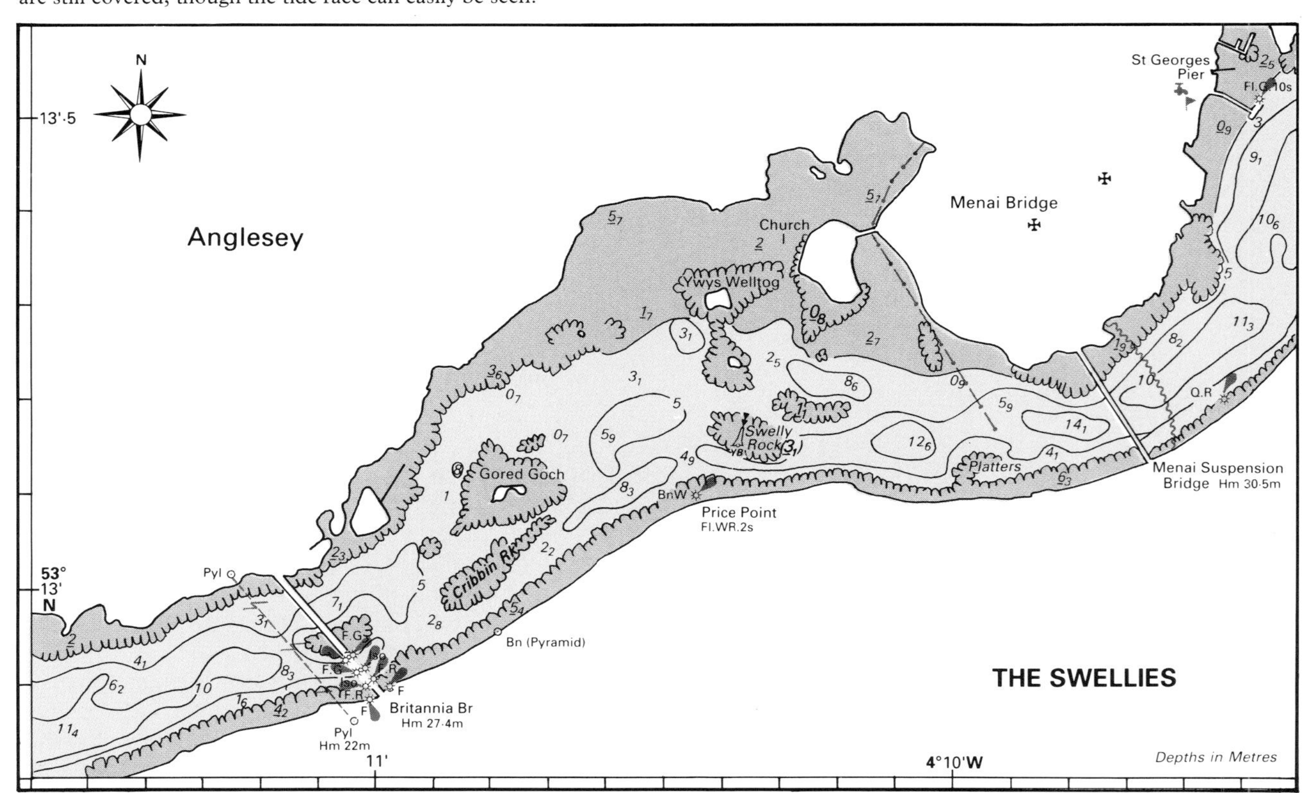

Before passing under the power lines (22m clearance) which span the strait preceding Britannia Bridge, the course must be laid to lead under the middle of the south span of Britannia Bridge, giving an adequate berth to Britannia Rock, lying mid-stream. A course is then steered onto a beacon 2 cables distant on the south shore, until the fixed white lights at the base of the bridge's south tower are in transit at 051°/231°. Keeping the lights in transit astern, the course then leads us between Swelley Rock S cardinal, marking Swelley Rock (dries 3·1m), and Price's Point, until Price's Point beacon (Fl.WR.2s5m3M) lies abeam. A course of due east should then be maintained for a cable or so, until Price's Point beacon is in transit with the centre tower of Britannia Bridge astern. Then steer onto the north tower of Menai Suspension Bridge until Swelley S cardinal bears due west, when a course may be laid (leading well clear of the Platters, to starboard) to pass through the middle of Menai Bridge, with 30m clearance. One of Telford's masterpieces, the bridge was started in 1819 and completed some 7 years later; it was widened and reinforced in 1939–41 so that it could cope with the vast amount of traffic which now uses it.

Heading north to south

From midstream, pass under the centre of Menai Suspension Bridge and then steer onto Swelley Rock S cardinal, keeping it just open on the port bow, until Price's Point beacon is in transit with the centre of Britannia Bridge. Then steer between Price's Point and Swelley S cardinal, heading towards the house on Gored Goch, until Price's Point is astern. You can then steer for the lights on the bridge's south tower until the beacon on the west shore is abeam, when the course is altered to pass under the southern span of Britannia Bridge.

Special note

At HW slack, which lasts approximately 20 minutes, there is 3m over the Platters, and therefore these can be ignored by the majority of craft.

Shoal-draught craft can even attempt the passage at slack LW, if adventurous.

Bangor

53°14'N 4°07'W

Charts

Admiralty 1464 (1:25,000)
Imray C52 (1:140,700)

Tides

Beaumaris HW Dover −0025
Caernarfon HW Dover −0105

Height in metres

MHWS	MHWN	MTL	MLWN	MLWS
3·7	6·1	3·9	2·5	0·8

Radio/telephone

Dickie's VHF Ch 16, 9, M
☎ Harbourmaster (0248) 722920

Once through the bridge, the channel follows the Anglesey side, keeping 1½ cables offshore, and passing Bangor, on the mainland, where one can anchor between the pier and Bangor Flats (go near the moorings for further shelter). Alternatively, provided that it is between 1½ hours either side of HW, one can tie up to the quay at Dickie's Boatyard, drying to mud, where chandlery, diesel and water are available. Early closing Wednesdays.

Beaumaris

53°15'·8N 4°05'·5W

Charts

Admiralty 1464 (1:25,000)
Imray C52 (1:140,700)

Tides

Beaumaris HW Dover −0025
Caernarfon HW Dover −0105

Height in metres

MHWS	MHWN	MTL	MLWN	MLWS
3·7	6·1	3·9	2·5	0·8

Lights

Beaumaris pier F.WG.5m6M Mast 212°-G-286°-W-041°-G-071°

Radio/telephone

☎ Harbourmaster (0248) 750057

At Gallows Point, some 3 miles distant from Menai Bridge, the channel becomes buoyed again. Good anchoring can be had between Gallows Point and Beaumaris, in sand and mud, near the many moored craft, or one can go a little further in and take the ground, if desired. Full supplies are available at Beaumaris (early closing Wednesdays), and there are boatyard facilities at Gallows Point, home of the Venturers Yacht Club, where advice may be sought regarding a temporary mooring.

Beaumaris (its name is thought to have been derived from 'beautiful marsh') is the location of Edward I's best castle, which, though never completed, is very picturesque and has a water-filled moat. It is also the home of the Blue Peter II inshore lifeboat, which many of my generation will have helped to pay for by saving sweet wrappers or some such thing.

Three miles to the north of Beaumaris is Penmon, the most easterly point of Anglesey, which provides a pleasant stroll in fine weather, passing St Seriol's 12th-century priory. From the headland, marked by a black and white hooped lighthouse, the weathered limestone crags of Puffin Island (Priestholm) open up across the channel, with the sweeping expanse of

Above Bangor Pier – showing Dickie's Boatyard centre right.

Below Beaumaris – showing Gallows Point bottom left.

Conwy Bay in the background. The island, as its old name suggests, was once the home of a monastic settlement, first built by St Seriol in the 6th century, though the ruined church dates from the 12th century. The only other building is a disused 19th-century semaphore station, by which Liverpool used to be informed of the arrival of a ship off Holyhead. Its main inhabitants these days are rats, who have put paid to the puffins and the other seabirds.

Conwy

53°18'N 3°50'W

Charts

Admiralty 1977 (1:75,000)
Imray C52 (1:140,700)

Tides

HW Dover −0015

Height in metres

MHWS	MHWN	MTL	MLWN	MLWS
7·6	5·9	4·1	2·3	0·7

Lights

Conwy river entrance S side Fl.WR.5s5m2M Black metal column 076°-W-088°-R-171°-W-319°-R-076°
Trwyn-Du Fl.5·5s19m15M Bell(1)30s White round castellated tower, black bands 101°-vis-023° F.R on radio mast 2M SW and R Lt on radio mast 3·3M W

The pontoon at Conwy Harbour.

Radio/telephone

VHF Ch 16, 14 (0900–1700. Mon–Fri only in winter).
☎ Harbourmaster (0492) 596253

The channel from Beaumaris is well buoyed until exit is made from the Strait by leaving Perch rock beacon, belonging to Puffin Island, to starboard, and the black and white lighthouse, Trwyn-Du, at

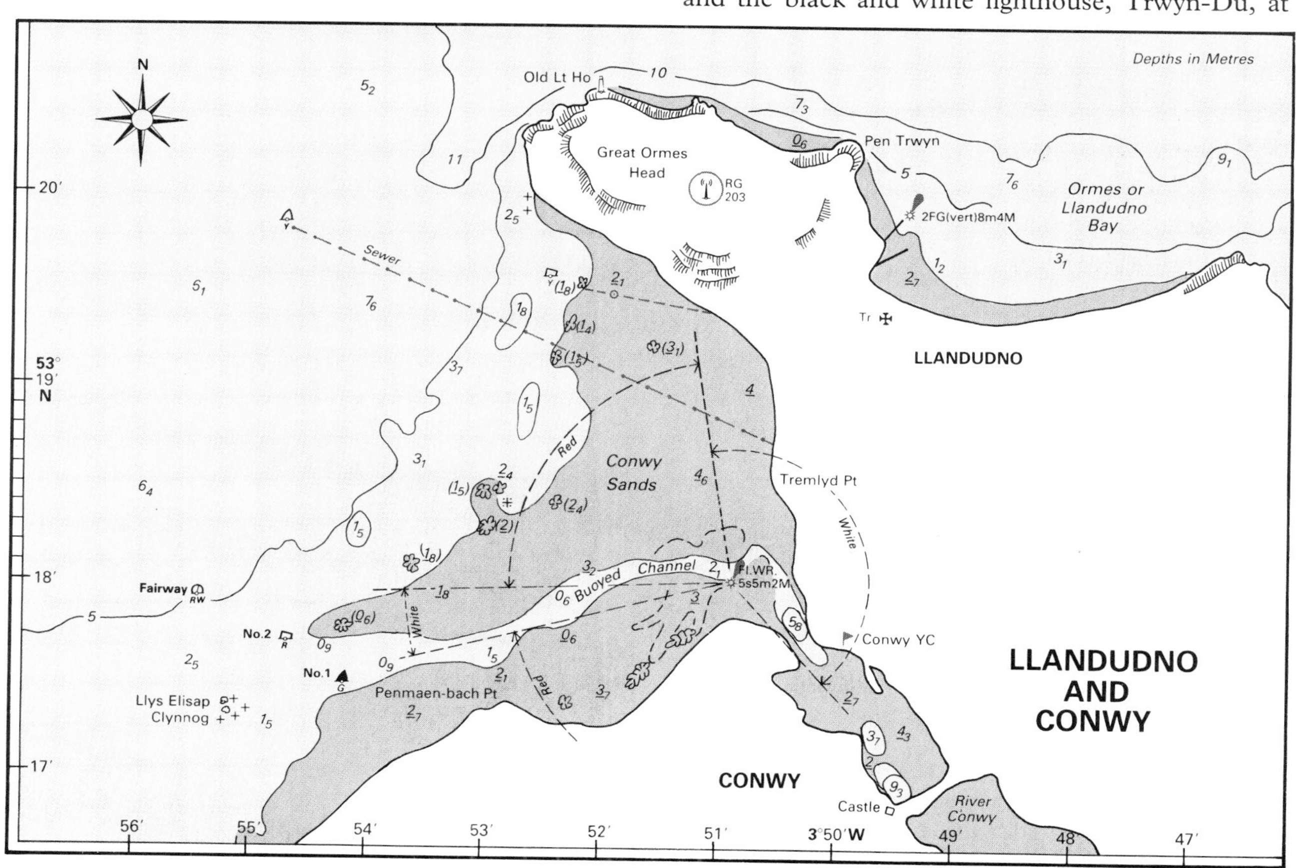

Yachts laid up for the winter at Conwy.

The black and white hooped lighthouse of Trwyn-Du, with Puffin Island in the background.

Penmon (Fl.5·5s19m15M Bell(1)30s) to port. (This may seem strange at first, considering that Conwy lies to the east, but the direct route across the shifting sands of Dutchman Bank (Penmaen Swatch) is best only attempted between 2 hours either side of HW).

Rounding Puffin Island, keeping a couple of cables offing, a course can be laid 110° onto Conwy Fairway RWVS buoy. The five-metre contour is well placed for use in reduced visibility, as it lies offshore of all major navigational hazards. From the buoy, entry can be attempted between −3 hours HW and +2 hours HW by setting a course of 114° onto No. 2 R can buoy, 9 cables distant. The channel is then marked by No. 1 G conical, Nos 4, 6 and 8 R can, and No. 3 G conical lateral buoys, which are unlit, though closely spaced, at 3–4 cable intervals. They lead towards Conwy light beacon (perch), Fl.WR.5s5m2M, which should be left 30m to starboard before heading off to the harbour entrance (heading approximately 139°). From the harbour entrance, the channel is buoyed up to Bodlondeb Point, from where deep water is to be found at all states of tide by passing between the harbour pontoons and the mooring trots.

A temporary vacant berth can be taken before contacting the harbourmaster, Mr Tony Mead (☎ (0492) 596253, VHF Ch 16, 6, 8, 12, 14, 71 and 80), whose office is situated on the town quay; he will allocate a more permanent berth.

Conwy Marina, just inside the harbour entrance, is now operational, and can be contacted 24 hours a day on VHF Ch 80, call sign *Camper Base*.

Currently there are 250 secure pontoon berths, with full services, and there are plans for a chandlery, a hoist, shops and a public house at a later date. Visitors should report to the marina office on arrival for allocation of a berth. Marine diesel and petrol are available 0700–2359. Toilets, showers and the launderette are temporarily based in purpose-built portacabins while work advances. (☎ 0492 593000).

Conwy is a small, very attractive town, completely enclosed by the great walls of the castle built in 1283 by, again, King Edward I. The main roads lead through the very narrow castle gates, which, until the recent opening of the A55 tunnel, led to very congested scenes in midsummer. The small, busy fishing quay is the site of the smallest house in Britain. Full stores are available from the town. Early closing Wednesdays.

Porth Dinllaen to Conwy, rounding Anglesey

Lights

Bardsey Island Fl(5)15s39m26M Horn Mo(N)45s White square tower, red bands Obscured by Bardsey Island 198°-250° and in Tremadoc Bay when bearing less than 260°

Llanddwyn Island S end Fl.WR.2·5s12m7/4M White tower 280°-R-015°-W-120°

South Stack Fl.10s60m23M Horn 30s White round tower

The Skerries Fl(2)10s.36m22M/F.R.26m16M Horn(2) 20s White round tower, red band (F.R 231°-vis-254°)

Point Lynas Oc.10s39m20M Horn 45s RC White castellated tower 109°-vis-315°

Trwyn-Du Fl.5·5s19m15M Bell(1)30s White round castellated tower, black bands 101°-vis-023° F.R on radio mast 2M SW and R Lt on radio mast 3·3M W

The tide races around the westernmost point of Anglesey at up to 6 knots at springs. It creates fierce tide-rips, extending 1½ miles NW of South Stack and ½ mile W of North Stack on the NNE stream,

Above Liverpool, Albert Dock.
Below Liverpool Marina.

Above Roa Island.
Below Castletown Bay looking SW towards Castletown harbour entrance. There is an anchorage SE of the pierheads, sheltered from between NW through N to E. *Peter Cumberlidge*

Above opposite Looking NE across Port St Mary, on the Isle of Man with Alfred Pier on the right and the inner harbour 2 cables to the NW. Anchor 50–100m NW of Alfred Pier, just inside a line taken between the two pierhead lighthouses. *Peter Cumberlidge*

Middle opposite Peel Bay, on the W coast of the Isle of Man. The harbour dries and is rather full of fishing boats, but the anchorage outside is sheltered from SW through S to E. *Peter Cumberlidge*

Below opposite Castletown Bay, Isle of Man looking SW towards Castletown harbour entrance. There is an anchorage SE of the pierheads, sheltered from between NW through N to E. *Peter Cumberlidge*

and ½ mile W of South Stack on the SSW stream. In severe conditions, the tide-rip extends over 6 miles to Holyhead deep, and seas in excess of 50ft have been reported.

Leaving Porth Dinllaen at around LW, and allowing an average speed of 4 knots for the 30-mile voyage, a course of 340° gives a good offing to South Stack and leaves to starboard the overfalls of Carrag Hen. Holyhead chimney (red lights), standing 146m high, and South Stack light (Fl.10s60m 28M) are excellent landmarks. This course is maintained until South Stack, a lighthouse with a tenuous link with the mainland, bears due east, when a course may be laid to round Holy Island, giving a wide berth to the rough water off North Stack. Alternatively (only during favourable conditions, of course), arrival at South Stack can be calculated to coincide with slack water, when a route close inshore can be taken.

Holyhead

53°19'·8N 3°37'·1W

Charts

Admiralty 1413 (1:25,000), 2011 (1:6,250)
Imray C52 (1:140,700)

Tides

HW Dover −0035
Height in metres

MHWS	MHWN	MTL	MLWN	MLWS
5·7	4·5	3·2	2·0	0·7

Lights

Breakwater head Fl(3)15s21m14M Siren 20s White square stone tower, black band F.R on chimney 2M SSE

Fish dock Admiralty pier off head 2F.G(vert)8m5M Bell(1)15s Concrete mast on dolphin

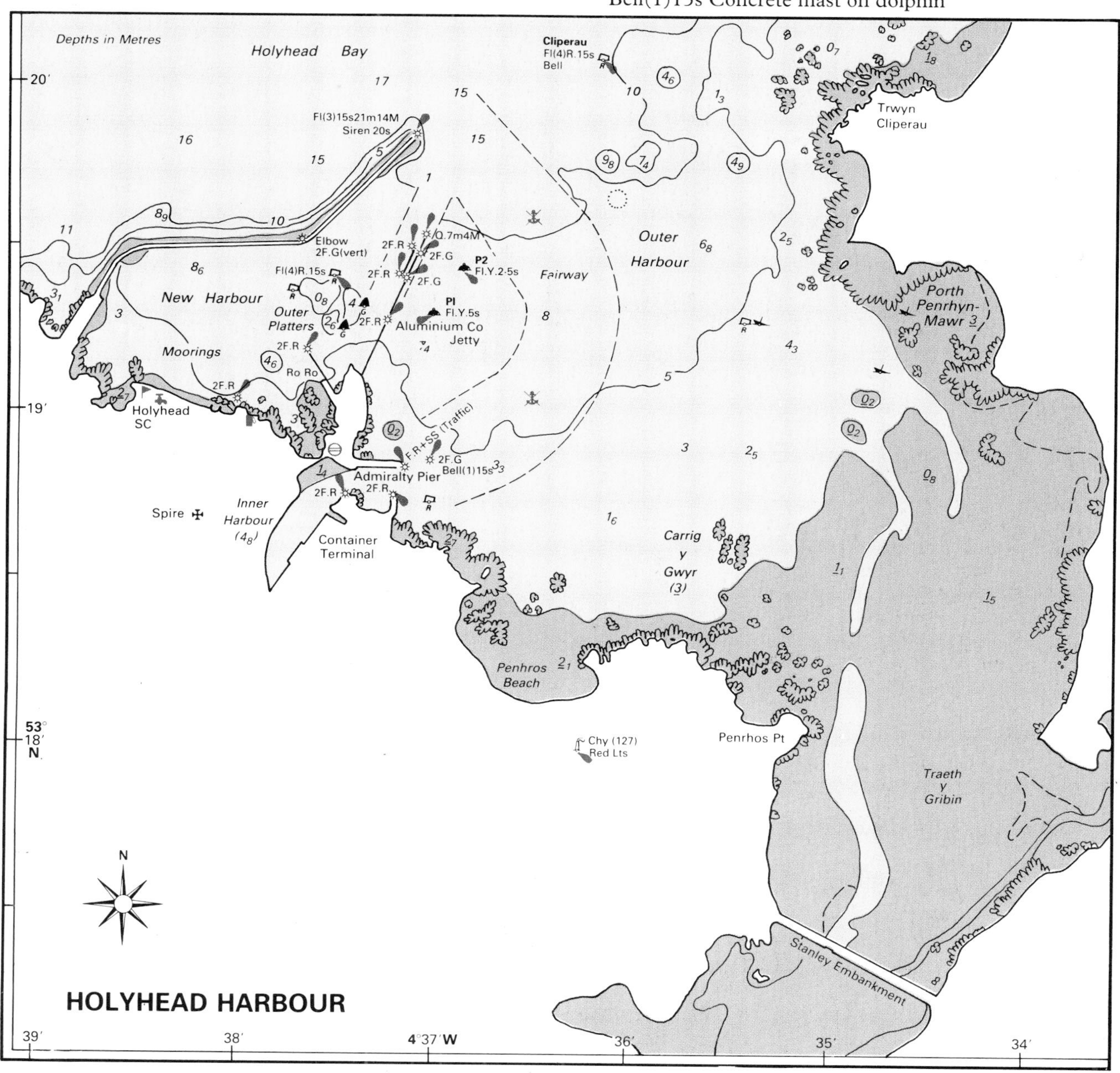

Holyhead Harbour – the massive Holyhead breakwater can be seen in the background.

Head F.R.7m1M White round tower 184°-vis-188° Traffic signal F, shows F.R when entrance is impracticable
S spur 2F.G(vert)
S pier head 2F.R(vert)7m Metal mast
Inner harbour dredged channel N side outer Fl.G.3s7m White metal column
Inner Fl.G.5s6m White metal column
Anglesey Aluminium Jetty head seaward dolphin Q.7m4M Horn 10s Dolphin
New harbour Mackenzie pier head 2F.R(vert)5m5M Post

Radio/telephone

VHF Ch 16, 14; sailing club Ch M
☎ Harbourmaster (0407) 762304

On rounding North Stack, the great Holyhead breakwater (approximately 1½ miles long), striking NE from the tip of Holyhead, opens up to the east. Leave the tip of the breakwater (Fl(3)15s14M Siren(1)20s), where there are off-lying rocks, well to starboard, and the R can buoy of Creigiau Cliperau (Fl(4)R.15s Bell) to port. The course then runs SW, leaving the Aluminium Jetty to port, into the New Harbour, where many yachts can be seen swinging at their moorings. The Holyhead Sailing Club boatman may be on hand to advise about a mooring, or one may decide to anchor just outside the last mooring trot. Alternatively, it is possible to berth temporarily along the inner arm of the breakwater, where there are frequent steps, so that arrangements with Holyhead Sailing Club can be made for a more permanent berth. This area, however, dries to uneven rock after 3 hours' ebb.

Holyhead Harbour is a natural deep-water harbour, with typical depths of 5–15 metres, and for centuries has been a departure point for Dun Laoghaire, in Ireland, 55 miles to the west. Construction of the great breakwater took some 33 years (it was completed in 1873). It gives the harbour complete shelter in all but NE winds, with which an uncomfortable, lumpy swell rolls in. It is fully equipped, with a boatyard and a 30-ton lift, fuel and water on the quay, and good supplies from the town, which has efficient bus and rail connections to the mainland. Holyhead harbourmaster ☎ (0407) 762304; VHF Ch 16, 14.

Moelfre Head anchorage

53°20'·1N 4°10'·5W

Lights

The Skerries Fl(2)10s36m22M+F.R.26m16M Horn(2) 20s White round tower, red band (F.R 231°-vis-254°)

Point Lynas Oc.10s39m20M Horn 45s White castellated tower 109°-vis-315°

Unless you wish to explore the northwestern coastline of Anglesey, or to spend a night at anchor in Cemlyn or Cemaes Bay, a course well outside the Skerries is desirable, as the tide runs very fiercely close inshore, reaching up to 6 knots and above at springs.

The voyage to Moelfre Head leads around the northwestern tip of the island, marked by a group of jagged rocks known as the Skerries. In 1841 Trinity House paid £500,000 to acquire the Skerries lighthouse, previously privately owned. It now has the characteristics Fl(2)10s36m22M and F.R.26m16M. Departing Holyhead, very good progress can be made by taking the NE-bound flood (5 knots springs) around the Skerries, leaving Ethel Rock N cardinal and Archdeacon Rock N cardinal to starboard – the sea can be quite disturbed shorewards of these.

A course can then be laid to round Point Lynas light (Oc.10s39m20M Horn 45s), keeping 1 mile offing to leave Middle Mouse and East Mouse, two rocky islets ½ mile off the north shore, to starboard. Point Lynas lighthouse dates back to 1835, and in the past was the main stop for liners taking on board a Liverpool pilot, the pilot launch having a berth on the east side of the point, near the jetty.

The course now sets to leave Ynys Dulas, a small offshore rock islet marked by a refuge tower, and the associated off-lying rocks of Garreg Allan, to starboard, before rounding the island of Ynys Moelfre and bringing up behind Moelfre Head; here there is good anchoring in mud/sand, near the lifeboat station, giving very secure shelter from the west.

Alternatively, there is a secure anchorage in Traeith Bychan, 1 mile to the south, giving shelter from NW–S, although this site is very popular with dinghy sailors and may be a little noisy. Fish and chips are available ashore, and there are a couple of hostelries to choose from. The scenery, although not picturesque, has its own charm, typified by very low-lying moorlands, with crazy-looking windblown trees growing almost at right angles.

Conwy lies 15 miles to the east; on leaving Puffin Island, marking the most easterly part of Anglesey, to starboard, entry can be made into Conwy Harbour, as explained in the text headed 'Porth Dinllaen to Conwy via Menai Strait' (see page 46).

IV. North Wales to Morecambe

River Mersey and Ribble Estuary

Charts

Admiralty 1977 (1:75,000), 1978 (1:75,000), 1953 (1:25,000)
Imray C52 (1:140,700), C62 (1:280,000)

Main coastal lights

Bar LtF Fl.5s10m12M Horn(2)20s Racon Red hull
Formby LtF Iso.4s.11m6M Red hull, white stripes
Isle of Walney Fl.15s21m23M RC Stone tower Obscured 122°-127° when within 3M of the shore
Halfway shoal Q.R.16m10M Racon Red and yellow chequered vertical on beacon
Walney channel Ldg Lts *Front* Q.7m10M Orange vertical on pile structure
No. 2 *Rear* 0·61M from front Iso.2s13m10M Orange vertical on pile structure

Submarine exercise area

A good look out must be kept at all times for submarines when navigating in north Irish Sea areas.

The section of coast from Conwy and North Wales sets along the NW coast of England, and is marked by a dramatic change in the geology of the shoreline. The coast becomes progressively flatter as the land falls slowly from a sandy foreshore into the sea, creating many sandbanks and mudflats which make navigation a little more difficult than previously.

The Dee Estuary

The large Dee Estuary, most of which dries, has little to offer the visiting cruising yachtsman. The tide runs strongly in the shifting channels, and whilst it is possible for shoal-draught power craft to navigate the upper reaches all the way to Chester, this requires extensive local knowledge.

The anchorages at the outer limits of the Dee Estuary are all exposed and rolling, and it is prohibited for yachts to use Mostyn Harbour unless forced to do so by an emergency.

Approaching from the west along the North Wales coast, the Inner Passage and Welsh Channel are marked by lit lateral buoys to Mostyn Deep. The tidal stream runs very hard in the channels, particularly when the banks are dry, and care must be taken when going ashore to Mostyn by tender for supplies. A warmer welcome awaits you if you are approaching from the north. Take Hilbre Swash Channel, which turns approximately S by W after passing HE1 E cardinal to starboard; this then leaves HE3 green conical to starboard and Hilbre Island beacon Fl.R.3s14m5M to port. There is a drying anchorage south of the marina lake, near the moorings. Contact West Kirby SC ☎ (0625) 5579 for friendly advice. Stores from West Kirby.

Liverpool

Pilotage notes supplied by Alec Rollinson

Liverpool is very much a commercial port, and as such has tended to be avoided by pleasure craft, with the exception of our local boats and vessels passing through to their winter berths. The opening of the Albert Dock and the Liverpool Marina at Brunswick and Coburg Docks has made the place much more attractive to visitors.

The approach to Liverpool should present no problems to yachts in reasonable weather. However, the Mersey Bar does have a poor reputation, and in strong onshore winds and spring tides the place needs to be treated with great respect.

Charts

Admiralty 1951 (1:25,000), 3490 (1:15,000)
Imray C62 (1:280,000)

Buoys

Bar LtF Fl.5s10m12M Horn(2)20s Racon Red hull 53°32'N 3°20'·9W

From the Bar, the sea channels are very well marked, by a mix of green conical buoys and cardinal marks on the starboard side, and large red can boat beacons on the port side. There are also safe-water mid-channel marks:

Formby LtF Iso.W.4s11m6M Red hull, white stripes 53°31'·2N 3°13'·1W
Crosby LtF Oc.W.5s11m8M Red hull, white stripes 53°30'·7N 3°06'·2W

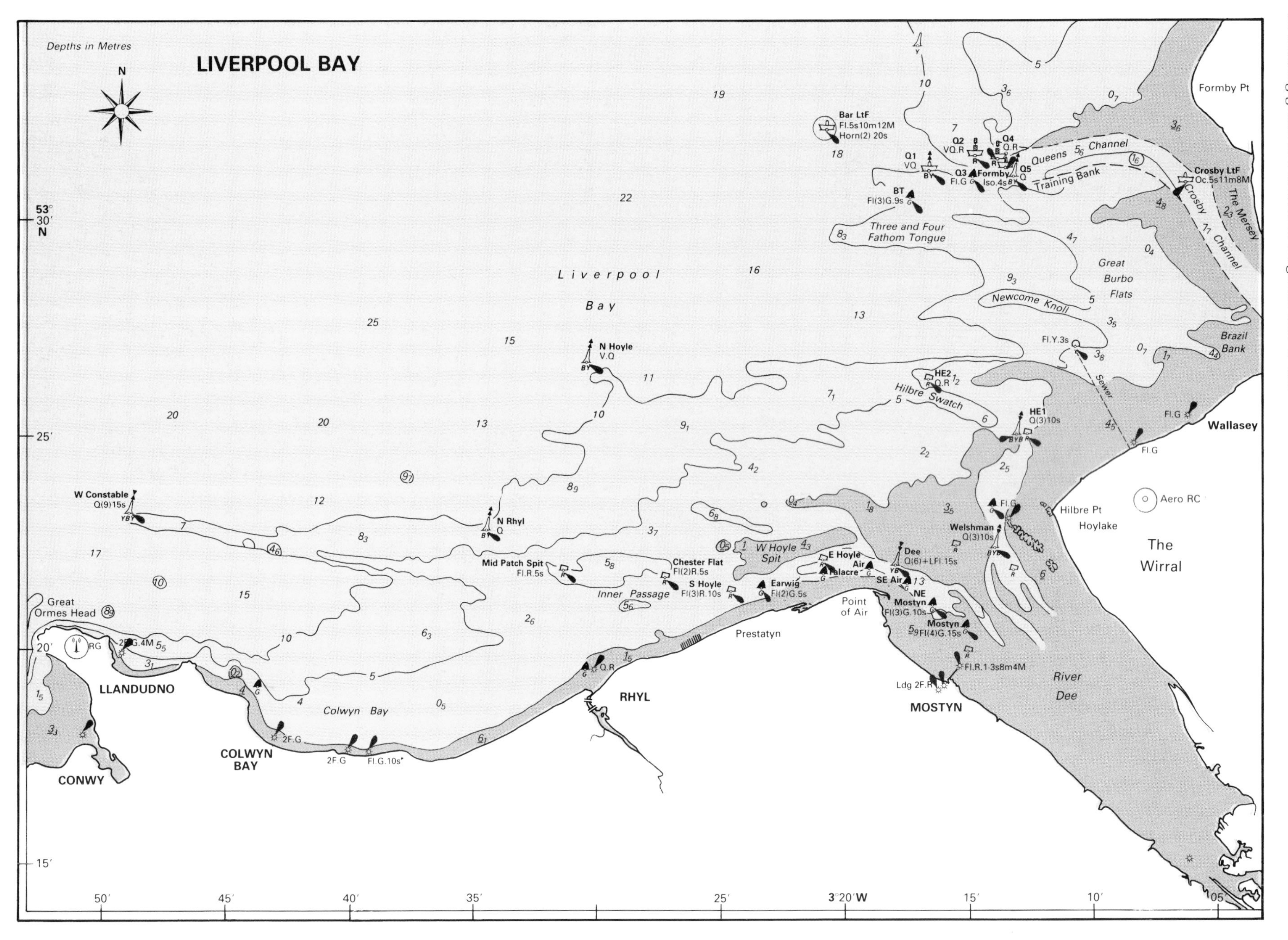

Depths in Metres
LIVERPOOL BAY
N
Formby Pt
Bar LtF
Fl.5s10m12M
Horn(2) 20s
Q1
VQ
Q2
VQ.R
Q3
Fl.G
Q4
Q.R
Q5
Q
Formby
Iso.4s
BT
Fl(3)G.9s
Queens Channel
Training Bank
Crosby LtF
Oc.5s11m8M
Crosby Channel
The Mersey
Three and Four Fathom Tongue
Great Burbo Flats
Newcome Knoll
Liverpool Bay
Fl.Y.3s
Sewer
Brazil Bank
Wallasey
Fl.G
N Hoyle
V.Q
HE2
Q.R
Hilbre Swatch
HE1
Q(3)10s
Aero RC
Hilbre Pt
Hoylake
The Wirral
W Constable
Q(9)15s
N Rhyl
Q
Welshman
Q(3)10s
W Hoyle Spit
E Hoyle
Air
Talacre
Dee
Q(6)+LFl.15s
SE Air
NE Mostyn
Fl(3)G.10s
Mostyn
Fl(4)G.15s
Mid Patch Spit
Fl.R.5s
Chester Flat
Fl(2)R.5s
S Hoyle
Fl(3)R.10s
Earwig
Fl(2)G.5s
Inner Passage
Point of Air
Great Ormes Head
RG
2F.G.4M
Prestatyn
Fl.R.1·3s8m4M
River Dee
Ldg 2F.R
LLANDUDNO
Q.R
RHYL
MOSTYN
Colwyn Bay
2F.G
COLWYN BAY
Fl.G.10s
CONWY
53° 30′ N
25′
20′
15′
50′
45′
40′
35′
25′
3°20′W
15′
10′
05′

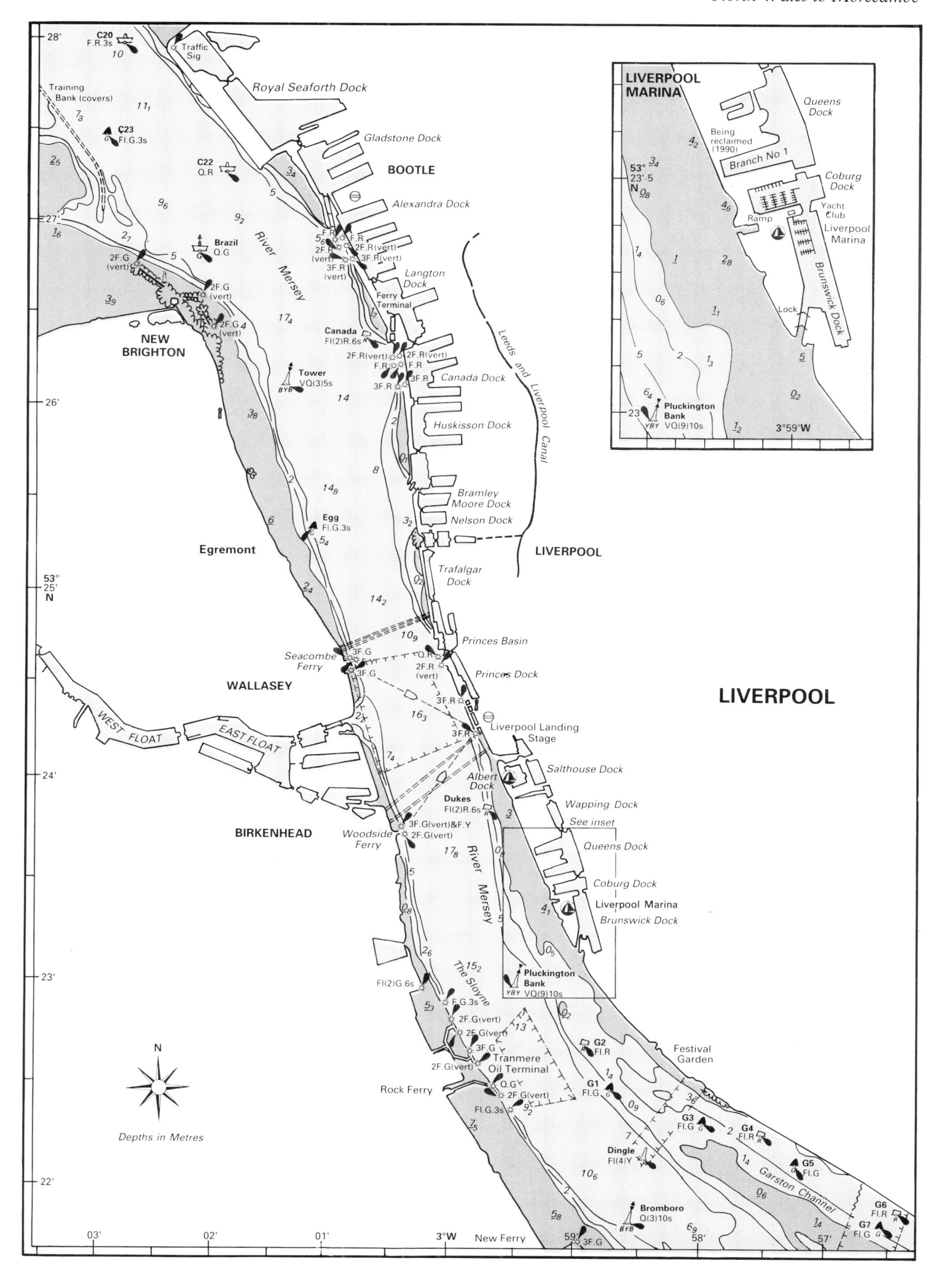

Royal Seaforth Dock
Gladstone Dock
BOOTLE
Alexandra Dock
Langton Dock
Ferry Terminal
Canada Dock
Huskisson Dock
Bramley Moore Dock
Nelson Dock
LIVERPOOL
Trafalgar Dock
Princes Basin
Princes Dock
Liverpool Landing Stage
Salthouse Dock
Albert Dock
Wapping Dock
See inset
Queens Dock
Coburg Dock
Liverpool Marina
Brunswick Dock
Leeds and Liverpool Canal
River Mersey
NEW BRIGHTON
Egremont
WALLASEY
WEST FLOAT
EAST FLOAT
BIRKENHEAD
Seacombe Ferry
Woodside Ferry
Rock Ferry
New Ferry
The Sloyne
Tranmere Oil Terminal
Festival Garden
Garston Channel
Training Bank (covers)
Traffic Sig
C20 F.R.3s
C23 Fl.G.3s
C22 Q.R
Brazil Q.G
Canada Fl(2)R.6s
Tower VQ(3)5s
Egg Fl.G.3s
Dukes Fl(2)R.6s
Pluckington Bank VQ(9)10s
G1 Fl.G
G2 Fl.R
G3 Fl.G
G4 Fl.R
G5 Fl.G
G6 Fl.R
G7 Fl.G
Dingle Fl(4)Y
Bromboro Q(3)10s
LIVERPOOL MARINA
Being reclaimed (1990)
Branch No 1
Ramp
Yacht Club
Lock
53° 23'·5 N
3°59'W
Depths in Metres

The distance from the Bar LtF, via the Queen's and Crosby Channels, to the Rock lighthouse, at the entrance to the river, is 14 miles.

Tides

Tide at the Bar light float floods at up to 2¼ knots and ebbs at 2 knots, setting approximately ESE on the flood and WNW on the ebb tide, and increasing to 3½ knots at New Brighton. The set is onto the starboard-hand buoys on the flood in Queen's Channel to Q11, and off the G buoys from Crosby to Burbo; the ebb tide is reversed.

The sea channels are dredged continually to maintain a 7m channel. At the time of writing, 6·7m (below chart datum) in patches close to the north of C7 is the least water to be found in Queen's and Crosby Channels.

Tides – river

The River Mersey is unusual in having its narrow part, only ½ mile wide between the stages, 2M in from the Rock lighthouse, widening out to 2·5M wide between Eastham and Garston, with over 20 square miles of drying banks to Runcorn. Large areas are over 6m above chart datum.

Chart datum for Liverpool is 4·93m below ordinance datum Newlyn, approximating to LAST (lowest astronomical spring tide).

Height in metres

MHWS	MHWN	MTL	MLWN	MLWS
9·3	7·4	0·0	0·9	2·9

Highest predicted Equinoctial Spring Tide 10·3–0·1m. The fastest rate of tide, from the chart, shows a spring rate of 5·4 knots just north of the stages at 1 hour's ebb. However, heavy rain in the Upper Mersey, coinciding with equinoctial springs, can cause that to be exceeded by a considerable amount.

Eddy tides form on both sides of the river before HW, while the flood in the centre is still going strongly to the south; this happens earlier on big tides.

Radio

The Port of Liverpool has a VTS system operated through Mersey Radio; direct calling on VHF Ch 12.

Traffic disposition broadcasts are made on VHF Ch 9 at 2 hours and 3 hours before HW. These give details of ship movements, lock entrance traffic, local weather station reports and local weather forecasts.

Although at the moment there are no arbitrary restraints on pleasure craft using the Mersey and approaches, a call to Mersey Radio, Ch 12, when passing the Bar inward, or leaving a lock outward, is appreciated, and assists the VTS operators in monitoring vessel movements. It may also be necessary for yachts to adjust their speed or wait to avoid interfering with the movements of large vessels.

Dock entrance information

Access to the Leeds Liverpool Canal for vessels small enough to negotiate a narrow canal system – draught limit 3ft (0.91m) – can be arranged via Stanley Dock, by telephoning British Waterways at Wigan, ☎ (0924) 42239.

Access to Stanley Dock itself requires permission from the dockmaster at Langton Lock: ☎ (051 922) 2020, or VHF Ch 21.

Entry to the Manchester Ship Canal, which gives access to Northwich (via the River Weaver), the Shropshire Union Canal, and Ellesmere Port Boat Museum, requires prior consent from the Manchester Ship Canal Company, Queen Elizabeth II Dock, Eastham, Wirral L62 0BB, ☎ (051 327) 1461, or VHF Ch 7.

Canning river entrance, immediately S of the Prince's Landing Stage, on the Liverpool side of the river, gives access to the Maritime Museum and the magnificently restored Albert Dock complex. There are pontoon berths in the Albert Dock, surrounded by bonded warehouses built during the Napoleonic Wars.

The sill at Canning entrance is 3·5m above chart datum, and the single gate can be opened between 2 hours before HW and HW. Canning Dock, being a half-tide basin, does not open on every tide; it opens only by prior arrangement with the Harbourmaster, Merseyside Development Corporation, ☎ (051 236) 6090.

Liverpool Marina occupies the next dock system to the south, accessed through a completely rebuilt Brunswick Lock, which has been provided with floating pontoons to make tying up in the lock easier. The sill at Brunswick lock is 4·5m ABD; the lock is manned on every day tide, working for as long as there is 2m over the sill, normally for 2 hours either side of HW. Locking can be provided on dark tides by prior arrangement only.

Inside, the marina provides 300 pontoon berths, with all facilities, including a 60-ton boat lift and a club house and restaurant. There are usually vacant berths, but a telephone call before venturing up the Mersey would make good sense. ☎ (051 708) 5228, VHF Ch M37, or, after 5pm, (051 709) 2683.

South of the marina, the river is buoyed as far as Garston on the east side and Eastham on the west side. There is a marina at Widnes Canal, beyond the Runcorn bridge, and a sailing club can be found at Fiddler's Ferry, but as the drying channels in the Upper Mersey are no longer buoyed, local knowledge would be required to proceed beyond Garston.

Sailing clubs

There are sailing clubs at:

Speke: Liverpool Sailing Club

Liverpool: Marina Yacht Club

Rockferry: Royal Mersey Yacht Club, Tranmere Sailing Club

New Brighton: Wallasey Yacht Club, West Cheshire Sailing Club

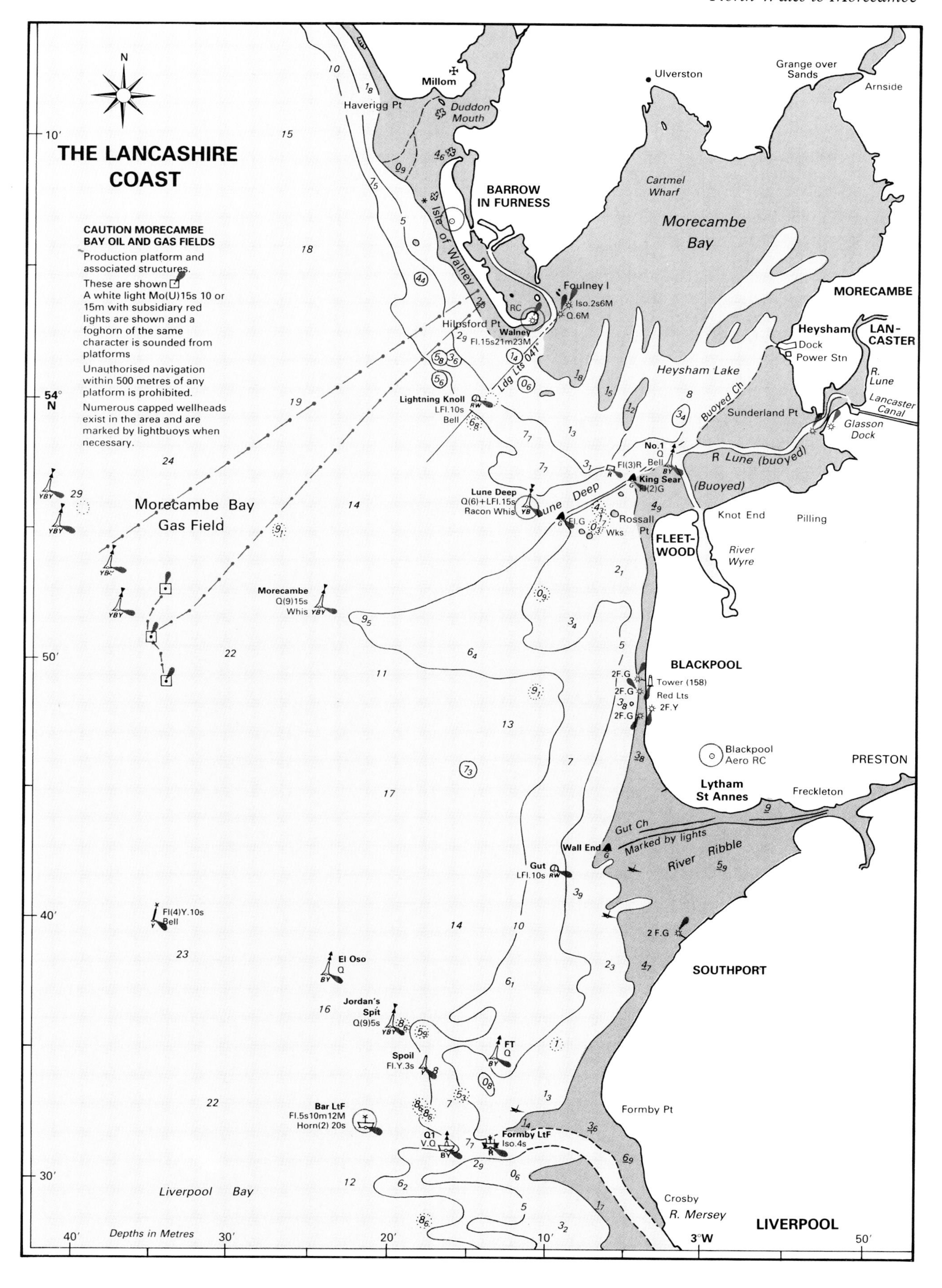
THE LANCASHIRE COAST
CAUTION MORECAMBE BAY OIL AND GAS FIELDS
Production platform and associated structures.
These are shown
A white light Mo(U)15s 10 or 15m with subsidiary red lights are shown and a foghorn of the same character is sounded from platforms
Unauthorised navigation within 500 metres of any platform is prohibited.
Numerous capped wellheads exist in the area and are marked by lightbuoys when necessary.
Morecambe Bay Gas Field
Millom
Haverigg Pt
Duddon Mouth
Isle of Walney
BARROW IN FURNESS
Foulney I
Iso.2s6M
Q.6M
Walney
Fl.15s21m23M
Hilpsford Pt
Ldg Lts 041°
Lightning Knoll
LFl.10s
Bell
Lune Deep
Q(6)+LFl.15s
Racon Whis
Morecambe
Q(9)15s
Whis
Ulverston
Grange over Sands
Arnside
Cartmel Wharf
Morecambe Bay
MORECAMBE
Heysham
Dock
Power Stn
LAN-CASTER
R. Lune
Lancaster Canal
Glasson Dock
Heysham Lake
Buoyed Ch
Sunderland Pt
No.1
Q
Bell
Fl(3)R
King Sear
Fl(2)G
R Lune (buoyed)
(Buoyed)
Knot End
Pilling
Rossall Pt
Wks
FLEET-WOOD
River Wyre
BLACKPOOL
2F.G
Tower (158)
Red Lts
2F.Y
Blackpool Aero RC
PRESTON
Lytham St Annes
Freckleton
Gut Ch
Marked by lights
River Ribble
Wall End
Gut
LFl.10s
Fl(4)Y.10s
Bell
El Oso
Q
Jordan's Spit
Q(9)5s
Spoil
Fl.Y.3s
FT
Q
SOUTHPORT
Bar LtF
Fl.5s10m12M
Horn(2) 20s
Q1
V.Q
Formby LtF
Iso.4s
Formby Pt
Crosby
R. Mersey
LIVERPOOL
Liverpool Bay
Depths in Metres
54° N
10′
50′
40′
30′
40′
30′
20′
10′
3°W
50′

The marina provides some short-stay moorings at Rockferry, marked LMYC. Except in the case of one of these, approval should always be sought before picking up an empty mooring, as it may be suspect.

Further information

Immediately north of the moorings at Rockferry is Tranmere Oil Terminal, with berths for tankers of up to 300,000 tons and 15m. Commercial traffic should always have right of way.

Should you choose to come to or leave Liverpool in the dark, no matter what you have been told to the contrary, please stay on your own side of the channel. Remember, to a pilot, even one who sails, you are just a light; a light in the wrong place causes adrenalin to flow, and no one likes to be frightened.

Conwy to Ribble Estuary

Leaving Conwy Fairway buoy, the course alters to leave the great limestone outcrop of Great Orme's Head ½ mile to starboard. From here it sets across Liverpool Bay, where the flood runs east at 1·5 knots and ebbs west at 1·5 knots at springs.

Round Great Orme's Head, leaving Constable W cardinal buoy, marking Constable Bank, which may be crossed in fine weather, close to starboard. The course lies 052°, leaving Jordan's Spit W cardinal to starboard, directly onto Gut RWVS buoy, and directly onto Blackpool Aero RC. (Bar LtF Racon Fl.5s10m12M, lying 9 miles to the west of Formby Point, gives added reassurance on a night passage.)

Morecambe Bay Gas Fields

This area is still under development, and gas platforms are often added to or relocated; they should therefore not be relied upon when fixing a position. Do not navigate within 5 cables of a platform.

River Ribble, Lytham and Preston

53°45'N 2°47'W

Charts

Admiralty 1981 (1:75,000)
Imray C62 (1:280,000)

Tides

HW Dover +0013

Lights

S side 14¼ mile perch Fl.G.5s6m3M Black framework tower and tripod
13½ mile perch Fl.G.5s6m3M Black metal framework tower on tripod
N side 13 mile perch Fl.R.5s6m3M Black metal framework tower on tripod
S side 12½ mile perch Fl.G.5s6m3M Black metal framework tower on tripod

Radio/telephone

☎ Preston harbourmaster (0772) 726711
☎ Preston Marina (0722) 733595

From Gut RWVS buoy (LFl.10s), the course sets 072° for 2 miles; from here the channel is well marked, at ½-mile intervals, all the way to Preston Docks , though all this area dries.

Since the closure of Preston as a commercial port in 1981, the official maintained channel into the river Ribble has been undredged, and it has silted so that it now dries 3·6m in places. It is nevertheless still viable for 1½ hours either side of HW if you set a course of 072°M from Gut RWVS. From here the channel is clearly marked at ½-mile intervals by lateral perches, some lit, which are actually driven into the training wall.

Alternatively, the South Gut Channel, which leads into the main channel via a breach in the south training wall, can be attempted for 3 hours either side of HW. Maintain a course of 087°M from Gut Fairway buoy until South Gut No. 4 buoy is abeam, when a course of 058°M will lead through the hole in the training wall, passing the unlit, steel-framed 'Tony's Perch' (marking the westernmost point of the hole) close to port.

Note No. 4 South Gut buoy is yellow and unlit. This is a local mark, and not indicated on Admiralty publications. It may be relocated as the channel shifts.

Lytham, the next landfall, lies on the north shore of the Ribble Estuary; there is anchoring in moderate holding in the pool near the 47ft Tyne class lifeboat (1m at chart datum), or off the low-lying wooden jetty near the lifeboat station, where a number of local craft lie at their drying moorings, sheltered from NW–N–E winds. It is a quiet town, characterised by Lytham Windmill, standing beautifully preserved on the village green. Full supplies are available ashore, and, if there are any golf clubs aboard, Lytham has four world-class courses.

As I have already mentioned, the shelter at Lytham is good in winds NW–N–E. If the wind freshens and moves to the W–S arc, however, a quick evacuation upstream is advisable, as there is a fetch straight across the Irish Sea. Secure anchoring at the mouth of the River Douglas to starboard, or at Freckleton to port, is possible, though both of these sites are remote and isolated. For an hour either side of HW, however, it is possible to pass 3 miles up the reaches of the River Douglas to Douglas Boatyard (☎ (0772) 812462), where you can berth alongside the pontoon (which dries) in the company of many local craft. Full boatyard facilities and chandlery are available, though stores have to be carried half a mile from the town. Access one mile up to Freckleton is also possible, for craft of moderate size and draught, by keeping a boat's width or two off the west bank, which is quite steep-to; one can then berth alongside a vacant stage, as appropriate, near the boatyard. The Ship Inn, at the top of the lane, takes care of the crew's more urgent needs, while Les, who owns the moorings, will issue

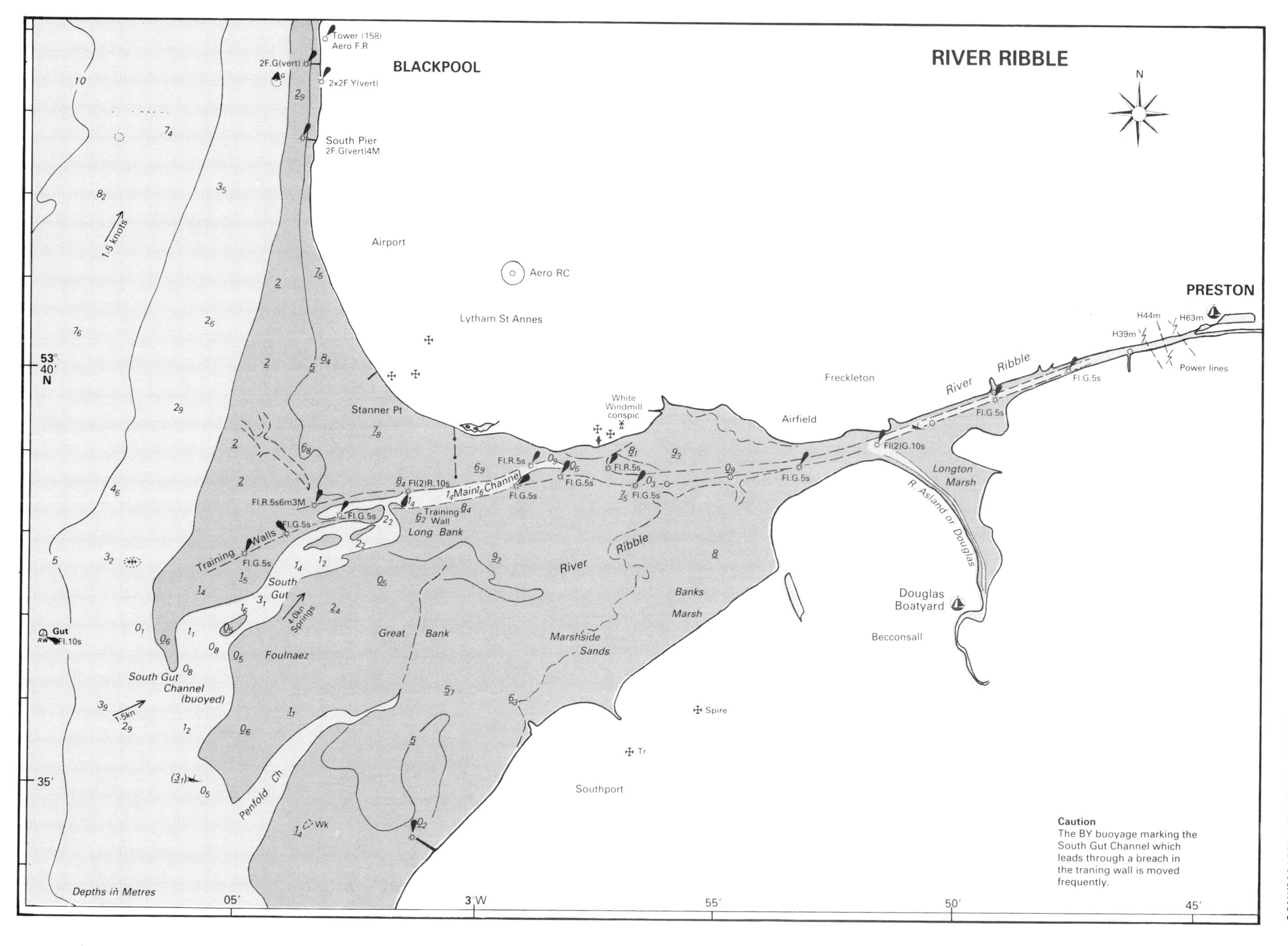
RIVER RIBBLE
BLACKPOOL
PRESTON
Tower (158) Aero F.R
2F.G(vert)
2x2F.Y(vert)
South Pier 2F.G(vert)4M
Airport
Aero RC
Lytham St Annes
Stanner Pt
White Windmill conspic
Freckleton
Airfield
River Ribble
Fl.G.5s
Fl(2)G.10s
Power lines
H44m
H63m
H39m
Longton Marsh
R. Asland or Douglas
Douglas Boatyard
Becconsall
Main Channel
Training Wall
Long Bank
Training Walls
Fl.R.5s6m3M
Fl(2)R.10s
Fl.R.5s
South Gut
4.0kn Springs
Great Bank
Marshside Sands
Banks Marsh
Foulnaez
South Gut Channel (buoyed)
Gut Fl.10s
1.5 knots
1.5kn
Penfold Ch
Wk
Spire
Tr
Southport
Depths in Metres
Caution
The BY buoyage marking the South Gut Channel which leads through a breach in the traning wall is moved frequently.

Above Douglas Boatyard at Hesketh Bank, looking upstream, showing the drying pontoon.

Below The Albert Edward Dock at Preston, River Ribble, looking downstream.

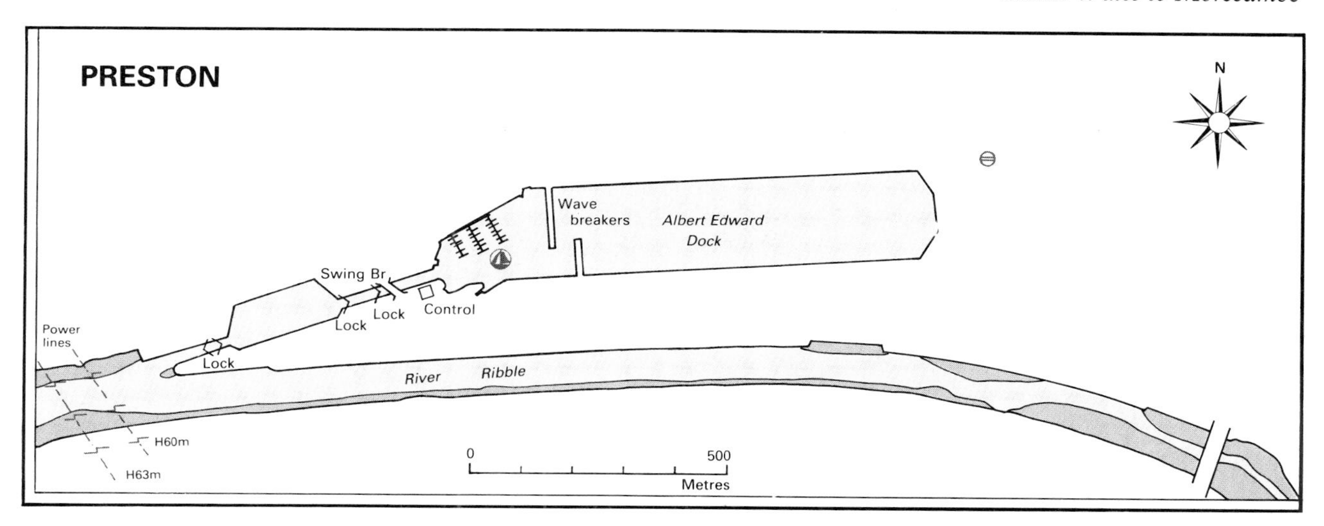

the visitor with a key to the toilet and shower on payment of a very modest berthing fee.

The Albert Edward Dock, approximately 10 miles up the Ribble from Lytham, has undergone a transformation, and is now the site of Preston Marina (☎ (0772) 733595). This has found favour with many local cruising folk, as a facility of this nature has long been needed along this stretch of coastline. Navigation up the Ribble is viable for 2 hours either side of HW, the channel being marked with perches and lights; the entrance channel will be found on the north bank (keep near the south quay on entering, as the north quay is silted). The outer lock gates are operated between 0700 and 2100, and are open for 1½ hours either side of HW. The inner lock and swing bridge, giving access to the marina, are operated by a lock-keeper; call Riversway VHF Ch 16, 14. Once the outer lock gates are closed, there is room to lie afloat along the south quay (the Bullnose) of the entrance channel, served by chain ladder, to await the next tide.

The marina offers secure berthing at modest cost, and the management, being yachtsmen themselves, are extremely helpful and accommodating. Diesel, water, chandlery and brokerage facilities are available, along with craning onto hard standing. It is a suitable place for crew changes, as Preston is served by the main inter-city network and the M6 motorway, and Manchester's international airport is just 1 hour's drive away. Food supplies are available from the local supermarket, and there is a choice of two waterfront hostelries, both with restaurants.

Membership of the newly founded Preston Yacht Club is free.

Southport

52°39'·4N 3°01'·4W

Lights

Southport pier head 2F.G(vert)6m5M White post 033°-vis-213°

Due south from Lytham, across the Ribble estuary, lies the seaside resort of Southport (the word 'port', where the NW coastline is concerned, isn't to be taken too seriously. It can mean anything from a very small indentation to no indentation at all). Southport doesn't see much of the sea nowadays; the pier (2F.G.6m5M) was made in a vain attempt to catch it as it receded, leaving behind mile upon mile of golden sand.

It is possible to anchor off Southport in good holding when the tide decides to come in, but care must be taken, as there is no shelter from onshore winds, and the highest tide is in excess of 10m above chart datum. This can leave an unwary skipper atop a sandbank the size of a small hill – rather like Noah, but not half as pleased with one's achievement. Ashore, Southport now has a large marine lake (if the mountain won't come to Mohammed...), and seems firmly set in its Victorian past, with wide expanses of flowering gardens, and hanging baskets along the main street, where good-quality supplies can be obtained – provided that the long hike back across the sands to one's craft seems worth the effort.

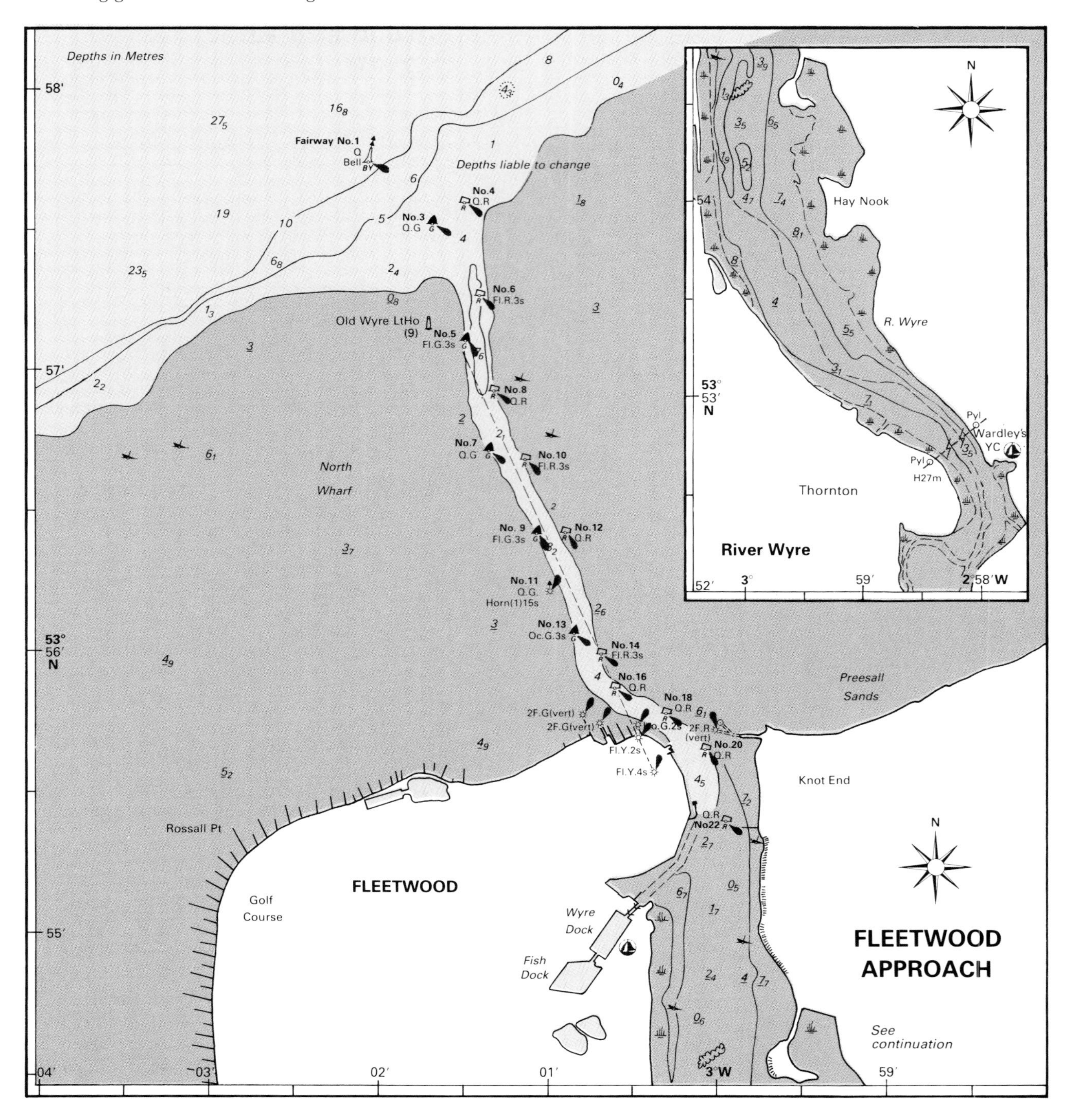
Depths in Metres
Fairway No.1
Q
Bell
Depths liable to change
No.4
Q.R
No.3
Q.G
No.6
Fl.R.3s
Old Wyre LtHo
(9)
No.5
Fl.G.3s
No.8
Q.R
No.7
Q.G
No.10
Fl.R.3s
North
Wharf
No. 9
Fl.G.3s
No.12
Q.R
No.11
Q.G.
Horn(1)15s
No.13
Oc.G.3s
No.14
Fl.R.3s
No.16
Q.R
No.18
Q.R
2F.G(vert)
2F.G(vert)
2F.R
(vert)
Fl.Y.2s
Fl.Y.4s
No.20
Q.R
Q.R
No22
Preesall
Sands
Knot End
Rossall Pt
FLEETWOOD
Golf
Course
Wyre
Dock
Fish
Dock
See
continuation
FLEETWOOD
APPROACH
Hay Nook
R. Wyre
Pyl
Wardley's
YC
H27m
Thornton
River Wyre
53° 56′ N
53° 53′ N
04′
03′
02′
01′
3°W
59′
2 58′W

Morecambe Bay

Despite its name, derived from the Roman *Sinus Moricambe* (Morecambe Sea), thinking of it as a sea can be very dangerous for a stranger to the area. The bay dries out almost completely, and has a strong tidal stream, in excess of 4·5 knots springs, which forms short, very steep seas – especially during SW gales, which have a 120-mile fetch from Ireland. It is also famed for its quicksand, which claims lives every year. If run aground in the bay, I would be very wary about jumping over the side for a walk around after the tide has retreated.

I once asked an old fisherman, 'How many folk have been lost on the sands in your lifetime?' He replied, 'None, as I can remember. Many have drowned, but they're usually found when the tide goes out.'

Leaving Lytham, the next haven along the coast lies just into the southern end of Morecambe Bay at the mouth of the River Wyre, a cruising distance of approximately 23 miles.

From Gut RWVS buoy, the course leads 355° though the majority of yachts can head inshore of the newly established gas platform, and steer directly for Shell Wharf G conical, to get a closer look at the renowned resort of Blackpool, with its piers and tower (158m).

The tidal drift is a little unusual along this small stretch of coast, and in many cases does not reach the expected values. Blackpool Tower and a very conspicuous chimney at Fleetwood, however, provide ample opportunity to fix one's position. Blackpool Aero RC and Walney RC may also be pressed into service.

Note In settled offshore weather it is possible to anchor close in, between the piers, at Blackpool, and take the ground. The kids can then have their fill of candy floss, toffee apples and funfair, while the rest of the crew enjoy fish and chips, and maybe a trip to the theatre between tides.

Fleetwood and Knot End

53°55'N 3°00'W

Charts

Admiralty 1552 (1:10,000), 2010 (1:50,000)
Imray C62 (1:280,000)

Tides

HW Dover −0015

Height in metres

MHWS	MHWN	MTL	MLWN	MLWS
9·5	7·6	5·3	3·1	1·2

Lights

Fleetwood Esplanade Lts in line 156° *Front* Fl.Y.2s14m Stone tower *Rear* 320m from front Fl.Y.4s28m Stone tower
Black Scar perch No.11 Q.G.4m Horn 15s Green ▲ topmark on beacon
Steep Breast perch Iso.G.2s3m2M Platform on black wooden post, black base
Victoria pier head 2F.G(vert)8m
Groyne 2F.G(vert)6m Platform on post
Knot End slipway head 2F.R(vert)3m2M Platform on column
New harbour berth N dolphin 2F.G(vert)6m1M
S dolphin 2F.G(vert)6m1M
Ferry berth S side 2F.G(vert)
RNLI berth 2F.G(vert)
Knot End sailing school jetty Lts in line 27m from head 2F

Radio/telephone

Fleetwood Control VHF Ch 16, 12
Fleetwood Docks VHF Ch 16, 12 (HW +2hrs)
☎ Harbourmaster (0253) 872323

On closing with Lune Deep S cardinal, the course is altered directly onto No. 1 Fairway N cardinal, bearing 073°, 5 miles distant, between Danger Patch R can to port and King Scar G conical to starboard, where the tide runs parallel to the channel at over 3·5 knots at springs. From here the channel is well marked with lateral buoys, all of which are now lit; it passes the skeletal framework of the old, disused Wyre lighthouse to starboard. Use the leading lights in line at 156° as a rough guide only, as the upper and inner reaches of the buoyed channel deviate from this course. There is a strong tidal drift directly across the outer reaches of the channel at around half tide, and care must be taken.

Entering the Wyre mouth between 3 hours either side of HW, there is plenty of room to manoeuvre out of the way of the large Pandoro Ro-Ro ferries, and the Sealink ferry which leaves Fleetwood for the Isle of Man. ('All ships' warnings are given for ferry movements, on VHF Ch 16, by Fleetwood harbour control.) The only major navigational problem is giving Knot End breakwater, which strikes due west from the point, a wide berth.

Note The Wyre Channel is viable at all states of tide to the Pandoro Ro-Ro dock, where there is a dredged pool.

Anchor anywhere on the Knot End side of the channel, keeping clear of the many moorings; most of the areas dry to level sand and mud after three hours' ebb. This site provides excellent all-round shelter, except from due north; when a wind from the north is behind it, the tide races in, creating a small bore, which may cause problems for centreboard craft lying on the bottom.

Land by tender, at Knot End Sailing School jetty (the tide runs at over three knots, so a reliable outboard or a very strong oarsman is required); there is usually room to leave the tender on the grass bank to the left of the school. On no account must it be left unattended on the jetty, since the school allows yachtsmen to use its jetty only as a concession.

Knot End village is small, and offers only minor provisions. There is a passenger ferry to Fleetwood (operating hourly from 0950 to 1750, 80p each way 1992), the home of Lofthouse's 'Fisherman's Friends', on the opposite bank, from where a regular tram service runs to Blackpool. Fleetwood is a young town, built on a rabbit warren in 1836 by the landowner, Hesketh Fleetwood, in an attempt to take advantage of the industrial revolution. It never took off as a major port, and most of the steam packets to Ireland and the Furness coast continued to use Liverpool as their main departure point. It did, however, have great success in the early 1900s as a fishing port, and boasted a fine fleet of around 300 trawlers in the 1920s, a fleet which has now, sadly, been reduced to a couple of dozen.

Recently, a channel dredged to dry 2m and viable for 2½ hours either side of HW has been cut, leading SW from the main deep-water channel to Wyre Dock, which is now under development as Fleetwood Harbour Village Marina (Wyre Dock Marina ☎ (0253) 872323). On my last visit, in spring 1991, the first phase of pontoons had been completed and were filled to capacity with local craft, making it necessary for visiting yachts to find a berth along the outside face of the pontoons. I got the feeling that the development was rushing a little ahead of itself, as, while all the pontoons were full, the only amenities consisted of two small porta-cabins. Nevertheless, Wyre Dock provides excellent shelter and security, and as the tidal Wyre now has relatively clear water, free from the smell of diesel and the litter found in a thriving commercial port, it may just be the lifeline that the town has been waiting for.

Five miles further up the reaches of the Wyre lies Skippool Creek, headquarters of Blackpool and Fleetwood Sailing Club. Unless one's craft is shoal draught or has a centre plate, however, local knowledge is required for the passage, as the continually shifting sandbanks are unbuoyed – talking with local skippers at Knot End, many of whom lay up at Skippool, may be helpful.

Swinging moorings at Knot End, the majority of which dry.

River Lune estuary

Charts

Admiralty 1552 (1:25,000), 2010 (1:50,000)
Imray C62 (1:280,000)

Lights

Lts in line 083·68° Plover Scar *Front* Fl.2s6m6M White stone tower, black lantern. Channel liable to change
Cockersand Abbey *Rear* 854m from front F.18m8M Red framework tower
Crook Perch No.7 Fl.G.5s3M Green ▲ topmark on mast
Bazil Perch No.16 Fl(3)R.10s3M Red vertical topmark on mast
Glasson Quay F.G.1M
Dock entrance E side F
Outfall Fl.W
Outfall Fl(2)R.6s

Buoys

Lune Deep S cardinal pillar Q(6)+LFl.15s Whis Racon; can Fl(3)R; conical Fl.G.2·5s; King Sear conical Fl(2)G; and No. 1 N cardinal pillar light buoy Q Bell

To the east of Knot End and further into Morecambe Bay, the River Lune estuary can be navigated all the way to Lancaster at HW, though the havens of chief concern lie at Sunderland Point on the north bank and Glasson Dock on the south bank, near the mouth of the estuary.

As the lock gates at Glasson are only open for the hour preceding HW, the usual course of action on leaving Knot End is to anchor near Sunderland Point, where one can await HW on the next tide in order to enter the dock. Sunderland Point is attainable for 2½ hours either side of HW, and so leaving Knot End when afloat, approximately 2 hours before HW, gives plenty of time for the 10-mile voyage.

Leaving Knot End, the buoyed Wyre Channel sets approximately 336° until, on passing Wyre lighthouse to port and making Fairway No.1 N cardinal, a course is laid onto the River Lune W cardinal, 1½ miles distant, from where the channel heads eastwards and is well buoyed. The leading lights, again, only give a rough guide, as this course would lead over the foul area of Sunderland Shoulder, marked on the chart as having numerous stakes.

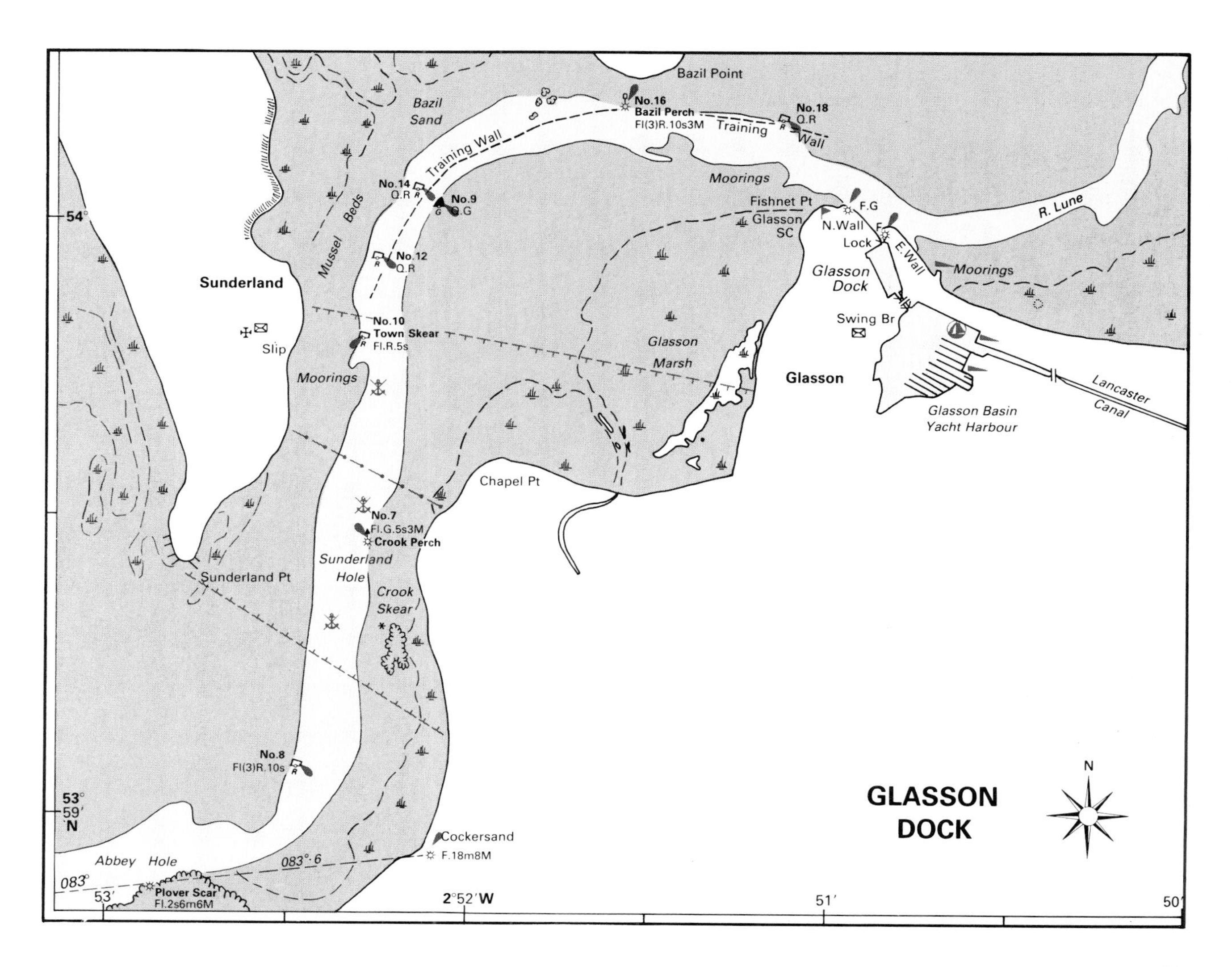

The famous 'Cotton Tree' of Sunderland Point.

Sunderland Point – the tide goes well out here!

Leave Abbey light, with its tide gauge showing the depth of water over the sill at Glasson, to starboard. The channel bears north between a R can and a G conical buoy, from where a small row of houses on the quay at Sunderland Point, and a number of moored craft, open to the northwest. There is room to anchor here (keeping clear of the prohibited areas) in good holding, drying to sand and mud. Shelter will be found from all but S–SW winds, in which a heavy swell sets in across the bay.

Ashore, Sunderland Point is a very small, well kept hamlet, with only one street. It was developed by a Quaker merchant named Robert Lawson as a port for his West Indian trade, though it never quite took off, owing to the nearby competition of Glasson. Alongside the old barn on the quayside grows the famous 'cotton tree'. (I thought cotton grew on a bush – shows what I know!) Folklore has it that a cotton seed fell from a bale of cargo and landed on the quay; it grew naturally, developing into a very unusual tree which produces cotton every year (don't take my word for it). Another tale is that of 'Black Sambo', the boy servant of a skipper trading with the West Indies, who was left behind when his master went away on business. It is said that he was so heartbroken that he died, and he now lies in the corner of the field. His epitaph, on a copper plate dating back to the 1790s, is, surprisingly, still decorated with posies of wild flowers by local children to this day.

Sunderland Point has only one road leading inland (indeed, it only has one road), which is cut off at HW – much to the chagrin of impatient motorists when they find themselves in over their bonnets. So when walking to the nearest pub, the Golden Globe at Overton (locally known as 'Snatchems', as many a local lad, the worse for drink, was press-ganged from here), a mile or so inland, one must ensure that the crew is back before HW. Or, a more popular choice with most crews, that they are away for the duration.

Glasson Dock

53°59'·8N 2°51'W

Charts

Admiralty 1552 (1:25,000), 2010 (1:50,000)
Imray C62 (1:280,000)

Tides

HW Dover +0020

Height in metres

MHWS	MHWN	MTL	MLWN	MLWS
6·6	4·4	–	–	–

Lights

Glasson quay F.G.1M
Glasson Dock entrance E side F
Outfall Fl
Outfall Fl(2)R.6s

Radio/telephone

VHF Ch 16, 08 (HW–2 to HW +1) Marina Ch 80
☎ Harbourmaster (0542) 751724

To enter Glasson Dock, which lies 1 mile to the east and upstream of Sunderland Point, departure should be taken 1½ hours before HW; this will give ample time to follow the training wall, to which the R buoys are moored, until the dock entrance is seen to starboard. Usually, local craft will be seen at anchor here, waiting to enter the dock.

Once inside the main basin, there is usually room to berth temporarily alongside the wall to port, though the main marina lies to starboard, with its well equipped boatyard, chandlery, and full laying-up facilities. For major food supplies, a bus trip into Lancaster, 4 miles to the north, is the best option.

Glasson Dock.

The lock gates at Glasson.

The dock is quite large, as it was built in the 1780s by local merchants to become the main port of Lancaster. It is also connected to the Lancaster Canal, which keeps the water level in the dock pretty constant.

Old Heysham and Morecambe

53°45'N 2°47'W

Charts

Admiralty 1977 (1:75,000)
Imray C52 (1:280,000)

Tides

HW Dover −0015
Height in metres

MHWS	MHWN	MTL	MLWN	MLWS
9·5	7·4	5·3	3·1	1·1

Lights

Morecambe sewer outfall Fl.G.2s4m2M Metal framework tower
Stone pier head F.12m Stone tower
Lts in line about 090° *Front* F.R.10m2M Green mast
Promenade *Rear* 140m from front F.R.14m2M Green mast
Heysham S breakwater head 2F.G(vert)9m5M Siren 30s White metal framework tower
SW quay Ldg Lts 102·25° *Front* F.Bu.11m2M Orange and black ◆ topmark on post (mark centre of dredged channel into the harbour)
Rear 137m from front F.Bu.14m2M Orange and black ◆ topmark on mast
S pier head Oc.G.7·5s9m6M White metal tower, red base
S outfall Fl(2)G.10s5m2M Metal post
N outfall Fl.G.5s5m2M Metal post
N pier head 2F.R(vert)11m2M Mast

Radio/telephone

VHF Ch 16, 14, 74

Entry signals

R Flag/Lt	No entry
No signal	No departure
2R Flags/Lts	No entry/departure

Tides run very strongly in the treacherous inner reaches of Morecambe Bay, and the anchorages at Old Heysham and Morecambe are both very exposed and dry. Departure from Sunderland Point should be timed so as to arrive at Heysham at around HW. The buoyed channel is followed until Lune W cardinal, when it sets 035° onto Heysham No. 1 G conical buoy; from here the channel is well defined with lateral light buoys, leaving to starboard the three pipelines which extend from the shore.

Heysham Harbour is a large commercial harbour, of little interest to cruising folk, though it could be used in an emergency. Its main features on closing are the large grey box-like nuclear power station and the long open-span framework of its south jetty. It is the main port for traffic to and from Douglas, in the Isle of Man, and right of way must be given to commercial and ferry traffic, as there is little room to manoeuvre in the main channel. Giving the south jetty a cable offing to starboard, the course sets to leave the W cardinal buoy and obstruction beacon (Fl.G) to port. After leaving the unlit G conical buoy (marking the end of a sewer outlet) to the NW of Trobshaw Point to starboard, a course may be laid into the bay, where there is good holding in sand, sheltered from S–E.

On landing, a narrow lane leads from the sandy bay into the quaint little village of Old Heysham. It was here that St Patrick came ashore in 440 AD, after crossing the Irish Sea in his frail curragh; he was followed, a century later, by other monks, who built St Patrick's Oratory on the headland. Of this, two stone walls and a stone arched window still stand – quite miraculous, considering its very exposed position. Also very unusual are the graves around the oratory, which have been hollowed from bedrock to the shapes of the occupants, with small holes at their heads where wooden crosses would have fitted.

The church of St Peter's, in the town, is quite new by comparison, being a mere 1,000 years old. It is still well worth a visit, however, if only to see the 10th-century Viking burial hogback, discovered in the churchyard by a gardener in the 1800s, which now takes pride of place in the church. Its sides are carved with dragons and wolves, providing a visual representation of the battle in which the Viking warrior lost his life.

The village itself is very well kept; there is little evidence now of its fishing past, though many village handicrafts are much in evidence. A number of quiet days can be spent here in settled weather, sampling a glass or two of the local delicacy, nettle beer.

Morecambe

54°04'·3N 2°53'·7E

Charts

Admiralty 1977 (1:75,000)
Imray C52 (1:280,000)

Tides

HW Dover −0015
Height in metres

MHWS	MHWN	MTL	MLWN	MLWS
9·5	7·4	5·3	3·1	1·1

Lights

Morecambe sewer outfall Fl.G.2s4m2M Metal framework tower
Stone pier head F.12m Stone tower
Lts in line about 090° *Front* F.R.10m2M Green mast
Promenade *Rear* 140m from front F.R.14m2M Green mast

Radio/telephone

Leaving Heysham, the course sets across Clarke Wharf, which dries to 3·5m in places, until the channel is reached. A course may then be laid to pass to starboard the light beacon, marking a sewer outlet, and the off-lying rock 3 cables to the WNW of the pier. From here one can round the central pier (2F.G(vert)), where there is plenty of room to anchor, in good holding, near the yacht moorings, though the site is very exposed and rolling.

Note The more direct route, heading due north from the anchorage at Old Heysham, is feasible for shoal-draught vessels, though the ground here is rocky and stony should one touch bottom. Deep-draught vessels not wishing to cross Clarke Wharf will have to retrace their steps along Heysham Channel, and take Grange Channel before bearing off for Morecambe.

Landing by tender at HW during onshore winds may leave you a little wet, and there are only a handful of landing sites along the stout sea wall. A better tactic is usually to wait for the tide to ebb a little before making a landing on the sands.

The pier is now sadly dilapidated and closed, though the stone jetty is open and houses a large tropical aquarium. Morecambe is an attractive town, without the hustle and bustle of Blackpool, and has its own illuminations from August to October. There are a fun fair and a Western Theme Park to keep the kids happy, while the rest of the crew's needs are catered for by theatres, restaurants and, of course, pubs. At sunset, the view across the glistening bay, with its flocks of seabirds and the backdrop of the Lake District mountains, can be breathtaking, though, alas, the fleets of nobbies (local cutter-rigged clinker smacks built to cope with the short, steep seas of the area) are now little in evidence.

V. The Cumbrian coast

Charts

Admiralty 2010 (1:50,000), 3164 (1:12,500), 1961 (1:75,000), 2013 (1:50,000), 1346 (1:100,000)
Imray C62 (1:280,000)

Main coastal lights

Isle of Walney Fl.15s21m23M RC Stone tower Obscured 122°-127° when within 3M of the shore
Halfway shoal Q.R.16m10M Racon Red and yellow chequered vertical on beacon
Walney channel Ldg Lts 040·68° No. 1 *Front* Q.7m 10M Orange vertical on pile structure
No. 2 *Rear* 0·61M from front Iso.2s13m10M Orange vertical on pile structure
Rampside Sands Ldg Lts 005·08° No. 3 *Front* Q.9m 10M White round GRP tower
No. 4 *Rear* 0·77M from front Iso.2s.14m6M Red brick column, white face
St Bee's Head Fl(2)20s102m21M White round tower Obscured shore-340° F.R lights on tower 14·6M SSE
Whitehaven pier head Fl.G.5s16m13M White round tower
Silloth East Cote F.G.15m12M White structure on piles 046°-vis-058°, intens 052°

Piel and Roa Island

54°06'N 3°12'W

Charts

Admiralty 3164 (1:12,500)
Imray C62 (1:280,000)

Tides

HW Dover −0030
Height in metres

MHWS	MHWN	MTL	MLWN	MLWS
9·1	7·1	5·0	2·8	1·0

Lights

Isle of Walney Fl.15s21m23M RC Stone tower Obscured 122°-127° when within 3M of the shore
Halfway Shoal Q.R.16m10M Racon Red and yellow chequered vertical topmark on beacon
Walney channel Ldg Lts 040·68° No. 1 *Front* Q.7m-10M Orange vertical topmark on pile structure
No. 2 *Rear* 0·61M from front Iso.2s13m10M Orange vertical topmark on pile structure

Buoys

Lightning Knoll safe-water RW buoy LFl.10s Bell
SEA 1 G conical light buoy Fl.G.2·5s
SEA 2 R can light buoy Fl.R.2·5s
SEA 3 G conical light buoy Fl(3)G.10s
Halfway Shoal beacon Q.R.16m10M port topmark, Racon B
SEA 5 G conical light buoy Fl(5)G.10s
Outer Bar R can light buoy Fl(4)R.10s
SEA 7 G conical light buoy Fl.G.5s
Bar R can light buoy Fl(2)R.5s
SEA 9 G conical light buoy Fl(3)G.10s
Walney R can light buoy Fl(4)R.10s
SEA 11 G conical light buoy Fl(5)G.10s
Haws Point beacon Q.R.8m6M
Haws Point East beacon Q.G.9m6M, port topmark
West Scar R can light buoy Fl.R.5s
East Scar G conical light buoy Fl.G.5s
Castle R can light buoy Fl.R.10s
Foulney G conical light buoy Fl(3)G.10s
Piel West R can light buoy Fl.R.2·5s
Piel East G conical light buoy Fl(5)G.10s

Radio/telephone

Barrow Ramsden Dock VHF Ch 16, 12

Piel Island and Roa Island lie at the northwesternmost corner of Morecambe Bay, and both have secure anchorages, protected from the north by the mainland, from the east by Foulney Island, and from the west by the large expanse of Walney Island.

Approaching Walney from the SW, the RWVS Lightning Knoll (LFl.10s Bell) marks the beginning of Walney Channel. From here a course is laid 041°, keeping the leading lights on Foulney Twist in transit, and passing Halfway R can and Outer Bar R can to port. On passing Bar R can, the course alters to head between Haws Point beacon, to port, and the G conical Haws Point East, to starboard. Piel Island, unmistakable with its ruined castle and moored-off craft – some schooners exceeding 45ft or so – then hoves into view off the port bow. Continue due north, leaving Scar G conical to starboard, before altering course NW and anchoring near the moored craft in Piel Harbour, out of the fairway; ferry to Roa Island. Alternatively, provided that it is between 2 hours either side of HW, the Piel R can buoy may be left to port and a course laid NNW; it is possible to anchor and take the ground outside the permanent moorings between Roa Island to the west and Foulney Island to the east, landing being made on the east side of Roa by tender.

Roa Island has the advantage over Piel, as it is linked to the mainland at Rampside by a causeway, and has a frequent bus service to Barrow, the main

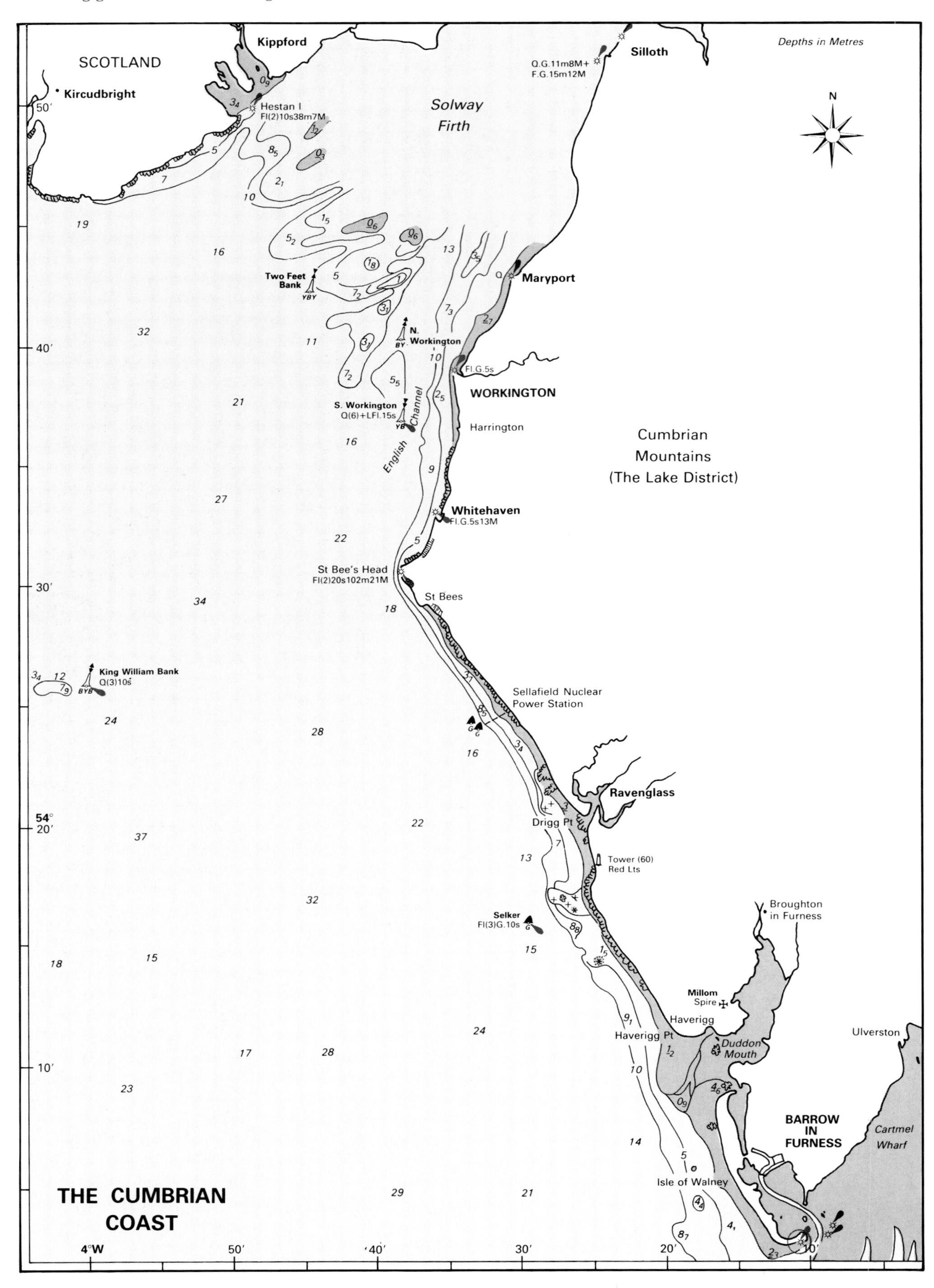
SCOTLAND
Kircudbright
Kippford
Hestan I
Fl(2)10s38m7M
Solway
Firth
Silloth
Q.G.11m8M+
F.G.15m12M
Depths in Metres
N
Two Feet Bank
YBY
Maryport
N. Workington
BY
Fl.G.5s
WORKINGTON
S. Workington
Q(6)+LFl.15s
YB
English Channel
Harrington
Cumbrian
Mountains
(The Lake District)
Whitehaven
Fl.G.5s13M
St Bee's Head
Fl(2)20s102m21M
St Bees
King William Bank
Q(3)10s
BYB
Sellafield Nuclear
Power Station
Ravenglass
Drigg Pt
Tower (60)
Red Lts
Selker
Fl(3)G.10s
Broughton
in Furness
Millom
Spire
Haverigg
Haverigg Pt
Duddon
Mouth
Ulverston
BARROW
IN
FURNESS
Cartmel
Wharf
Isle of Walney
THE CUMBRIAN
COAST
50′
40′
30′
54°
20′
10′
4°W
50′
40′
30′
20′
10′

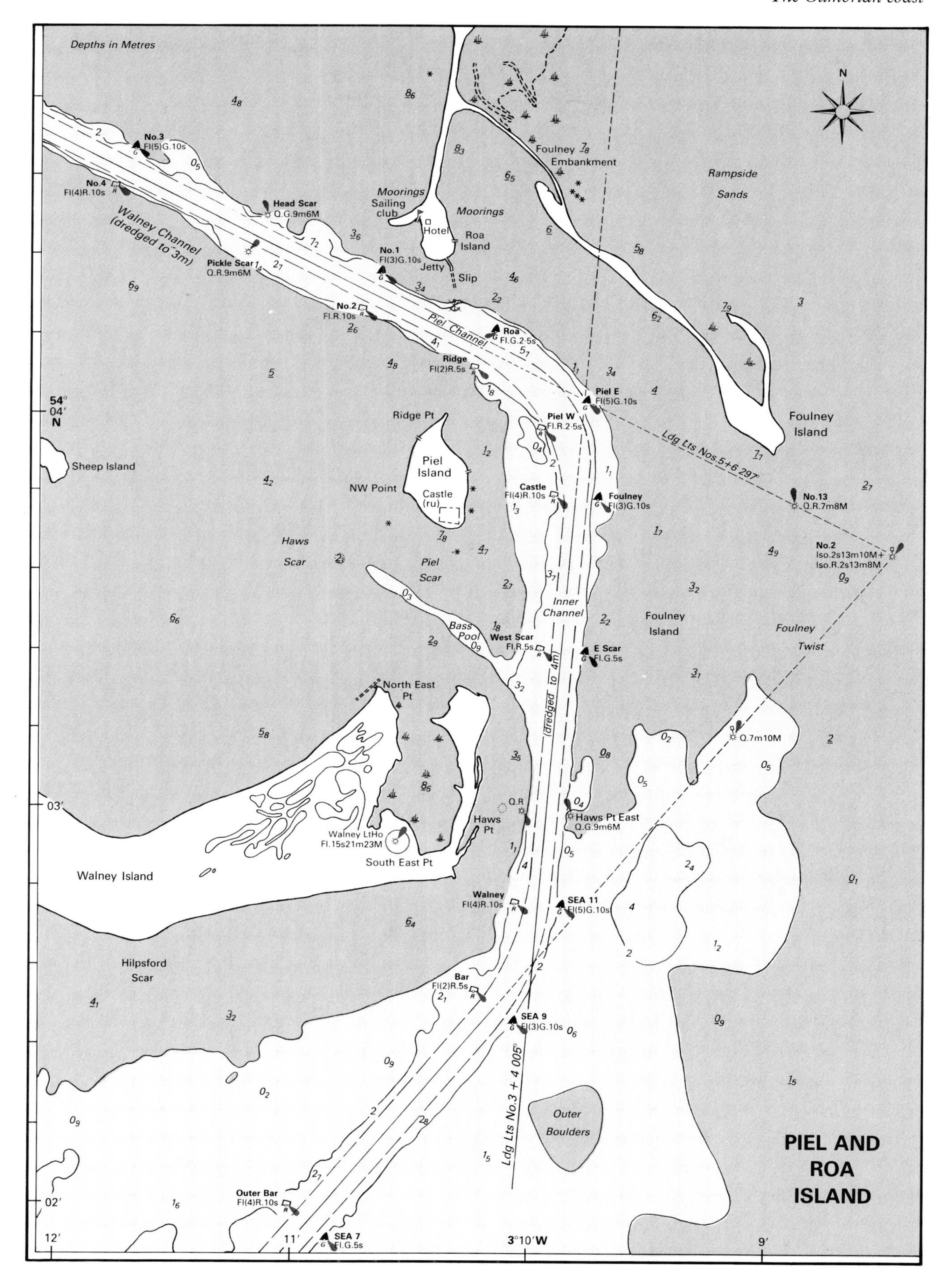
Depths in Metres
No.3
Fl(5)G.10s
No.4
Fl(4)R.10s
Head Scar
Q.G.9m6M
Walney Channel
(dredged to 3m)
Pickle Scar
Q.R.9m6M
Moorings
Sailing club
Moorings
Hotel
Roa Island
Jetty
Slip
No.1
Fl(3)G.10s
No.2
Fl.R.10s
Piel Channel
Roa
Fl.G.2·5s
Ridge
Fl(2)R.5s
Foulney Embankment
Rampside Sands
Piel E
Fl(5)G.10s
Piel W
Fl.R.2·5s
Ridge Pt
Piel Island
Castle (ru)
NW Point
Sheep Island
Foulney Island
Ldg Lts Nos.5+6 297°
Castle
Fl(4)R.10s
Foulney
Fl(3)G.10s
No.13
Q.R.7m8M
No.2
Iso.2s13m10M+
Iso.R.2s13m8M
Haws Scar
Piel Scar
Inner Channel
Foulney Island
Foulney Twist
Bass Pool
West Scar
Fl.R.5s
E Scar
Fl.G.5s
(dredged to 4m)
North East Pt
Q.7m10M
Q.R
Haws Pt East
Q.G.9m6M
Haws Pt
Walney LtHo
Fl.15s21m23M
South East Pt
Walney Island
Walney
Fl(4)R.10s
SEA 11
Fl(5)G.10s
Hilpsford Scar
Bar
Fl(2)R.5s
SEA 9
Fl(3)G.10s
Ldg Lts No.3 + 4 005°
Outer Boulders
Outer Bar
Fl(4)R.10s
SEA 7
Fl.G.5s
54° 04′ N
03′
02′
12′
11′
3°10′W
9′
N
PIEL AND ROA ISLAND

Above Piel Island, with its ancient ruined castle and infamous Inn.

Below Roa Island, connected to the mainland by causeway.

Roa Island

town of the district. It is an entity in itself, boasting a pub, a post office, a small café, a yacht club, and a handful of houses. Life here is lived at a leisurely pace, though recently the island has become a venue for the sailboard fraternity, who congregate at the conjuncture of Roa and Foulney Island, adding a lot of colour to the place. Foulney itself is very low lying, almost awash at HW, and is a favourite breeding ground for many species of bird. Piel Island's main feature is its ruined castle, built by King Stephen, and further strengthened and refurbished by the abbots from the local abbey to protect their trading against pirates and privateers. The island lies across the main channel from Roa, and boasts several houses and a famous inn, whose landlord bears the title 'King of Piel'. This dates from an age-old tradition by which the king has the power to grant seafarers the honoured title 'Knight of Piel' – after due ceremony, of course, the candidates swearing to be of good behaviour, steady at all times, attentive to the opposite sex, and willing to aid the king in boat racing, pigeon shooting and cock fighting. In return, a knight, if wrecked or drowned, is at liberty to demand free lodging and sustenance at the inn – a little difficult if drowned, I should think!

Barrow

Lights

Isle of Walney Fl.15s21m23M RC Stone tower Obscured when within 3M of the shore

Walney channel Ldg Lts 040·68° No. 1 *Front* Q.7m 10M Orange vertical topmark on pile structure

No. 2 *Rear* 0·61M from front Iso.2s13m10M Orange vertical topmark on pile structure

Rampside Sands Ldg Lts 005·08° No. 3 *Front* Q.9m 10M White round GRP tower

No. 4 *Rear* 0·77M from front Iso.2s14m6M

Anchoring at Piel or Roa is usually very quiet, being well sheltered from the west by the large expanse of Walney Island, a low-lying natural breakwater. (The name comes from the Norse, and means Killer Whale Island – though I haven't seen any recently.) With a SE wind, however, a swell sets right in from across the bay, when it may be wise to evacuate, and follow the well buoyed Walney Channel between Vickerstown and Barrow, before the road bridge. There one can take the ground on the sand and shingle bank directly to port, where many craft lay up for the winter, or pick up a vacant mooring. The site, though very noisy, is completely sheltered, and gives easy access to Walney Island and the mainland, where full supplies are available.

Walney to Ravenglass

Lights

Isle of Walney Fl.15s21m23M RC Stone tower Obscured 122°-127° when within 3M of the shore

St Bee's Head Fl(2)20s102m21M White round tower Obscured shore-340° F.R lights on tower 14·6M SSE

Buoys

Selker green conical Fl(3)G.10s Bell

From Walney Channel, the next port of call for craft able to take the ground lies at Ravenglass, approximately 20 miles away. There are few navigational problems along this coastline, the main consideration being to time arrival at Ravenglass during daylight hours (night entry is virtually impossible) and between 1 hour either side of HW, as whilst the harbour is attainable for 2 hours either side of HW, the tidal stream experienced once inside the harbour can be very strong and unpredictable, and can quite easily take one unawares. When awaiting favourable tidal conditions for departing from Walney, anchoring off Piel in Piel Harbour enables departure to be made via the buoyed channel at any state of tide.

Rounding Walney's SE point (Walney light Fl.15s 21m23M), and leaving Bar red can Fl(2)R.5s to starboard, a short cut can be made (provided it isn't at the bottom of a spring) by heading 245° for 2 miles to clear Hilpsford Spit and Hilpsford Bank; the course may then be laid along the coast, keeping a good offing to leave to starboard the drying areas 1 mile to seaward of Vickerstown, which lie within the obscured sector of Walney light. On the whole of this voyage the tide will be found to run quite weakly, with a rather uncertain set, which makes accounting for it in one's navigation very difficult. As a general rule, however, it sets northbound at 0·4–0·8 knots between −1 and +5 hours Liverpool, after which it turns to run southbound at the same rate. The course is now laid onto Selker green conical Fl(3)G.10s, twelve miles distant, passing the wide expanse of Duddon Estuary. This is marked at its northern edge by the mass of Black Combe, a very dark mountain tinged purple with heather, standing some 596m high.

The road bridge connecting Barrow in Furness to Walney Island.

From Haverigg Point the coast becomes progressively more rugged, with ruddy-looking cliffs. The course leaves to starboard Black Leg Rock (dries 0·9m) and Selker green conical buoy; this buoy marks the reef of Selker Rocks, to shoreward, which lies within the obscured sector of St Bee's Head light (Fl(2)20s102m21M), 15 miles to the north.

Duddon estuary

As the estuary completely dries, and the channel is unmarked and constantly changing, local knowledge is essential.

There is anchorage at Haverigg, a pier at Askam and a tiny drying harbour at Hodbarrow. Ask local yachtsmen at Roa Island or Barrow for advice.

Ravenglass

54°21'N 3°25'W

Charts

Admiralty 1346 (1:15,000)
Imray C62 (1:280,000)

Tides

HW Dover −0015

Height in metres

MHWS	MHWN	MTL	MLWN	MLWS
8·3	6·4	4·5	2·5	0·9

Lights

Ravenglass F.G (occas) Blockhouse

Buoys

Selker G conical Fl(3)G.10s Bell

Unfortunately, the approach to Ravenglass from seaward is devoid of conspicuous landmarks and features, though the sloping sides of Whitfell (569m) and Ulpha Fell (483m), to the SE of the village, may give some indication of its position.

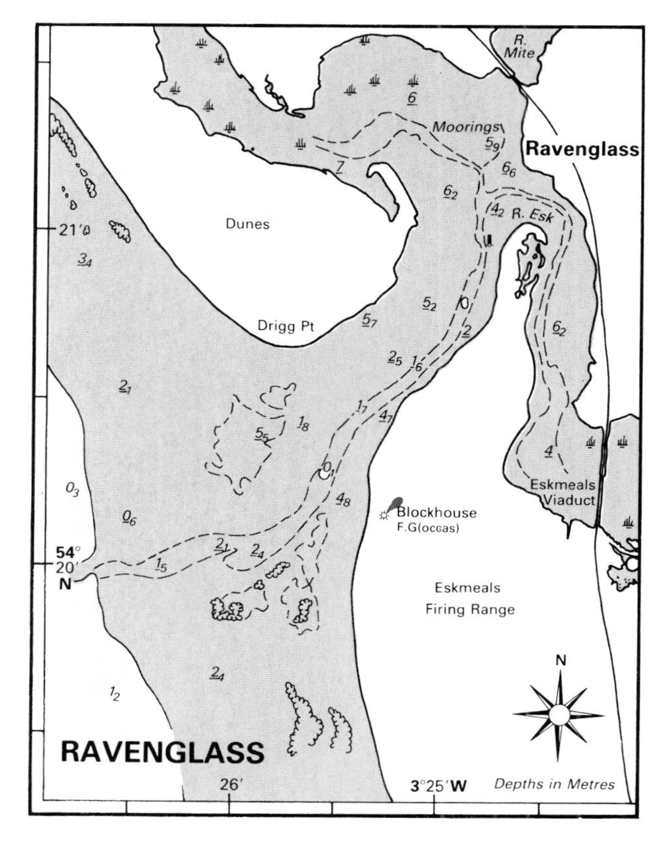

From Selker G conical, a course may be laid to close slowly with the coast, keeping well to the north of Selker Rocks, until the estuary can be distinguished, and the village of Ravenglass opens up with its many moored-off craft, a course being laid to anchor just outside the permanent moorings.

The villagers once earned their living from fishing, the estuary formed by the rivers Irt, Esk and Mite providing excellent shelter for their craft, which were designed to take the ground. Nowadays, however, due to pollution and a change in fishing methods, the fishing has all but ceased, and one is more likely to encounter tourist traffic during the summer months, attracted by the Ravenglass and Eskdale Narrow Gauge Railway, which runs for 7 miles through beautiful countryside, and the ancient Roman villa/baths of Walls Castle.

For the yachtsman/woman, Ravenglass provides a secure haven drying in quiet surroundings, with some supplies available ashore at the local store, the post office, and, of course, the fish and chip shop.

Ravenglass to Whitehaven

Lights

St Bee's head Fl(2)20s102m21M White round tower Obscured shore-340° F.R lights on tower 14·6M SSE
Whitehaven west pier head Fl.G.5s16m13M White round tower
North pier head 2F.R(vert)8m9M White round tower
North wall quay head 2F.R(vert)8m2M White column
Old quay head 2F.G(vert)8m2M

Signals

R Flag – Gun test at Esmeals

Whitehaven lies some 17 miles up the coast. Like Ravenglass, the harbour dries, so either a very fast passage will have to be made in order to arrive at Whitehaven while there is still enough water to enter, or the right conditions should be chosen so that one may anchor off to the west of Whitehaven in 7 metres, or in Saltom Bay in 4 metres, to await the tide.

Leaving Ravenglass and the Esk estuaries, the course is set to give a good offing to Drigg Rock, to the NW of Drigg Point. The offing is then maintained to leave to starboard Kokoarrah Scar (dries 2·4m), Barn Scar (dries 3·4m), and the two G conical buoys marking the outfall from Calder Hall power station, whose cooling towers are quite a prominent feature (on a night passage, keeping St Bee's Head light open leads well outside these dangers).

The coast now becomes progressively more rugged as one closes with St Bee's Head, where the red sandstone cliffs rise to 137m, topped with a tall white lighthouse. The course passes inshore of Carlo wreck G conical (Fl.G.10s), with 7·2m over it. St Bee's Head can be rounded close-to if conditions allow, though in a fresh onshore wind the rebound effect creates a turbulent sea reminiscent of a tide-rip, when a course further offshore should be taken until Whitehaven, unmistakable with its mass of chimneys, masts and towers, opens up. The harbour should be entered between the white tower of the west pier head (Fl.G.5s16m 13M) and the white tower of the east pier head (2F.R). Keep close to the west pier head if entering with the flood, because of the strong E-bound tidal set across the harbour mouth, which reverses at HW, and can make the harbour unattainable in fresh westerly winds against the tide, when an ugly sea may develop.

Whitehaven

54°33'N 3°36'W

Charts

Admiralty 2013 (1:7,500)
Imray C62 (1:280,000)

Tides

HW Dover +0015
Height in metres

MHWS	MHWN	MTL	MLWN	MLWS
8·2	6·3	4·5	2·4	1·2

Lights

Whitehaven west pier head Fl.G.5s16m13M White round tower
North pier head 2F.R(vert)8m9M White round tower

Above Whitehaven Harbour.

Below Drying moorings at Whitehaven's southern harbour.

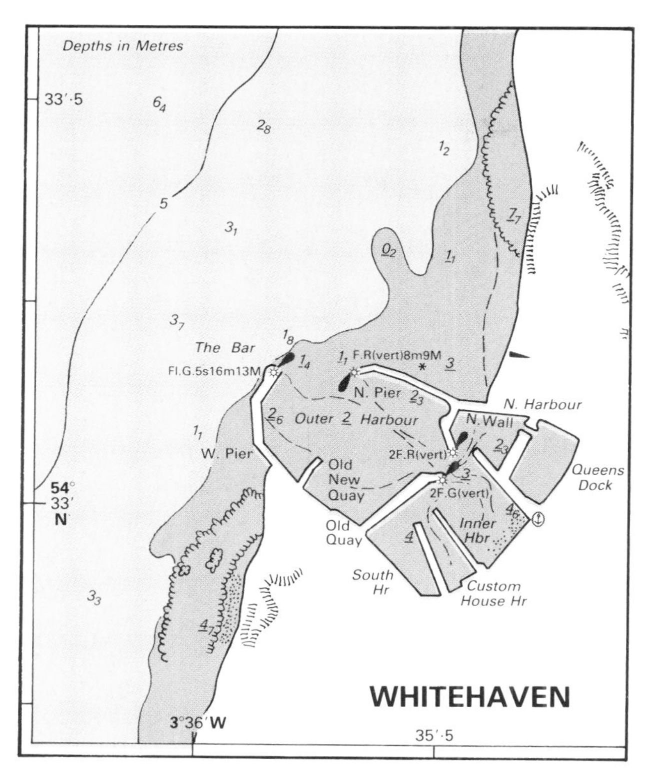

North wall quay head 2F.R(vert)8m2M White column
Old quay head 2F.G(vert)8m2M

Radio/telephone

VHF Ch 16 (HW −2½ to HW +2½)
☎ Harbourmaster (0946) 692435

Inside, the harbour, drying to beyond the pier heads, provides complete shelter for craft able to take the ground, and if quay space is unavailable some drying moorings for visiting craft may be available in the southern harbour. It must be stressed, however, that Whitehaven is a very busy commercial harbour, developed from a tiny hamlet into a major port in the 17th century for the export of coal; because of this, right of way must be given at all times to commercial traffic. Larger vessels unable to take the ground may, by prior arrangement with the harbourmaster (☎ (0946) 692435), be allocated a berth in Queen's Dock. This is a busy wet dock entered from the north harbour, through the lock gates, which are open for 1 hour either side of HW. Water and diesel are available from Fish Quay, and full provisions are available from the town; early closing Wednesdays.

Whitehaven Harbour entrance.

Whitehaven to Harrington and Workington

Harrington

54°37'N 3°34'W

Charts

Admiralty 2013 (1:50,000)
Imray C62 (1:280,000)

Tides

HW Dover +0025

Telephone

Moorings ☎ (0900) 823741

The next major harbour en route is Workington, 6 miles distant, though there is also the small harbour of Harrington, used by Harrington Sailing Club. This is approximately halfway between Whitehaven and Workington; enter between the stone pier to the south, and the wooden breakwater and red perches to the north. A secure berth is usually available along a section of the north quay reserved for visiting craft, after which the Ship Inn, close by, caters for the crew's inner needs. For the trailer sailor, there is also a concrete slip, available for two hours either side of HW.

Trailer sailors should note that Harrington, Whitehaven, and likewise Workington lead straight out into a very rough sea area, with strong tides and races around the harbour mouths. Whilst I have nothing but admiration for those seasoned sea dinghy sailors who cover tremendous distances in their small craft, I would strongly discourage those with little experience of sea sailing from using these sites.

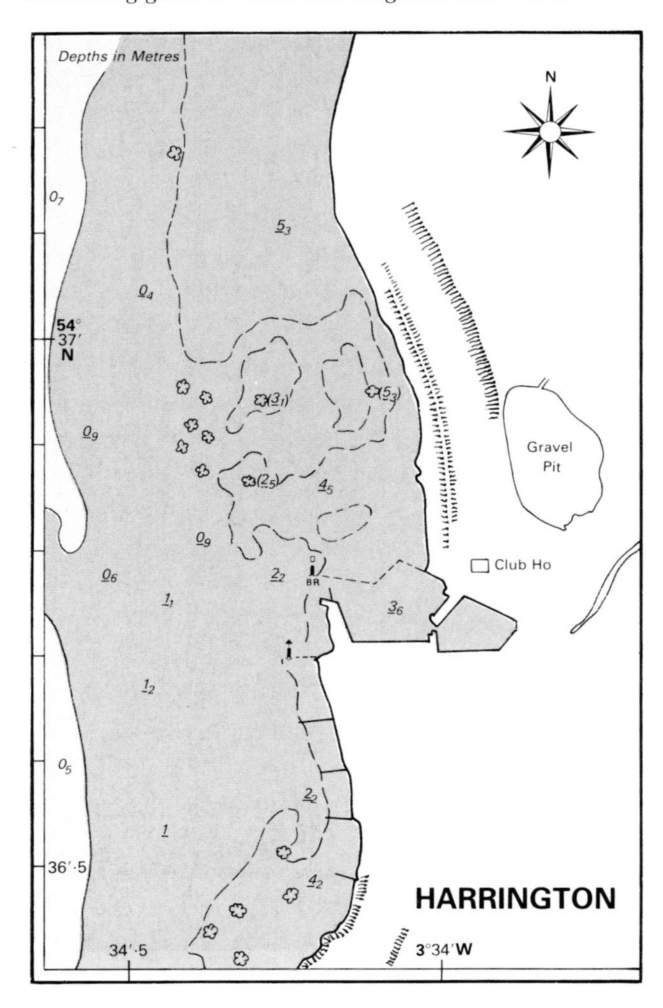

Workington

54°39'N 3°34'W

Charts

Admiralty 2013 (1:7,500), 1346 (1:100,000)
Imray C62 (1:280,000)

Tides

HW Dover +0025
Height in metres

MHWS	MHWN	MTL	MLWN	MLWS
8·4	6·4	4·6	2·5	0·9

Lights

S pier Fl.5s11m8M Siren 20s Red brick building
Head Q.G.5m Orange metal mast
N jetty head 2F.R(vert)7m Metal column
Bush perch Q.R. Metal mast
Ldg Lts 131·82° *Front* F.R.10m3M White pyramidal tower, orange band
Rear 134m from front F.R.12m3M White pyramidal tower, orange band
N side of channel Lts in line 131·82° *Front* F.Bu
Rear 70m from front F.Bu
S side of channel Lts in line 131·82° *Front* F.Bu
Rear 44m from front F.Bu

Radio/telephone

VHF Ch 16, 11, 14 (HW −2½ to HW +2)
☎ Harbourmaster (0900) 602301

On passage to Workington, the tide becomes progressively stronger, as this area is effectively the entrance to the lower reaches of Solway Firth, though as the tide still sets along the coast it is easily accounted for. There are no navigational hazards on this short leg (unless one's craft is of exceptionally deep draught, and it is the bottom of a spring tide, when the English Channel between Workington Bank and Workington may have to be used). The coast becomes progressively less rugged, until the

The small drying harbour of Harrington.

Workington Harbour.

Workington Harbour. The drill is very much 'find a berth where you can'. The tidal harbour, top right, is now guarded by a fixed railway bridge with very little clearance.

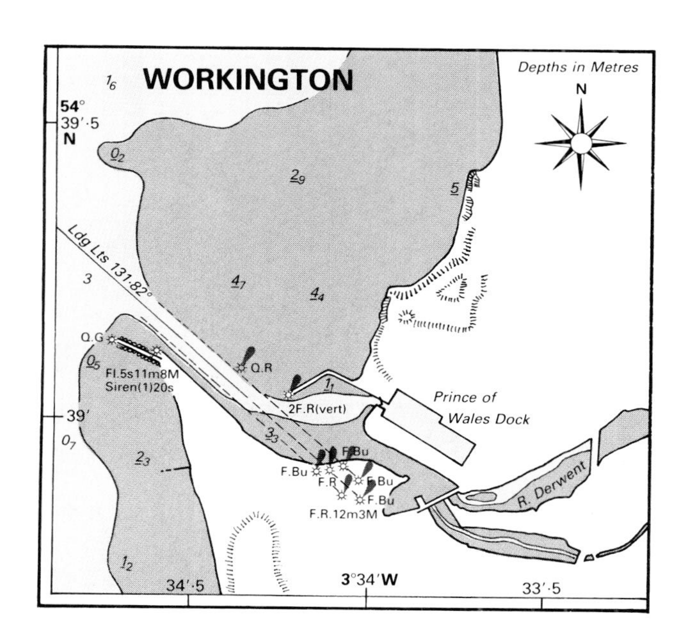

approach of the harbour is heralded by a conspicuous chimney and by Chapel Hill, ½ mile to the south of the entrance. Entry is made into the harbour between S Pier (Fl.5s11m8M), which extends 2½ cables NW from the south of the River Derwent, and the N jetty, which extends W from the north of the river and then angles SW to shelter the harbour – the leading lights 131° lead straight in. As at Whitehaven, the tide sets very quickly across the harbour mouth, and so the same drill of entering near the south pier on the flood, or entering near the north pier on the ebb, is wise, in order not to be taken by surprise.

Workington is the major port of Cumbria, but as the harbour dries all the large commercial traffic lies in the Prince of Wales dock, whose lock gates are opened for 1½ hours either side of HW. Despite this, however, berths for visiting yachts are not as freely available as one would wish, since the old harbour to the west of the tidal harbour is used exclusively by fishing craft, as is much of the quay

Above Workington tidal inner harbour, guarded by fixed railway bridge.

Below The small drying harbour of Harrington.

space, and the tidal harbour, which once afforded access via a swing railway bridge, is now of little use to sailing craft because the bridge has been fixed, with very little clearance.

The drill is very much 'find a berth where you can' – a very short-sighted attitude for the authorities to take, especially considering the developments which have been made at Maryport, our next destination. Despite the harbour's shortcomings, however, and the town's air of an industrial area in decline, I have a soft spot for the place. And, being a northerner myself and forever an optimist (look what they have done with my home town of Wigan – a tourist attraction!), I look forward to the day when the harbour's true potential can be realised.

Workington to Maryport

When I began to write the first draft of this pilot, I began my introduction to Maryport:

'Once a thriving seaport for the export of coal and iron; now officially closed (all craft are warned that they use the port at their own risk), and so silted by deposits of the River Ellen as to prevent its use by large craft. It continues to be a favourite heavy-weather haven with cruising skippers, however. Maryport has the advantage over Whitehaven and Workington that entry into it is much quieter in an onshore breeze, and there is plenty of room to manoeuvre, as it is no longer used by commercial traffic; there are acres of quay space to choose from.'

Whilst the above is still largely true of the rest of the harbour, I was very surprised on visiting early last year to find that a new marina development was well under way in Senhouse dock, which was then already approximately half full of yachts, even though work had only just begun on the proposed boatyard, chandlery, and marina-front properties. On full completion, which will probably coincide with the publication of this guide, the marina will boast 200 deep-water pontoon berths, with water and electricity, toilets and showers, a launderette, a boatyard with 80-ton slipping capability, and a chandlery.

Maryport

54°43'·1N 3°30'·5W

Charts

Admiralty 2013 (1:10,000), 1346 (1:100,000)
Imray C62 (1:280,000)

Tides

HW Dover +0038

Height in metres

MHWS	MHWN	MTL	MLWN	MLWS
8·4	6·6	4·7	2·5	0·9

Lights

Maryport S pier head Fl.1·5s10m4M Metal framework tower

Radio/telephone

VHF Ch 16, 12 (occas)
☎ Maryport Marina Ch 16M (0900) 813331
☎ Maryport harbour authority (0900) 812646

Leaving Workington before HW, the course sets again along the coast, keeping 1 mile offing, as the coast is foul with rocks, until Maryport is abeam. A course can then be laid to enter the harbour between the S pier (Fl.1·5s.10m4M), to starboard, and the open framework of the N pier, to port. Keeping the corner of Elizabeth basin and the centre windows of a large, conspicuous house at the bottom of Shipping Brow in transit ensures that one keeps to the centre of the 25m-wide channel, which dries to 1m. This leads into the basin, where, after giving a wide berth to the innermost end of the S pier (marked by a light tower), where there is an

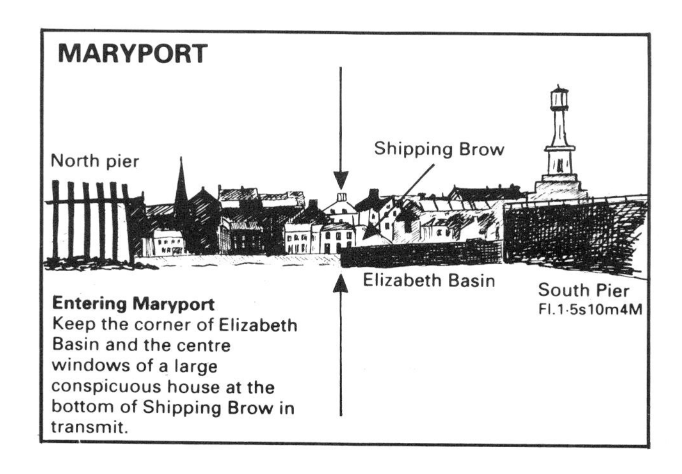

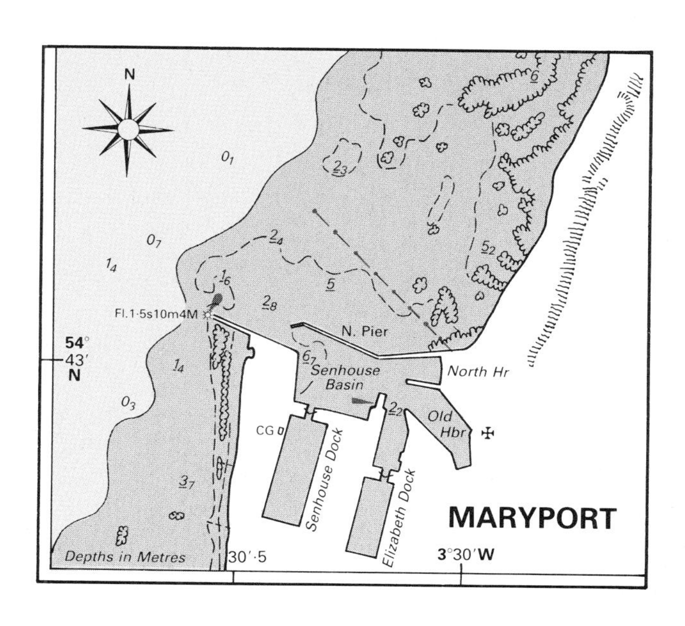

Maryport's Elizabeth Dock, where yachts used to moor before the marina was built in the Senhouse Dock. Maryport is now a useful harbour in the NW corner of the Irish Sea, and convenient for a passage to the Isle of Man. *Peter Cumberlidge*

extensive shoal area, a berth can be taken alongside the quays as desired (though you are warned that you do this at your own risk). Alternatively, if preferred, a course can be laid west of south directly into the 240-berth marina; the lock gates are open for two and a half hours either side of HW, when there is a least depth of 2m over the sill. The marina offers a full boat repair service, can cater for craft of up to (21m) 70ft, drawing a maximum of (3m) 10ft, and can slip craft of up to 80 tons by arrangement.

There is 24-hour security; access to the pontoon and shower block is by a swipe-card system. Gas and diesel are available from the marina office, there is a well stocked chandlery, and lightship 14, berthed in the dock, houses an à la carte restaurant and the yacht club.

Full stores are available from the town (early closing Wednesdays), and water is available from some of the old quays. For the trailer sailor, there is a concrete slip, available for 2 hours either side of HW, at the rear of the coastguard station.

Maryport Harbour, showing the Marina Development in Senhouse Dock.

VI. Southwest Scotland

Kirkcudbright Bay to Portpatrick

Kirkcudbright Bay to Portpatrick

Charts

Admiralty 1346 (1:100,000), 1826 (1:200,000), 2094 (1:100,000)
Imray C62 (1:280,000)

Main coast lights

Silloth East Cote F.G.15m12M White structure on piles 046°-vis-058°, intens 052°
Little Ross Fl.5s50m12M White tower Obscured in Wigtown bay when bearing more than 103°
Crammag head Fl.10s35m18M White tower
Mull of Galloway Fl.20s99m28M White round tower 182-vis-105 3F.R on radio mast 16M ENE

Maryport to Kirkcudbright Bay

Charts

Admiralty 1346 (1:100,000), 1826 (1:200,000)
Imray C62 (1:280,000)

Navigation north of Maryport Roads into the inner reaches of the Solway Firth is not normally undertaken by cruising craft. Silloth, a busy commercial harbour, lies within the Firth, but has no facilities for visiting yachts, which have to anchor off the harbour in Lees Scar in 4m, exposed to SW. The trip requires local knowledge, as pilotage is made very tricky by the shifting sands, the fierce tides, and the eddies and overfalls, at their worst just after LW, when the eastbound flood meets the outbound stream from the bay.

Silloth

54°52'N 3°24'W

Charts

Admiralty 2013 (1:10,000)
Imray C62 (1:280,000)

Tides

HW Dover −0050
Height in metres

MHWS	MHWN	MTL	MLWN	MLWS
9·2	6·9	4·8	2·3	0·8

Lights

Lees Scar Q.G.11m8M White structure on piles 005°-vis-317°
East Cote F.G.15m12M White structure on piles 046°-vis-058°, intens 052°
Groyne head 2F.G(vert)4m4M Dolphin. Fl.Bu traffic signal exhibited from New Dock Signal Mast
Outfall 2F.G(vert) Green triangle on beacon
New Dock channel Ldg Lts 115·25° *Front* and *Rear* F White masts (Vert strip lights)

Radio/telephone

VHF Ch 16, 12 (HW −2½ to HW +2½)
☎ Harbourmaster (06973) 31358

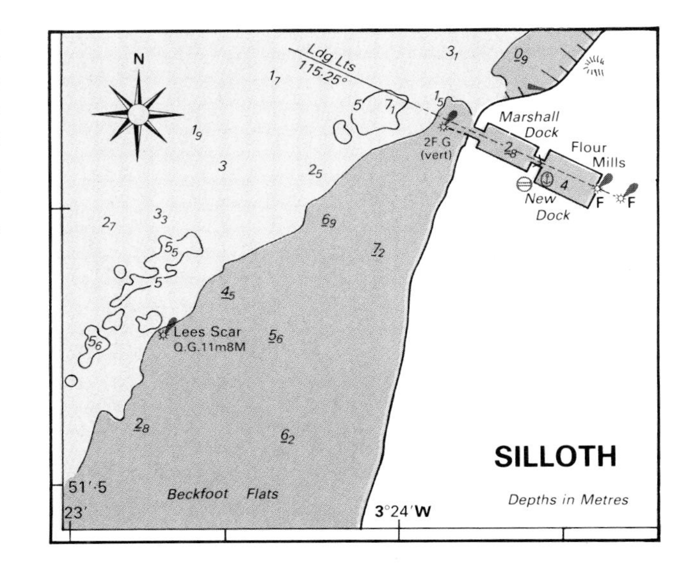

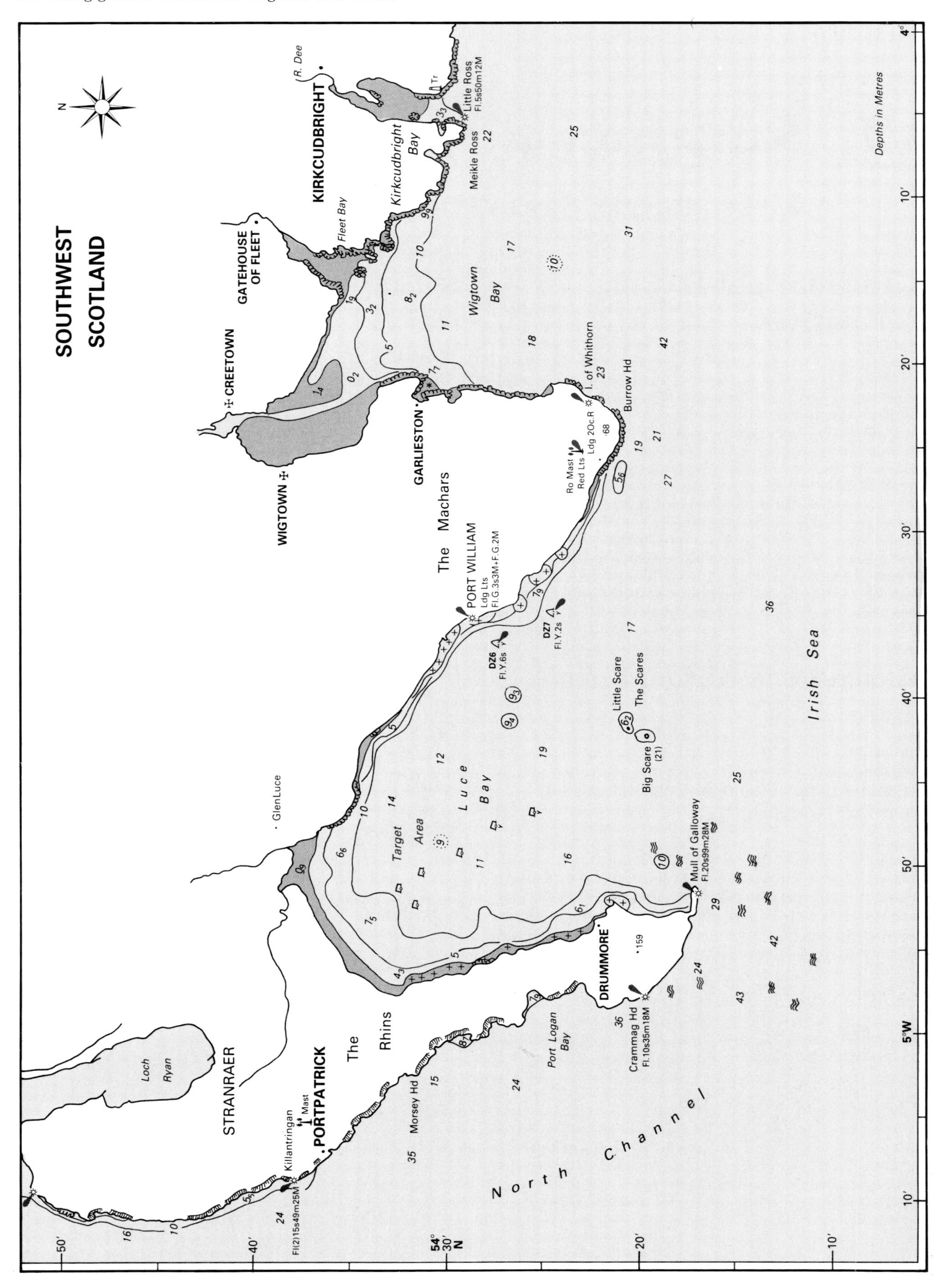
SOUTHWEST
SCOTLAND
KIRKCUDBRIGHT
R. Dee
Kirkcudbright
Bay
Little Ross
Fl.5s50m12M
Meikle Ross
Fleet Bay
GATEHOUSE
OF FLEET
CREETOWN
WIGTOWN
GARLIESTON
Wigtown
Bay
I. of Whithorn
Burrow Hd
Ldg 2Oc.R
Ro Mast
Red Lts
The Machars
PORT WILLIAM
Ldg Lts
Fl.G.3s3M+F.G.2M
DZ6
Fl.Y.6s
DZ7
Fl.Y.2s
Little Scare
The Scares
Big Scare
(21)
Irish Sea
GlenLuce
Luce
Bay
Target
Area
DRUMMORE
Mull of Galloway
Fl.20s99m28M
Crammag Hd
Fl.10s35m18M
Port Logan
Bay
The
Rhins
Loch
Ryan
STRANRAER
PORTPATRICK
Mast
Killantringan
Fl(2)15s49m25M
Morsey Hd
North Channel
Depths in Metres
4°
10'
20'
30'
40'
50'
5°W
50'
40'
54°
30'
N
20'
10'

Kippford

Radio/telephone

☎ Solway Yacht Club (0056) 62312

On the Scottish coast, shelter is a little better. Kippford, in the upper reaches of the Urr estuary, is the most easterly haven in the Solway Firth, but it dries out completely at LW. It is also plagued by shifting sands, necessitating the frequent repositioning of the channel buoys, and by strong tidal streams (the rapid rise from LW on a spring tide with a brisk southerly behind it can take one completely by surprise!) It is wise to enquire amongst local yachtsmen, or to contact Solway Yacht Club (☎ (0056) 62 312), before a first attempt.

There are no leading marks at the mouth of the estuary between Hestan Island (Fl(2)10s38m7M) to the west and Castle Point to the east, and care must be taken to give a wide berth to the Craig Roan Rocks, which form a drying reef extending a half mile or so off the south shore, just east of Castle Point.

Kippford has quite a large yachting population, and there is usually a vacant berth to be found upon enquiring ashore. Full supplies are available, along with a boatyard, chandlery, fuel and water. Solway Yacht Club offers a welcome to visitors by sea, and here toilets and showers are available.

Kirkcudbright Bay

Kirkcudbright Bay, in Galloway, lies across the approaches to the Solway Firth, northwest of Maryport; there sheltered anchoring can be found in all but southerly winds.

Note Prior to departure from Maryport, the Ministry of Defence firing range near Abbey Head, which fires out to sea Monday–Friday, creating a danger zone which extends some 14 miles out, should be contacted, by telephoning Dundrenna (055) 723 236, or, if already at sea, by calling the range patrol vessel *Gallovidian* on VHF Ch 16.

Departing Maryport Marina when afloat, the direct route to Little Ross, the small island guarding the western entrance into Kirkcudbright Bay, can be laid (Ministry of Defence permitting); it leads over Two Feet bank, with 1m over it. This has the advantages that the tidal streams encountered when crossing the Solway Firth will not be at their maximum, and that the allowances made for the NE flood (−2 to HW) and the SW-bound ebb (HW to +2) will tend to cancel each other out. On the negative side, however, arrival at the entrance to Kirkcudbright Bay will be too late to allow navigation up the stretches of the bay to Kirkcudbright itself. This will make it necessary to anchor in the lower reaches of the bay, where there is a strong tidal rate (4 knots springs), with a very uncomfortable swell in winds from the north or southeast.

After closing with Little Ross, with its conspicuous white lighthouse standing at its southeastern corner, a course can be laid directly into the bay between Little Ross to port and the high and rocky Gypsy Point to starboard; the latter can be taken close-to if desired. The first anchorage lies just two cables to the north of Little Ross in 6m; keep well to the east of the spit which runs from the northwestern tip of the island in the direction of Manor Point, and well to the southeast of Sugarloaf Rock (dries 0·8m). This anchorage is very remote, and wide open to the SE, however, and the alternative anchorage, in one of the pools just to the north of the lifeboat slip on the eastern shore, in 3m, may be more desirable.

Craft which are capable of taking the ground can gain much better shelter by anchoring in Ross Bay, ½ mile to the north of Little Ross, on the western shore, in sand and mud. Alternatively, they can anchor and take the ground on Manxman's Lake, to the southeast of St Mary's Isle, in good holding.

The River Dee channel to Kirkcudbright is navigable from 2 hours before HW for craft of moderate draught, and is well buoyed from the lifeboat house onwards.

From Little Ross, a course can be steered directly onto the lifeboat house; keeping the lighthouse and beacon on Little Ross in transit astern ensures that the free-standing rock (dries 0·5m) lying a cable off the eastern shore, between Torrs Point and the lifeboat house, is left well to starboard.

From No. 2 red can, the channel is well buoyed and follows the course of the river in a northwesterly direction, separating the drying banks of Manxman's Lake to starboard and Milton sands to port, before turning north after passing the rocky southern point of St Mary's Isle. After passing Fish House and Gibb Hill sawmill on the west bank, the channel eventually turns east at No. 24 red can onto Kirkcudbright.

Kirkcudbright

54°47'·7N 4°03'·7W

Charts

Admiralty 1344 (1:100,000)
Imray C62 (1:280,000)

Tides

HW Dover +0030

Height in metres

MHWS	MHWN	MTL	MLWN	MLWS
7·5	5·9	4·1	2·4	0·8

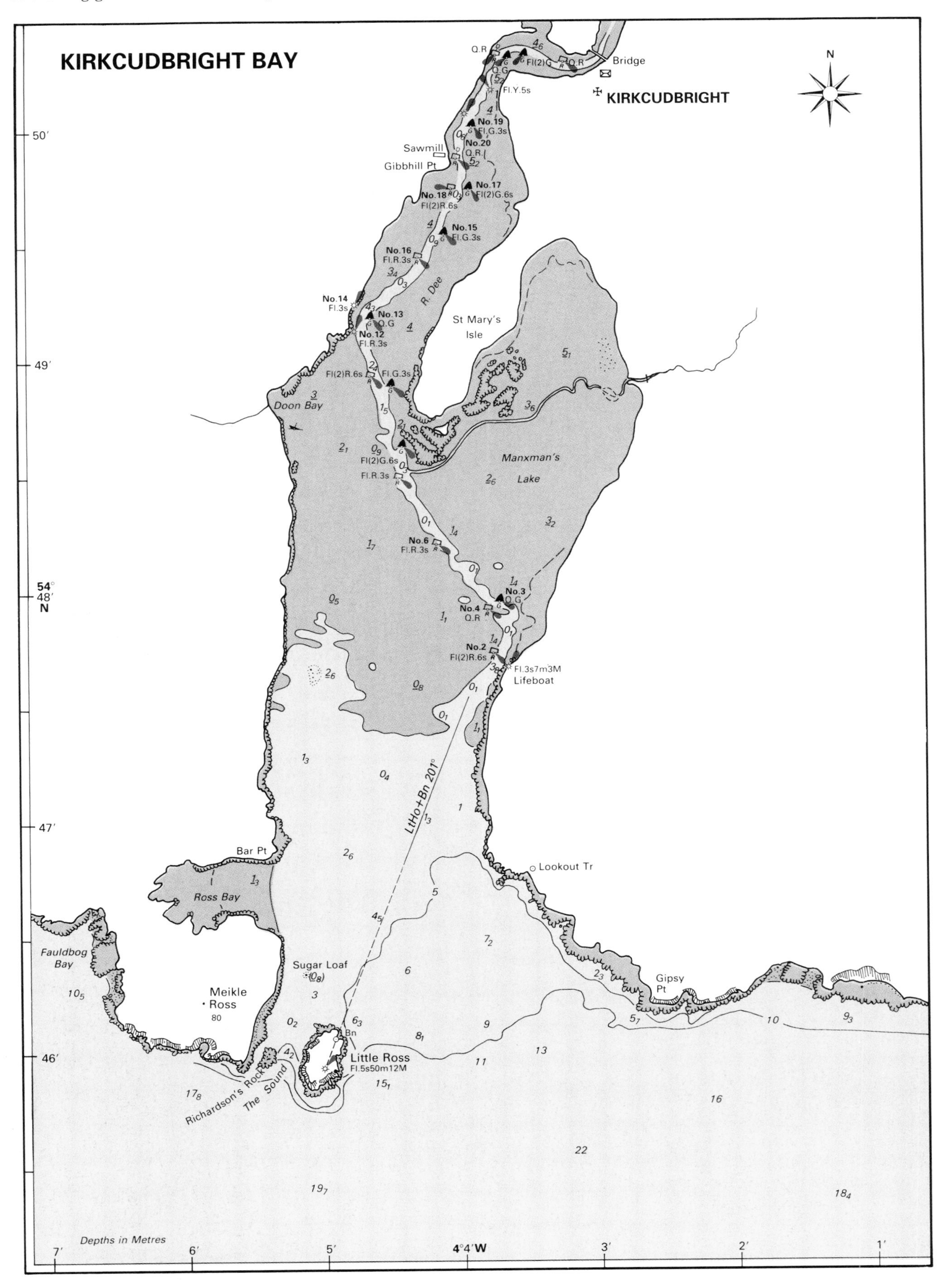
KIRKCUDBRIGHT BAY
KIRKCUDBRIGHT
Bridge
Sawmill
Gibbhill Pt
R. Dee
St Mary's Isle
Doon Bay
Manxman's Lake
Lifeboat
Lookout Tr
Bar Pt
Ross Bay
Fauldbog Bay
Meikle Ross
Sugar Loaf
Little Ross
Fl.5s50m12M
Richardson's Rock
The Sound
Gipsy Pt
LtHo+Bn 201°
Depths in Metres
4°4′W
54° 48′ N

Above Kirkcudbright, showing the stone wharf which dries to mud. Availability of a berth can be confirmed by contacting the harbourmaster.

Below Garlieston Harbour. Yachts may berth alongside as space allows.

Lights

Little Ross Fl.5s50m12M White tower Obscured in Wigtown bay when bearing more than 103°
Kirkcudbright Bay No. 1 Lifeboat house Fl.3s7m3M
No. 12 Fl.R.3s3m perch
No. 14 Fl.3s5m perch
No. 22 Fl.R.3s2m
Outfall Fl.Y.5s3m2M Yellow framework tower
Hestan Island E end Fl(2)10s38m7M White house

Radio/telephone

VHF Ch 16, 12 (HW ±2)
☎ Harbourmaster (0900) 31135

Kirkcudbright is a small port used mainly by coasters and fishing vessels, though there is usually a berth to be found alongside the stone wharf, near the middle of town, which dries to mud. The availability of a berth can be confirmed by contacting the harbourmaster (☎ (0557) 31135). Failing this, it is possible to anchor off the old wooden jetty, a cable below the warehouses, in 2m, though it is a wise precaution to buoy the anchor and, as one is in the channel, to exhibit an anchor light at night.

For the trailer sailor, a stone slip is viable for up to two hours either side of HW; there is also a concrete slip available for up to three hours either side at Gibb Hill sawmill, if preferred.

Ashore, the harbour frontage is lined with 17th and 18th-century merchants' houses, in stark contrast to the noisy and gaily coloured clutter of day-trippers which descends during mid-season.

The Stewartry Museum, illustrating life in bygone ages, is well worth a visit, while for one's more urgent needs there are shops, a post office, and some general chandlery. Early closing Thursdays.

Garlieston

54°47'N 4°21'W

Charts

Admiralty 2094 (1:100,000)
Imray C62 (1:280,000)

Tides

HW Dover +0100
Height in metres
MTL 3·8m

Lights

Isle of Whithorn harbour E pier head Q.G.4m5M Grey column
Ldg Lts 335° *Front* Oc.R.8s7m7M Orange ◆ topmark on orange metal mast
Rear 35m from front Oc.R.8s9m7M Orange ◆ topmark on orange metal mast. Synchronised with front
Garlieston pier head 2F.R(vert)8m3M Column

Radio/telephone

☎ Harbourmaster (07876) 259

Garlieston lies midway along the western shore of Wigtown Bay, a wide bay between Little Ross and Burrow Head. The tide can run very fast at the mouth of the bay (4 knots springs), with the flood setting ENE, and the ebb setting W then SW; there is up to one hour of slack and semi-slack at local HW and LW respectively.

Sailing directly from Kirkcudbright to Garlieston, a distance of only 14 miles, is feasible provided that a quick passage can be made. Allowing an average boat speed of 4 knots and departing Kirkcudbright 2 hours before HW, arrival off Garlieston should be made at HW +2/+3, when it is still possible to enter. This is cutting things a little fine, however, and if mistimed may necessitate a quick detour to the Isle of Whithorn (see below), or anchoring off Garlieston Bay. All of this dries, and is rather exposed – especially from S–SE, where there is a fetch of some 100 miles from the North Wales coast.

Garlieston Bay is only ½ mile wide, and is protected by a rocky ledge, extending three cables SE from Eggerness Point, and by a single drying rock outcrop (0·8m) halfway between the point and the breakwater. This makes entry from the NE a little taxing at low heights of tide.

Entering from the SE is perhaps the best course of action, using clearing bearings to lead safely between the rock outcrop to starboard and the breakwater to port, and then steering to pass one cable off the end of the pier, which is foul, before rounding up into the harbour.

There is approximately 2m inside the harbour at half flood in the channel, which runs close to the harbour wall, avoiding the mudbank which lies on the other side. Yachts may berth alongside as space allows, or take the ground 25m out from the wall in firm mud.

Though small, the port is quite busy, with a moderate amount of coasting traffic. Water is available at the quayside, while stores and petrol are available from the town. Early closing Wednesdays. For major supplies, Wigtown, the largest town on the Machars, may well be worth a visit.

Isle of Whithorn

54°42'N 4°22'W

Charts

Admiralty 2094 (1:100,000)
Imray C62 (1:280,000)

Tides

HW Dover +0035
Height in metres

MHWS	MHWN	MTL	MLWN	MLWS
7·5	5·4	4·0	2·1	0·7

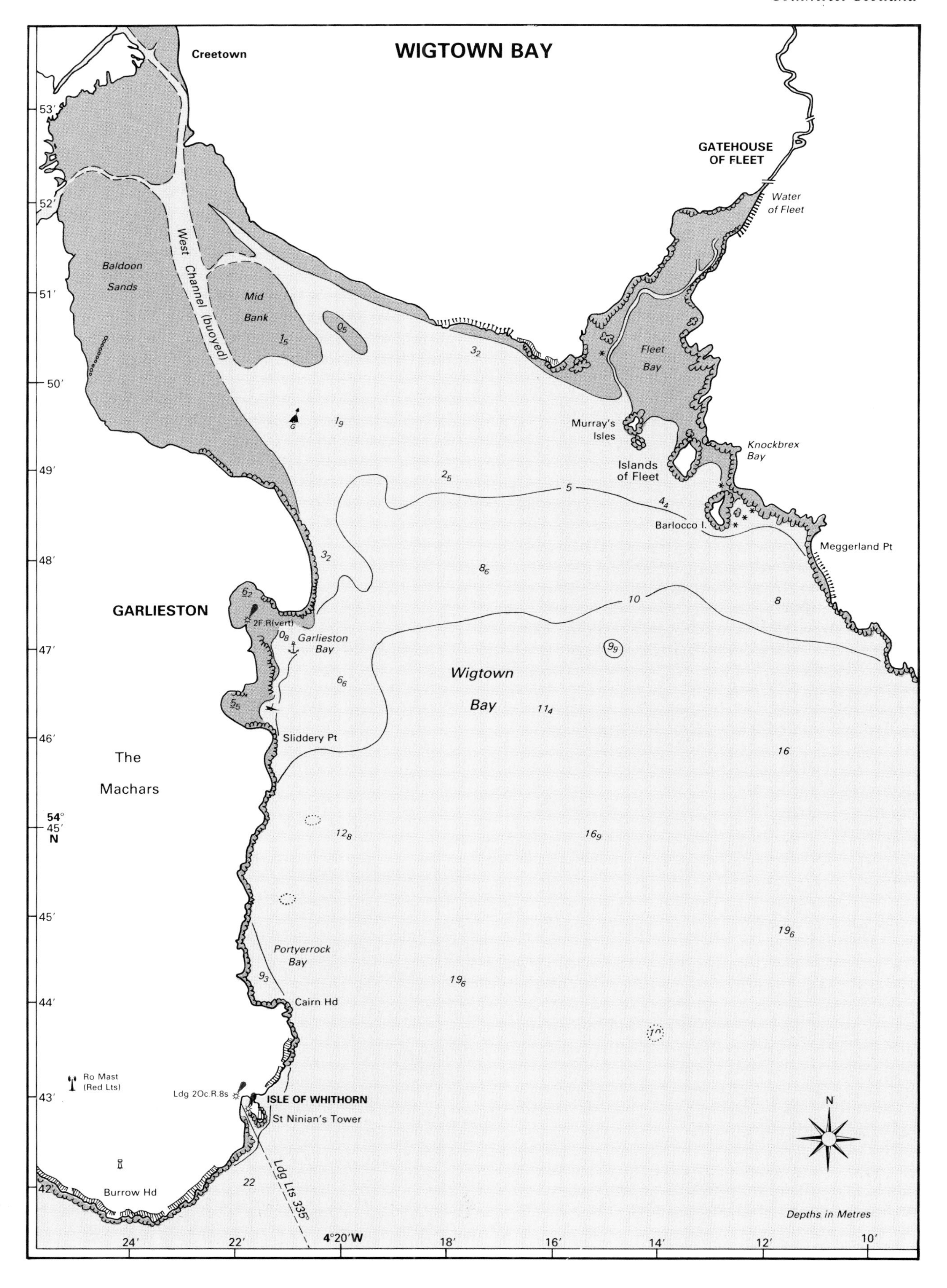
WIGTOWN BAY
Creetown
GATEHOUSE OF FLEET
Water of Fleet
Baldoon Sands
West Channel (buoyed)
Mid Bank
Fleet Bay
Murray's Isles
Islands of Fleet
Knockbrex Bay
Barlocco I.
Meggerland Pt
GARLIESTON
2F.R(vert)
Garlieston Bay
Wigtown Bay
Sliddery Pt
The Machars
Portyerrock Bay
Cairn Hd
Ro Mast (Red Lts)
Ldg 2Oc.R.8s
ISLE OF WHITHORN
St Ninian's Tower
Burrow Hd
Ldg Lts 335°
Depths in Metres
4°20′W
54° 45′ N

Lights

Harbour E pier head Q.G.4m5M Grey column
Ldg Lts 335° *Front* Oc.R.8s7m7M Orange ◆ topmark on orange metal mast
Rear 35m from front Oc.R.8s9m7M Orange ◆ topmark on orange metal mast. Synchronised with front

Radio/telephone

☎ Harbourmaster (09885) 3246

The Isle of Whithorn lies just 6 miles to the south of Garlieston, on the other side of Cairn Head, which is cliffy and steep-to.

It provides excellent shelter inside the harbour for craft capable of taking the ground, though the approach may be unattainable in a fresh to strong blow from the south, as there is a strong south-westerly tidal drift across the harbour mouth (up to 4 knots springs) from HW −4 to HW +4 (around LW the rate is very weak, and the set uncertain).

Approaching from the north, giving the coast a half-mile offing for comfort, the isle, now connected to the mainland by a large causeway, shows itself as a grassy peninsula, conspicuously capped by the white, low-lying St Ninian's Tower at its southeastern end.

The leading lights, bearing 335°, lead directly into the bay, between the island, which has a small off-lying rock ½ cable to the SW of its southernmost point, to starboard, and the Skerries, a rocky reef striking a cable east from the west shore, marked by a perch, to port. However, a course more to the east of mid-channel, to allow for the drift onto the Skerries, is wise.

Entering around LW has much to recommend it, particularly on one's first visit, as the rate and set of the tide are negligible, and the channel between Whithorn Island and the Skerries can easily be distinguished. It is then possible to anchor off the old slip, 2 cables to the south of the pier, in 3–4 metres, to await the tide.

The harbour lies behind its protecting pier, which extends some 75m WNW from the causeway, and can be entered at half tide by vessels drawing 2m; find a berth along the inside of the quay where space allows before contacting the harbourmaster (☎ (09885) 3246).

A concrete slip is available at the north of the harbour, viable for two hours either side of HW, for launching trailer sailors and dinghies. Water is available at the quay, and there is also a quayside hostelry where you can take a leisurely pint while keeping an eye on your craft as she settles on the first tide. The boatyard and chandlery are only a 'cock stride' away, and fuel and general stores are available from the town.

The island itself is well worth exploring, as it is the site of the ruined 12th-century St Ninian's Chapel, devoted to Scotland's first saint, who landed at this site in the 4th century.

Drummore

54°41'·5N 5°55'W

Charts

Admiralty 2094 (1:100,000)
Imray C62 (1:280,000)

Tides

HW Dover +0045
Height in metres

MHWS	MHWN	MTL	MLWN	MLWS
5·9	5·4	–	2·0	0·6

Luce Bay Firing Area

Virtually the whole of Luce Bay is now used as an RAF bombing range, indicated by yellow DZ light buoys. This effectively prevents exploration of the bay, except for two mile-wide strips of water along the east and west shoreline, which allow access to Port William, on the eastern shore (the main quay is now cordoned off, due to heavy subsidence, and the harbour itself offers little to the cruising yachtsman), and to Drummore.

Departing from the Isle of Whithorn bound for Drummore, a voyage of approximately 20 miles, two routes are open for rounding Burrow Head; the choice is largely dependent upon the weather and the state of tide.

- During settled conditions and times of moderate tide, a passage close-to can be taken, to lead inshore of the major tide disturbances off the head.
- During periods of fresh westerly weather opposing a westbound tide, a course well to seaward should be laid, to lead well offshore of the severe race which can build up off the head – a dangerous race, insufficiently indicated on the charts – before altering course and leaving to starboard B (Fl.Y.10s) light buoy. This is par-

Drummore. An excellent place to await favourable conditions for rounding the Mull of Galloway.

ticularly well placed from the yachtsman's point of view when on a night passage (well done RAF), as it marks the Scars, a reef of unlit rocks lying to the north, and also acts as a welcome waypoint in an area of very strong tides.

Special navigational note During the eastbound flood, a back eddy is set up at Burrow Head which will assist the passage of craft wishing to explore the eastern shoreline of Luce Bay. Unfortunately, this is of little use to us on our westbound passage, as what we gain from the eddy will soon be lost in beating against the main flood when crossing the bay.

From B light buoy, a course is laid into Drummore Bay, leaving well to port the 10m shoal patch 1½ miles NE of the Mull of Galloway, where severe overfalls may be encountered, and the foul Cailliness Point.

The tide sets progressively along the coast on closing with DZ8 (Fl.Y.2s) light buoy until, off Drummore Bay, near the large unlit mooring buoy, it runs approximately NNW on the flood and ebbs SSE at up to 3 knots springs.

Drummore Harbour, which dries to mud, is sited in the southern end of the bay, and it is possible to anchor in the bay to await the tide in good holding, sheltered from the west. The harbour is protected by a quay, which extends in a northwesterly direction, terminating in a groyne marked at its end by a beacon, and by a breakwater, which extends north-eastwards from the pier head to tame further the heavy seas which roll into Luce Bay in a strong southerly blow.

Entry can be made at half tide by vessels of moderate draught. Approach on a heading of SW until the inner side of the pier opens (the seaward side is reserved for the RAF range boat), when a course can be laid into the harbour; keep close to the quayside, where the channel is dredged to 2m, and berth alongside as space allows.

Water is available from the quay; although the village is quite small, there are also stores, fuel, and a post office. It is an excellent place to await favourable conditions for rounding the Mull of Galloway.

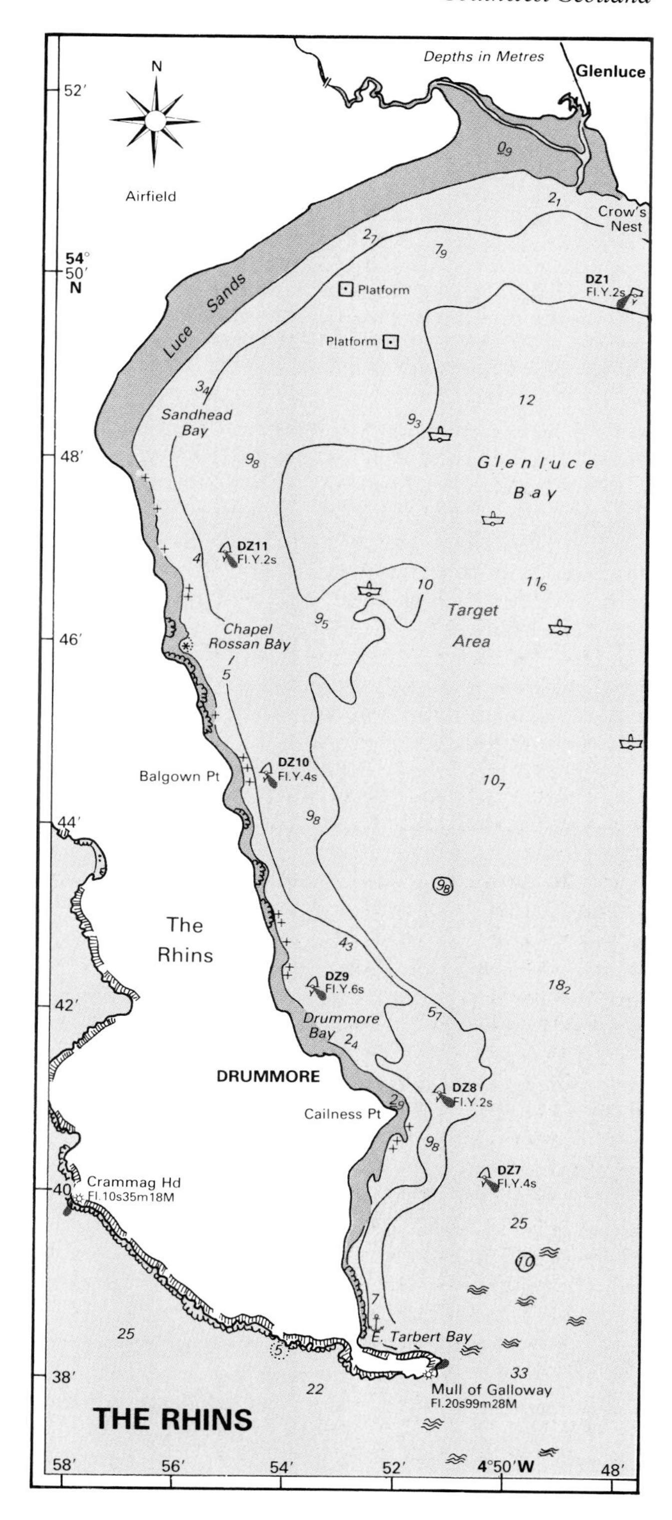

Rounding the Mull of Galloway

Main coastal lights

Mull of Galloway SE end Fl.20s99m28M White round tower 182°-vis-105°. 3 F.R on radio mast 16M ENE
Crammag head Fl.10s35m18M White tower
Mew Island Fl(4)30s24M Black tower, white band
Killantringan Black Head Fl(2)15s49m25M White tower, west side of balcony. F.R lights on radio mast 3·6M N

The Mull of Galloway is a bold headland standing some 83m high, and well signposted from the sea by its white-towered lighthouse, with a 28-mile range, standing 99m above MHWS. It is the sheer height of this lighthouse which is in fact its downfall, however, as during many a dark and windy night its light is hidden by low cloud, and is therefore neither 'use nor ornament'.

As may be deduced from its position and from the *Tidal Streams Atlas* (spring rate 4·5 knots), the major navigational problem when rounding the Mull is not fixing one's position, but negotiating the associated race, which extends 2 miles NE on the flood and 3–4 miles S–SW on the ebb, producing extremely heavy seas, particularly in wind against tide.

The ferocity of this race cannot be overstated, and this is supported by the Admiralty Pilot, which states that the race off the Mull of Galloway is 'Violent and may be dangerous to small vessels' – the Admiralty regards minesweepers and destroyers as small vessels!

In my opinion, the wisest course to steer is a wide one, giving a good three-mile offing to the headland. As there is no question of beating against the tide, unless one has a hefty auxiliary and very deep pockets, one has to go with the flow.

Departing from Drummore two hours before HW allows a good offing to be made to the SSE of the Mull, during the comparative slack before the ebb gains momentum, and drives us toward our next destination of Portpatrick.

Note As the Mull of Galloway is steep-to, a passage can be made close inshore during times of fine weather and neap tides – I am told that many local craft do this regularly. If this is for you, I would strongly suggest seeking local advice at Drummore, timing your departure to arrive at the Mull at slack water.

This course of action does suffer from the inherent problem, however, that if conditions begin to deteriorate when you are on passage, you are pretty much committed, 'trapped between the devil and the deep blue sea', as it were, whilst the course further out, although longer, keeps options open.

Portpatrick

50°50'·5N 5°07'W

Charts

Admiralty 2198 (1:4,000)
Imray C62 (1:280,000)

Tides

HW Dover +0032

Height in metres

MHWS	MHWN	MTL	MLWN	MLWS
3·8	3·0	2·1	0·9	0·3

Lights

Ldg Lts 050·5° *Front* F.G (occas) Orange stripe on sea wall. Private
Rear 68m from front F.G.8m (occas) Building, orange stripe. Private

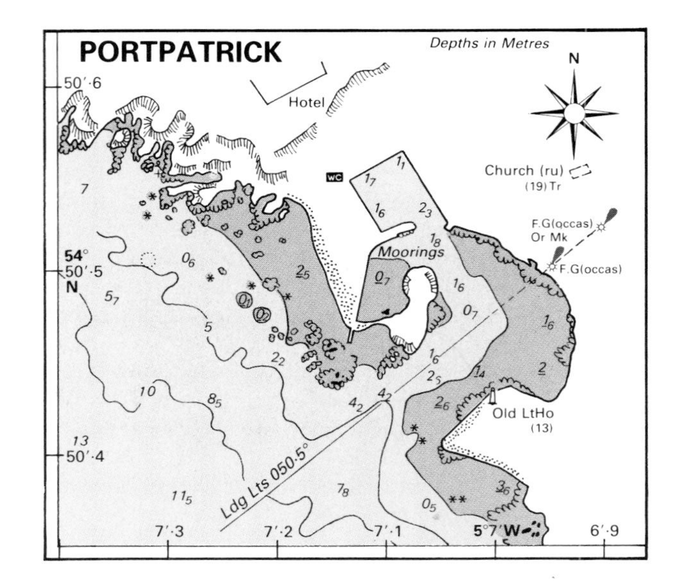

Portpatrick inner harbour, overlooked by the very conspicuous hotel.

Portpatrick north harbour.

Radio/telephone

VHF Ch 16, 14 (Stranraer)
☎ Harbourmaster (077 681) 355

The small natural harbour of Portpatrick lies approximately midway along the western shore of the Rhins, just two miles to the south of Black Head, and is unmistakable during clear weather, thanks to a conspicuous TV mast standing in the background.

Approaching on a course of 050° keeps the leading lights in transit, though this is almost impossible to maintain due to the strong tidal drift which sets along the shore, requiring an adequate allowance to be made in one's pilotage at a very early stage.

Entering between the north pier and the south pier, which has an old lighthouse at its inland end, the course keeps mid-channel to clear Half Tide rock, marked at its northeasternmost end by a barrel, and then leads NNW into the inner harbour, where one may berth alongside or raft up as necessary. Ensure that adequate fendering and springs are used, as a defence against the rolling swell which may enter during a prolonged southwesterly blow.

Water is available at the harbour, and stores and fuel can be obtained from the town (early closing Thursdays), while larger supplies are available from Stranraer by bus. There is a concrete slip near the disused lighthouse which is viable for two hours either side of HW, though it is unsuitable for any craft larger than a Seahawk (16ft).

The town was once the district's major ferry port for Ireland, though it has long since been succeeded by Stranraer, and little can now be seen of the original harbour, built in 1820. It is a light and cheerfully noisy place, however, especially during the summer months, and this is echoed by the many gaily colour-washed holiday villas and hotels which encircle the harbour.

VII. The Isle of Man

The Isle of Man, an island 33 miles by 12 miles at its widest, giving a coastline of 80 miles, is a favourite watering place for many craft from NW England, Wales and Ireland. Understandably, it is not quite so popular with skippers of cruising yachts from the south coast.

It has a treacherous coastline which is not for the inexperienced skipper, or, for that matter, the experienced one whose idea of paradise is to be berthed in a new marina with electricity and water on tap. The truth is, there isn't one, and this is true of the many areas of coastline bordering the east and west of the Irish Sea. All the harbours in the Isle of Man were built primarily for fishing, which has tragically declined.

With the exception of Douglas, all dry out, most with a tidal rise of over 6m. Anchoring off is possible in a number of places, but there are no havens which afford shelter from all points, and most of the coastline is very rocky. It isn't surprising, therefore, to find that most yachts visiting the Isle of Man are able to take the ground, bilge keelers being the most common, though a number of traditional deep keelers can still be found on 'legs'. Fin keelers have usually to anchor off in a heavy swell. This proved disastrous for a friend recently, when he misjudged the depth his craft had under her; at low water the rolling seas which are characteristic of this coastline, continually lifting and dropping his craft on a rock bottom, broke the keel off. She sank in 5ft of water (the small crop of rocks was not indicated on the chart).

So when anchoring off, it pays to anchor well off, and maybe test the bottom with some tallow on a lead and line (a practice that seems to have been lost in these days of electronic gizmos).

The Irish Sea is notoriously fickle and, owing to its shallowness and strong tidal streams, can develop short, steep, nasty seas in no time at all. Another hazard peculiar to the Isle of Man is sea mists or Mannin Mists, which tend to appear without any warning at all, cutting visibility to about 300 metres.

According to the age-old tradition of all pilot books, now that the skipper has been scared witless, it is time to extol the virtues of this beautiful island, which has its own particular olde worlde charm. As the *Tourist's Picturesque Guide to the Isle of Man* (1881) puts it:

'The Isle of Man as a watering place is one of the most popular resorts in Great Britain, and there are undoubtedly few spots within easy reach of the great centres of population in the UK, where a month or two of the summer season can be more agreeably and advantageously spent.'

For the yachtsman, it provides an opportunity for sheer peace and quiet, if anchored in a remote creek, or the hustle and bustle of making fast inside a large town, stepping off your craft and onto the main street, as in Castletown. There's something for everyone, even fish'n'chips, toffee apples and candy floss at Douglas, this being the only main tourist town.

Tides

The main tidal streams of the North Irish Sea are quite straightforward (see page 4). HW at Liverpool is only 13 minutes ahead of HW Dover; Calf Sound is 18 minutes ahead, Ramsey 17 minutes, and Douglas 9 minutes.

The main flood sets north, funnelling up St George's Channel, then spreads out from the tip of Anglesey, where it heads north to the Isle of Man and east into Liverpool and Morecambe Bay. The southbound flood funnels down the North Channel between Scotland and Ireland, where it divides into a south and a southeast-running flood. The southeast-running flood flows into Solway Firth and Morecambe Bay, while the southbound flood meets the northbound flood at Contrary Head (which gets its name from the way the tides meet), on the west of the Isle of Man, and at Maughold Head, on the east of the island, where some very ugly seas can be thrown up in a brisk westerly.

Looking at the island in more detail, then (see plan 106), the main northbound stream splits at Calf Island to pass either side of the Isle of Man. The weaker stream sets to the west, while the stronger stream sets along the east coast, causing a very strong stream and overfalls off Chicken Rock, and through Calf Sound, where it reaches 3·5 knots. The main flood stream continues along the east of the island, reaching 5 knots off Langness and 2 knots off Douglas, until it meets the south-going flood at Maughold Head.

The southbound flood, though a little weaker, is split at the Point of Ayre, the northernmost tip of the island; here it flows at 3 knots over Strunakill Bank, where white water can always be seen. The flood to the east of the island causes a bore in Ramsey Bay, the flood to the west of the island meeting the northbound at Contrary Head. The ebb is a reversal of this flow.

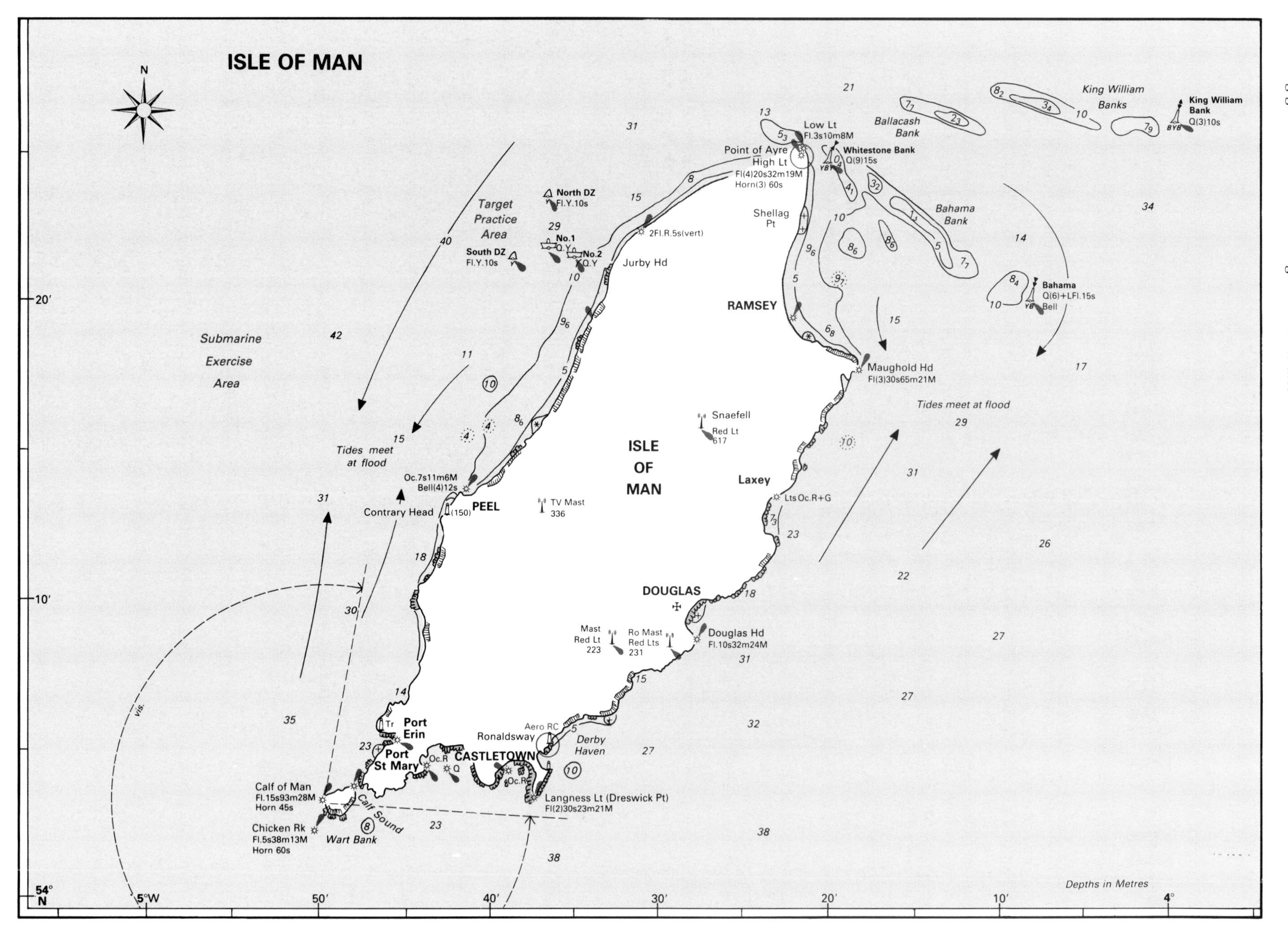
ISLE OF MAN
N
Submarine Exercise Area
Target Practice Area
North DZ Fl.Y.10s
South DZ Fl.Y.10s
No.1 Q.Y
No.2 Q.Y
Tides meet at flood
Contrary Head
Oc.7s11m6M Bell(4)12s
(150)
PEEL
TV Mast 336
Jurby Hd
2Fl.R.5s(vert)
Point of Ayre
High Lt Fl(4)20s32m19M Horn(3) 60s
Low Lt Fl.3s10m8M
Whitestone Bank Q(9)15s
Ballacash Bank
Bahama Bank
King William Banks
King William Bank Q(3)10s
Bahama Q(6)+LFl.15s Bell
Shellag Pt
RAMSEY
Maughold Hd Fl(3)30s65m21M
Tides meet at flood
Snaefell Red Lt 617
ISLE OF MAN
Laxey
Lts Oc.R+G
DOUGLAS
Douglas Hd Fl.10s32m24M
Mast Red Lt 223
Ro Mast Red Lts 231
Aero RC
Ronaldsway
Derby Haven
CASTLETOWN
Oc.R
Q
Langness Lt (Dreswick Pt) Fl(2)30s23m21M
Tr
Port Erin
Port St Mary
Calf Sound
Wart Bank
Calf of Man Fl.15s93m28M Horn 45s
Chicken Rk Fl.5s38m13M Horn 60s
vis.
Depths in Metres
54° N
5°W
50'
40'
30'
20'
10'
4°
20'
10'

Main lights

The eastern side of the island (see page 00) is well furnished with lights, and there should be little trouble approaching at night in good visibility. Running south down the coast, they appear as follows:

High Light Point of Ayre marking the most northern tip of the island Fl(4)20s32m19M Horn(3)60s

Maughold head has a very strong signal, and can be picked up easily approaching from the east Fl(3)30s65m21M

Douglas head Fl.10s32m24M can now be confused with Langness light and care must be taken

Langness Lt (Dreswick Point) Fl(2)30s23m21M

Calf Lt Fl.15s.93m28M Horn 45s 274°-vis-190° (276°) is by far the most splendid light on the island

Chicken rock now a shadow of its former self. Fl.5s38m13M Horn 60s

On the western side of the island there is only Peel light (Oc.7s.6M Bell(4)12s) of any significance between the Point of Ayre and Calf Isle, underlining how sparse the traffic on this side of the island is.

Ramsey

54°19'·4N 4°22'·4W

Charts

Admiralty 2696 (1:10,000), 2094 (1:100,000)
Imray C62 (1:280,000), Y70 (85,150)

Tides

HW Dover +0020

Height in metres

MHWS	MHWN	MTL	MLWN	MLWS
7·3	5·8	4·1	2·4	0·8

Lights

S pier head Oc.R.5s8m4M Bell(2)10s White tower, red band, black base

N pier head Oc.G.5s9m5M White tower, black base

Toe of Mooragh bank Iso.G.4s3m White post, violet band, on dolphin (For guidance of vessels inside the harbour. Not visible seaward. 2 F.R(hor) marks the centre of each side of the swing bridge.)

Radio/telephone

VHF Ch 16, 12 (0830–1630)
☎ Harbourmaster (0624) 812245

Ramsey is as good a place as any to begin a clockwise circumnavigation of the island (see page 106), since it is usually the first port of call for craft from the Morecambe Bay area.

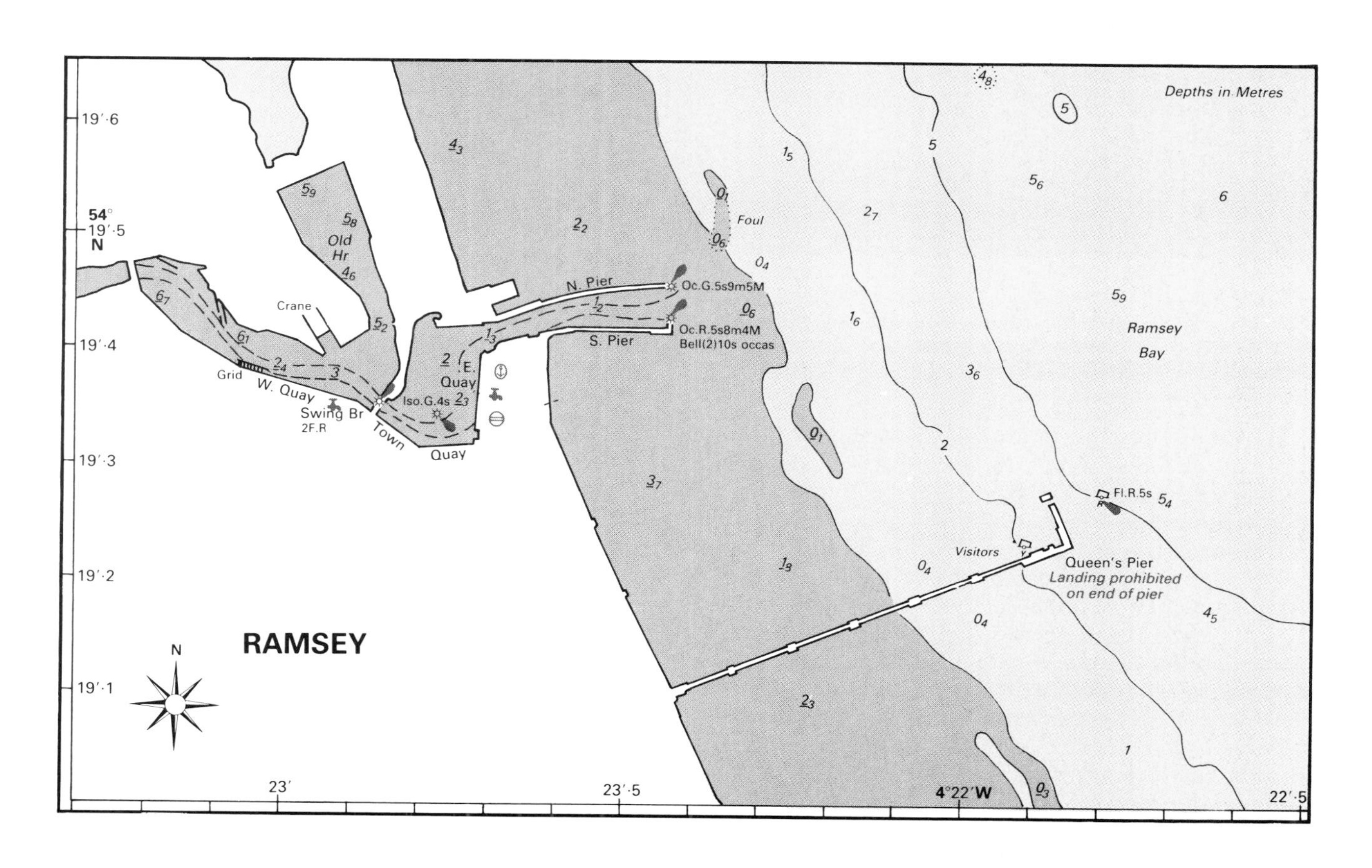

West Quay at Ramsey, beyond the swinge bridge.

The inner quay at Ramsey, on the NE coast of the Isle of Man. The harbour dries about 1·8m and is accessible 2hrs either side of HW, but the outside anchorage offers good shelter in any westerly weather. *Peter Cumberlidge*

At low water, the sandy beach at Ramsey dries out for about 400 metres, well beyond the pier heads. The harbour can really only be entered for 3 hours either side of high water.

The usual procedure, therefore, is to anchor off, in what may be an uncomfortable swell, and wait for the tide. There are no major hazards here, but if you are anchoring a good distance off you will need a radar reflector and anchor light after dark, since you will be in the fairway for local trawlers.

The beach between Queen's pier and the harbour piers is as good a place as any for taking the ground, though careful attention must be paid to the shipping forecast before doing so; it is not the place to be caught in a rising easterly.

There was once a delta islet of considerable size at Ramsey; over the centuries this has been destroyed by the tidal bore in Ramsey Bay. The town now stands on a fragment of it, and derives its name from it (Viking: *hrafn-raven*, hence Isle of Ravens). On entering the harbour (taking care not to be taken unawares by the tidal stream, which sets across the entrance from HW −2 to HW +6), a beach where craft may be dried out lies ahead, though the fairway turns sharply to port here, leaving a stout stone dolphin marking the Mooragh Bank to starboard.

Many craft lie along the Town Quay here, though it is important to go alongside a craft of equal draught, since there is a rise and fall of 5 metres to sand. The harbourmaster's office is to the north of East Quay, and should be contacted for payment of harbour dues, and for arrangement of a more permanent berth. East Quay is best avoided, since trawlers and coasters tend to berth there.

It is possible to berth alongside the inside arms of the north and south pier in settled weather, though the flood surge may make it a little bumpy. All supplies can be taken on board here, and there are a number of hostelries to choose from. Slips and cranage facilities, and laying up, in the old harbour, can also be arranged.

Maughold Head, Laxey and Garwick Bay

Departing from Ramsey, it is prudent to leave port half an hour before HW, so that you arrive at Maughold Head, where the tides meet, at slack water. You can then catch the ebb, which runs at 2 knots at springs, southwards to the next port of call. On leaving Ramsey, the coastline becomes steadily more rugged and steep; at Maughold Head it rises from the sea to a height of 114 metres, with a sheer granite precipice of 70 metres.

Half a mile further on is the inlet of Port Mooar, where it is possible to land, in settled weather, by tender. From here, a narrow path leads up the hillside to the ancient St Maughold churchyard.

Holding a course half a mile off the coast, it is possible to make very good progress with the ebb along the four miles of rugged cliff coastline to Laxey Head, and, tucked snugly behind the head, the harbour itself.

Laxey

54°13'N 4°23'W

Charts

Admiralty 2696 (1:10,000), 2094 (1:100,000)
Imray C62 (1:280,000), Y70 (85,150)

Tides

HW Dover +0025
Height in metres
HW 6·4m (approx), MTL 4·0m

Lights

Pier head Oc.R.3s7m5M White tower, red band Obscured when bearing less than 318°
Breakwater head Oc.G.3s7m White tower, green band
Maughold head Fl(3)30s65m21M White tower

Laxey Harbour, although very sheltered, is not very convenient, since all the moorings are private. There is very limited space, and it dries to uneven rock. On entering the harbour, leaving the jetty to starboard and the pier to port, a submerged training wall, leading the Laxey River from the harbour, must be left to starboard – its presence is indicated by three green starboard-hand perches with conical topmarks.

The town itself is remote and quiet, consisting of a few shops and a local hostelry, while only a short walk away are the Laxey mines and water wheels, which are well worth a visit.

In this neighbourhood of protruding granite, there are rich veins of minerals such as lead, silver and copper, and mining these became quite a source of income for the island. The disadvantage was that most of the metallic waste produced was carried down the Laxey River to the sea. The mines were last worked 60 years ago.

It is possible in calm weather to anchor off Laxey and go in by tender, though the holding ground is poor, and it would be prudent to leave an anchor-watch on board. A much safer anchorage is in Garwick Bay (Wick from the Norse *vik*, meaning creek), at the southern end of Laxey Bay, where the holding ground is much better, and there is reasonable shelter from north through west to south.

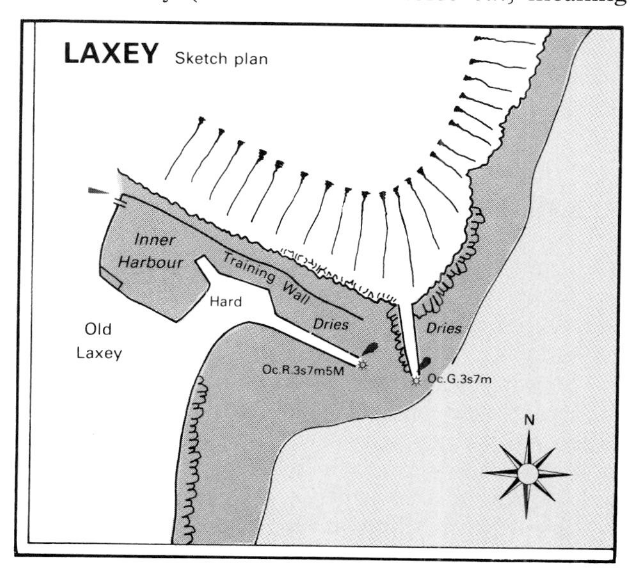

The entrance to Laxey Harbour, showing the training wall marked by three green starboard-hand perches. This area dries to uneven rock.

On leaving Garwick Bay and rounding Clay Head, 127m high, the course continues southwest along the coast. It is possible to sail quite close in here, since there are no major navigational hazards; on rounding Onchan Head, the crescent of Douglas Bay opens up, with its Blackpool-like boarding houses spreading up the hillside. Directly to starboard here is a cove, at the northern edge of Black Rocks, where it is possible to anchor with a reasonable degree of shelter from N through to SW.

When crossing Douglas Bay it is important to keep a keen look out, as Douglas is the main port of call for most of the ferry traffic to the Isle of Man. Bearing this in mind, and remembering also that there is a 2-knot tide stream running across the bay at springs, it is best to enter under engine. St Mary's rock (Connister rock), the scene of numerous shipwrecks in the past, is now marked by the Refuge Tower erected by Sir William Hillary, founder of the RNLI; it should be left well to starboard.

Douglas

54°08'·9N 4°28'W

Charts

Admiralty 2696 (1:10,000), 2094 (1:100,000)
Imray C62 (1:280,000), Y70 (85,150)

Tides

HW Dover +0009
Height in metres

MHWS	MHWN	MTL	MLWN	MLWS
6·9	5·4	3·9	2·4	0·8

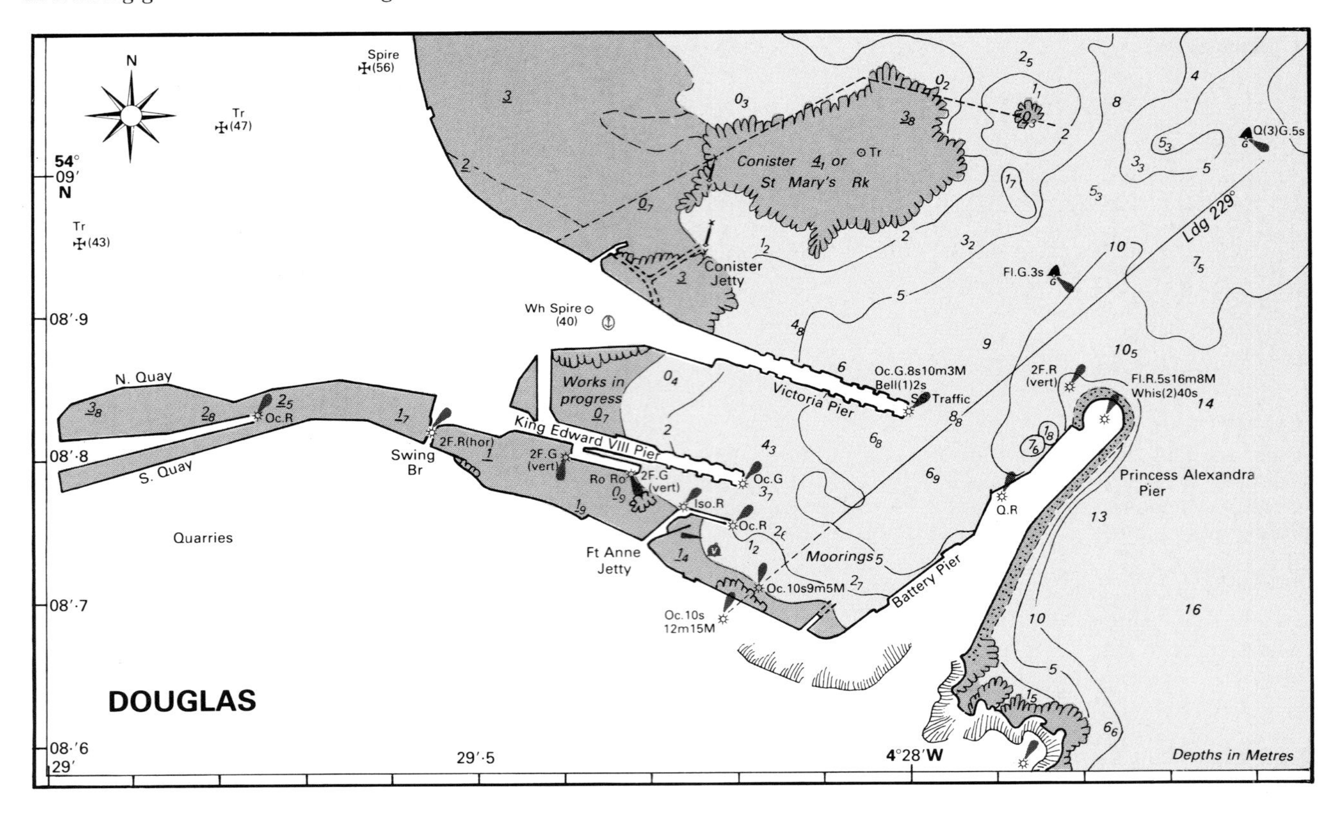

Swinging moorings at Douglas Harbour. Showing the large visitors' mooring, centre.

Lights

Douglas head Fl.10s32m24M White tower and buildings Reduced range shore-220° Obscured when bearing more than 037°. F.R lights on radio masts 1 and 3M W

Princess Alexandra pier head Fl.R.5s16m8M Whis(2) 40s Red metal mast

Battery pier 140m from breakwater head Q.R.12m1M White tower, red band 038°-vis-218°

Ldg Lts 229·3° *Front* Oc.10s9m5M White ▲ topmark, red border, on metal mast on concrete column. For use west of 4°26'W only

Rear 62m from front Oc.10s12m5M White ▼ topmark, red border, on metal mast. Synchronised with front

Dolphin 2F.R(vert)10m2M Red mast on concrete dolphin 038°-vis-310°

Victoria pier head Oc.G.8s10m3M Bell(1)2s White column 225°-vis-327° International Port Traffic signals

Fort Anne jetty head Oc.R.4s6m2M White tower, red band 107°-vis-297°

Elbow Iso.R.4s5m1M White and red post 095°-vis-275°

King Edward VIII pier S side head Oc.G.4s6m2M 253°-vis-005° White framework tower, green band. F.R on each side of swing bridge, 365m west, when closed. 2F.G(vert) marks SE and SW corners of pier link span 160m west

Inner harbour The Tongue head Oc.R.6s4m White post, red band

Radio/telephone

VHF Ch 16, 12 (24hrs)
☎ Harbourmaster (0624) 623813

Because of the heavy ferry traffic, entry to the harbour should be as brisk as possible, between Victoria pier to starboard and Battery pier to port. It is wise to radio telephone Douglas Harbour control (Ch 12) to enquire about ferry movements before entering.

There is a very small pontoon, where perhaps six moderate-sized yachts can raft up, at the inner end of Battery pier; alternatively, the visitors' mooring, a large black buoy, can be used. This is located to the right of the leading lights, where many local boats swing on their permanent moorings.

Battery Pier, Douglas Harbour.

The drill here is to moor 'Mediterranean style', taking a stern warp to the buoy, motoring out, dropping the hook, then bringing the craft stern-on to the buoy again, putting the engine into reverse to dig home the hook, if preferred. In this way, many craft are able to moor to the same buoy.

The outer harbour is quite sheltered, except from the north to northeast; with winds from these directions, a very nasty swell running straight into the harbour can make life uncomfortable. It is not the place for a long stay. If you plan to remain for a few days, go into the sheltered inner harbour areas, via the swing bridge. This bridge is now left open from 2300 to 0700, and also swings upon request. You can make arrangements to use it when seeing the harbourmaster to pay harbour dues (also payable if you are on visitors' moorings). In the inner harbour, the yacht may be moored to the South Quay or to the Tongue, and left in complete safety – though you should watch her settle down on the first tide, which dries to sand and mud. The Douglas Motor Boat and Sailing Club is situated on the South Quay, where showers and toilet facilities are available throughout the day. Berths may now also frequently be had on the inner end of North Quay, due to the dwindling population of trawlers.

This is rather a noisy place to stay, since it is in the heart of the town, but supplies are good, and there are a chandlery and a boatyard. Douglas' main landmark is Castle Mona, which is of no great historical interest. It was built in 1820 by the Duke of Athol, last Lord of Man, who ended his reign by selling his feudal rights to the Crown of England.

Derby Haven

54°04'·5N 4°37'W

Charts

Admiralty 2696 (1:10,000), 2094 (1:100,000)
Imray C62 (1:280,000), Y70 (85,150)

Tides

HW Dover +0030

Lights

Derby Haven breakwater SW end Iso.G.2s5m5M
White tower, green band

Radio/telephone

☎ Harbourmaster (0624) 823549

Langness lighthouse, a prominent mark at the S tip of the Isle of Man. *Peter Cumberlidge*

Leaving Douglas and heading south, departure should be taken at HW slack, so that the ebb may be taken to Derby Haven, 7 miles distant.

A mile and a half on, heading south from Douglas Head, Little Ness (Little Nose), a rocky spit, is passed. Behind it a small cove opens up, named Port Soderick, and boasting a licensed café and amenities. The holding round here is poor. Although there is no beach, there is a serviceable slipway.

Rounding Santon Head, with at least ½ mile offing because of Baltic Rock, another little creek hoves into view, with Port Grenaugh a mile to the west of the head. Here there is a shingle/sand bay giving good holding, with about a cable to swing. A quiet night may be spent here, but note the submarine cable to the east.

Another mile further on may be found another small creek, Port Soderick (Norse: Sun Creek), where the high rugged coast falls to a sandy shore. This is a very quiet spot, with a footpath leading upwards to the remains of an old fort.

Derby Haven is a well sheltered anchorage, and was a favourite shelter for windbound vessels during the days of sail, since its only open aspect is to the northeast. To port on entering the haven is St Michael's Island, connected by a causeway to Langness. To starboard is a breakwater made on top of a crop of rocks, behind which lie many local craft on their drying moorings. Drying out in this area requires the utmost caution, however, as there are many rocky outcrops in the sand. It is wisest to anchor in deep water near the handful of private moorings laid in the northern half of the haven, where there is plenty of room to swing.

Making a landing by tender on the smooth rocky shore of St Michael's Island, where there is a small concrete pier, is quite easy, as it is usually well sheltered, though it could be wise to carry a spare shear pin in case the prop accidentally touches bottom. Here, as well as a ruined fort built by the Earl of Derby when he held the Isle of Man against Parliament in 1644–51, lie the ruins of a 12th-century chapel, from which the island gets its name.

Derby Haven village once had a thriving kipper industry. It now boasts a small chandlery, and a bar and hotel 'Castletown Golf Links' which lies adjacent to the outer anchorage.

Castletown

54°04'·3N 4°39'W

Charts

Admiralty 2696 (1:10,000), 2094 (1:100,000)
Imray C62 (1:280,000), Y70 (85,150)

Tides

HW Dover +0025
Height in metres
MTL 3·4m

Lights

New pier head Oc.R.15s8m5M White tower, red band
N side of entrance Oc.G.4s3m White metal post on concrete column
Irish quay Oc.R.4s5m5M White tower, red band 142°-vis-322 2F.R(hor) mark swing bridge 150m NW
King William college tower Aero F.R (occas) Obstruction
Langness Lt (Dreswick Point) Fl(2)30s23m21M White tower

Radio/telephone

VHF Ch 16, 12
☎ Harbourmaster (0624) 823549

Langness (Norse: Longnose) is a large, flat, slate formation, cropping out to sea from limestone beds (see page 113). Being no more than a few metres in height, and having a tide race of up to 5 knots around the point at springs, it has been the setting for innumerable shipwrecks. Its presence is now indicated at night by the Langness (Dreswick Point) light, Fl(2)30s21M.

As with all the passages around the island, it is best to use the tide (although this is not always possible), leaving Derby Haven just before HW slack. Round St Michael's Island, where the ruined circular fort can be seen clearly, and head SSW along the two-mile stretch of Langness. Keep half a mile off for comfort, although there are no major obstructions along this stretch. A stone tower standing 32m in height, erected as a marker in 1811, can be seen for the entire journey. Further on, the Langness (Dreswick Point) light, at 23m, marks the southernmost part of this reef. The course then alters to due west for half a mile to round Langness Point; keep half a mile offing here to clear Dreswick Rock and Skerranes. A wider offing should be given if an uncomfortable sea is visible off Langness and Dreswick Point.

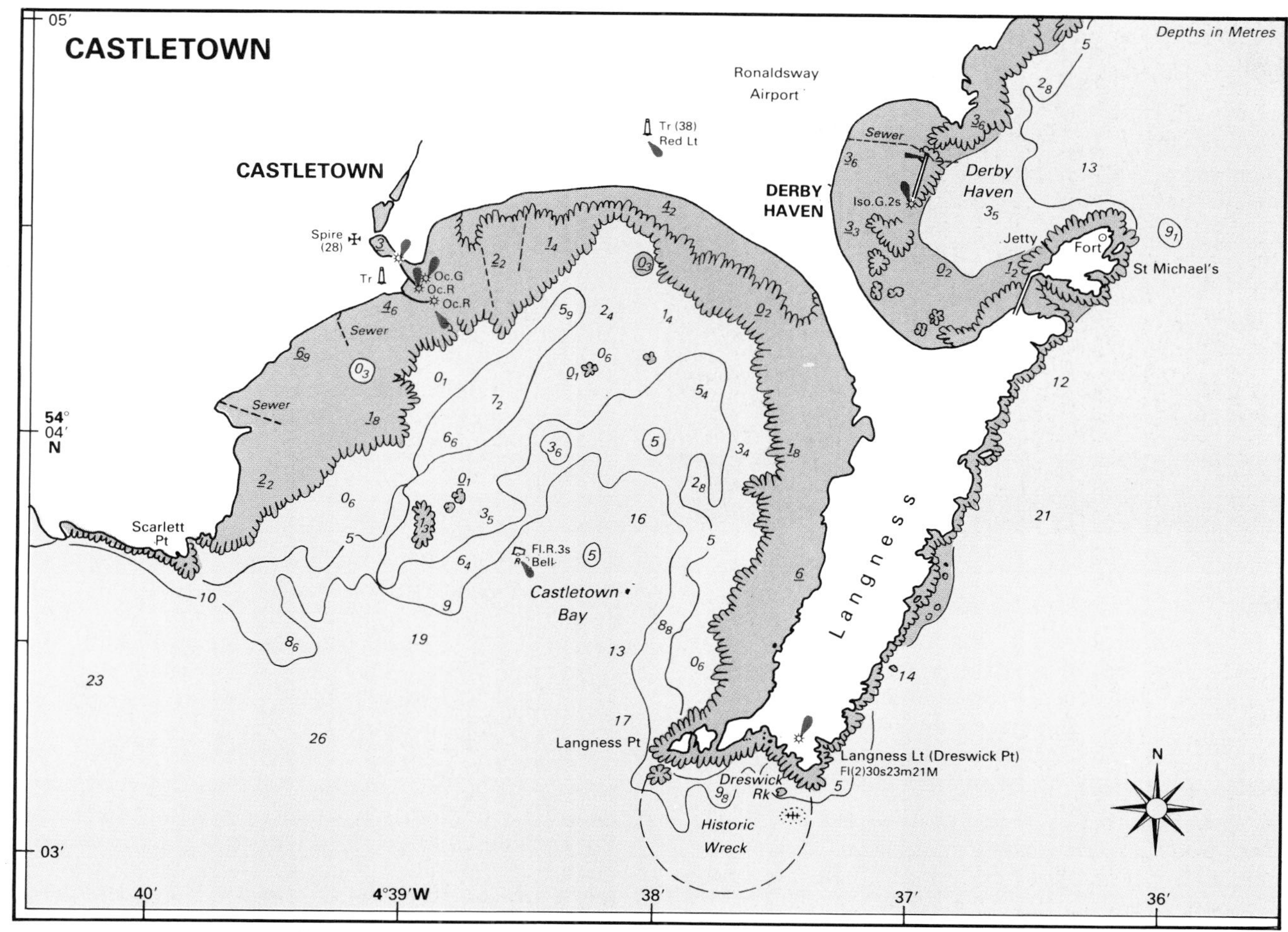

The course now leads NNW into Castletown Bay, where the tide sets weak, and stock may be taken of the situation before we wind our way through the lobster pots and head into Castletown.

After locating the red can buoy (Fl.R.3s Bell) and leaving it to port, a direct course may be laid off for the pier head at Castletown, unmistakable with Castle Rushen looming in the background. Castletown Harbour dries, and can only be entered for about 2½ hours either side of HW, hence the need to leave Derby Haven just before HW slack. There is room to anchor to the north of the fairway, between the pier head and Boe Norris Rocks, to await the tide, though anchoring for any length of time here may be uncomfortable in winds from a southerly arc.

Entrance

On entering, the outer harbour lies to port, beyond the outer arm of the pier and the light tower of Irish Quay. It is enclosed on three sides, and dries to even sand, though there are rock outcrops not far beneath the surface. It is largely unused, and ample space will be found; it is again wise to watch the boat down on the first tide. This is not the place to leave the craft unattended for any length of time, since with strong winds a heavy swell may cause a good deal of bumping. Tony, the harbourmaster, can be contacted on VHF Ch 16 change 12 for 2 hours either side of HW, and makes the shower in his office available to visiting yachtsmen.

Castletown inner harbour with swing bridge, centre.

Between the white with red hoop tower of Irish Quay to port and the all-white tower on an outcrop of rocks to starboard is the entrance to the inner harbour, guarded by a swing bridge. There is usually room to moor alongside Irish Quay, but you must make arrangements with the harbourmaster if you wish to enter the inner harbour, as this entails swinging the bridge, which has only 4m clearance at HW. The swing bridge is manually operated by the harbourmaster.

Castle Rushen, overlooking Castletown inner harbour.

In the inner harbour, there is usually room to berth alongside anywhere to port, or on the upper reaches to starboard, near the old brewery site. Passage into the upper harbour is barred by a fixed road bridge. (This, though, is an excellent place for laying up, once the mast has been stowed).

After berthing in the inner harbour, you can walk off the docks into the centre of what was once the capital of the island, since the harbour lies under the walls of Castle Rushen. Castletown was the seat of the Kings of Man before 1265, and the administrative centre of the Lords of Man thereafter. It is an olde worlde town whose grey limestone buildings have changed little since its heyday, evoking a quaint peacefulness which is echoed by its Maritime Museum. This is built around the old schooner *Peggy* (built in 1793), and is a pilgrimage for all cruising folk.

I can recommend the Ship Inn for very reasonably priced nourishment and libation. The coastal path to Port St Mary, perhaps five miles long, provides ample opportunity to stretch one's legs in some very fine scenery.

Port St Mary

54°04'·7N 4°43'·1W

Charts

Admiralty 2696 (1:10,000), 2094 (1:100,000)
Imray C62 (1:280,000), Y70 (85,150)

Tides

HW Dover +0020

Height in metres

MHWS	MHWN	MTL	MLWN	MLWS
5·9	4·7	3·2	1·7	0·6

Lights

The Carrick Q(2)5s6m3M ⁞ on black pillar, red band
Alfred pier head Oc.R.10s8m6M Bell(3)12s White tower, red band
Inner pier head Oc.R.3s8m5M White tower, red band

Radio/telephone

VHF Ch Port St Mary Hbr 16, 12 (0830–1630)
☎ Harbourmaster (0624) 833206

Port St Mary is only a brief 5 miles distant; leave Castletown at HW, using one of two possible routes. Either leave the red can buoy to starboard before heading west past Scarlett Point, or take the shallower channel between Lheeah-rio rocks and the mainland, giving a good offing at Scarlett Point to clear the stack which juts southwards for a cable or so from the point.

On rounding Scarlett Point, Bay ny Carrickey (Carrick Bay) opens up, with the Carrick, a rock formation drying to 4m, dead centre, marked by an isolated danger beacon (Q(2)5s6m3M). This should be left to starboard; make an approach to the light tower on the outer pier, standing 8m. A 133m TV mast behind Port St Mary, carrying red lights, is now a valuable navigation aid at night.

Enter Port St Mary harbour between Alfred pier and Cathure rocks, marked by a beacon. The outer harbour is immediately to port, drying to rock, with Pot rock and Little Carrick the main offenders, and has a rise and fall of over 6m. The 150ft breakwater has 2·5m at LWS, and although it is used by local trawlers, a good berth is possible except in northwesterlies, provided that you ensure that your lines go ashore if you are rafted alongside a resident craft, and that your craft is attended at times of fishing fleet movements.

The inner harbour, on the other hand, is very sheltered and dries to even sand. The problem is that most of the area is now taken up by permanent fore and aft moorings, and that much of the quay is also taken. The harbourmaster may be able to find a berth; his office is at the top of the inner wall near the Isle of Man Yacht Club, a favourite port of call. Failing this (or perhaps preferably), a good anchorage can be found in the north of Chapel Bay, with adequate shelter except from S to E. It is possible for a bilge keeler to take the ground here, on firm sand, only a short walk from the town centre. Fin keelers must either anchor further out, with less shelter and much rolling, or pick up one of six visitors' moorings at the outer limits of Chapel Bay.

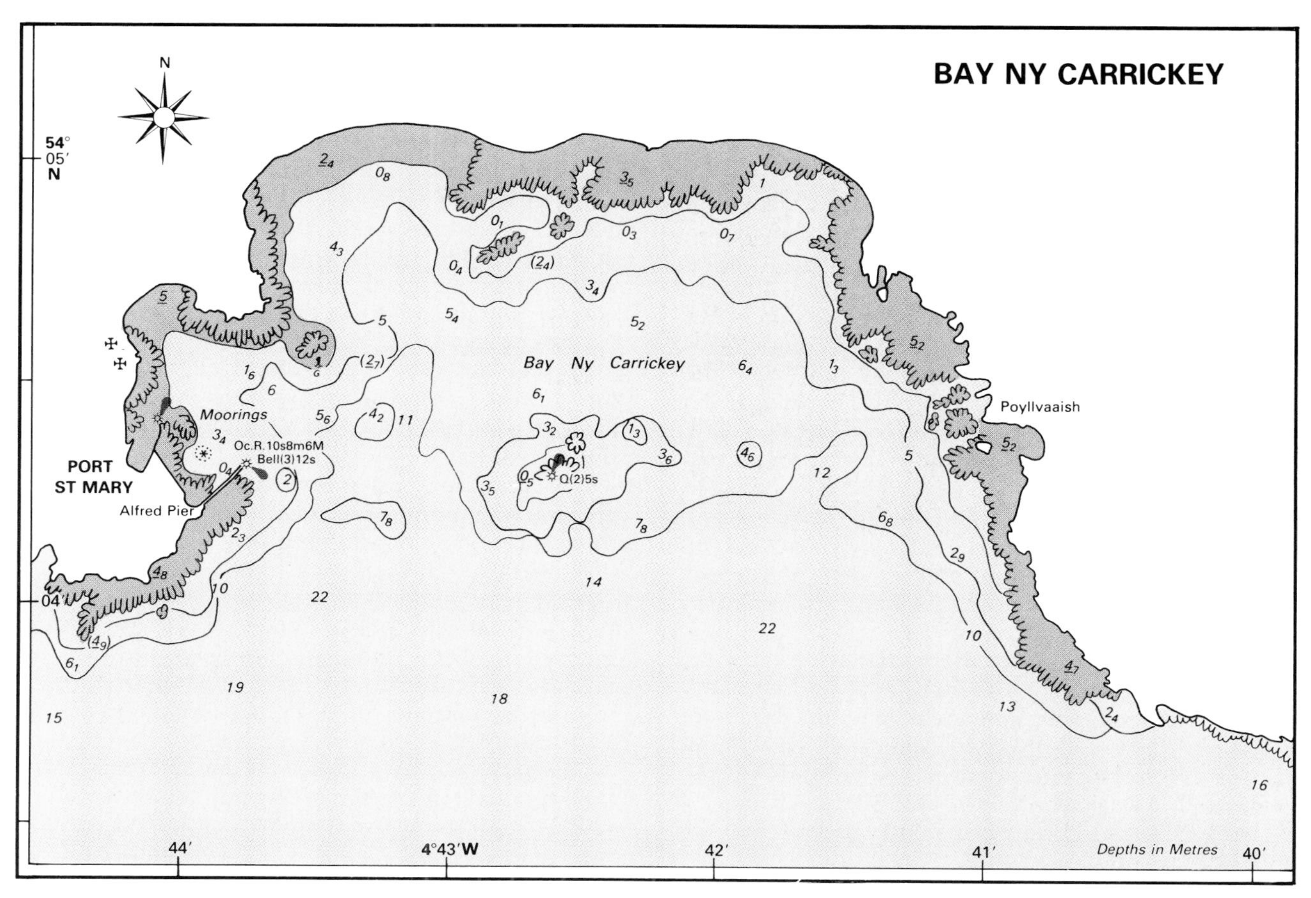

Calf Sound

From Port St Mary to Port Erin, on the western side of the island, is a trip of only 5 miles via Calf Sound, a short stretch of water, perhaps 2 cables long and 1 cable wide, leading between the Calf of Man (a plateau of approximately 800 acres, with precipitous crags all around) and the two islands of Kitterland near the mainland.

This stretch of water appears inoffensive on the charts, but this belies the fact that it has been the scene of innumerable shipwrecks and much loss of life. It has a fierce reputation with Manxmen, land-based and seafarer alike, as the most dangerous piece of water in the Irish Sea. The chart shows a spring tidal race of 3·5 knots (up to 8 knots if the locals are to be believed), and not much less at neaps, with no slack to speak of. This, along with the confined space in the sound, leads either to very short, steep, foamy seas with a westerly of Force 4 or above blowing against the tide, or to large, towering, toppling seas running with the tide, with rocky crags all round.

After this horror story, it won't be surprising that most skippers elect to take the longer route around Chicken rock, though this, as will be seen later, isn't always a particularly calm alternative.

Calf Sound is a viable route, provided that the conditions are absolutely right. But the more conditions deviate from this proviso, the more uncomfortable the passage will become, until it becomes impossible.

The wind may be from any direction as long as it is calm (Force 3 or under). I would never undertake the sound under sail alone unless forced to, since there is precious little room to tack. This brings us to the auxiliary, which must be reliable, and capable of a turn of speed in excess of 5 knots. Even such an auxiliary would only make good 1·5 knots against the 3·5-knot race if attempting to push through

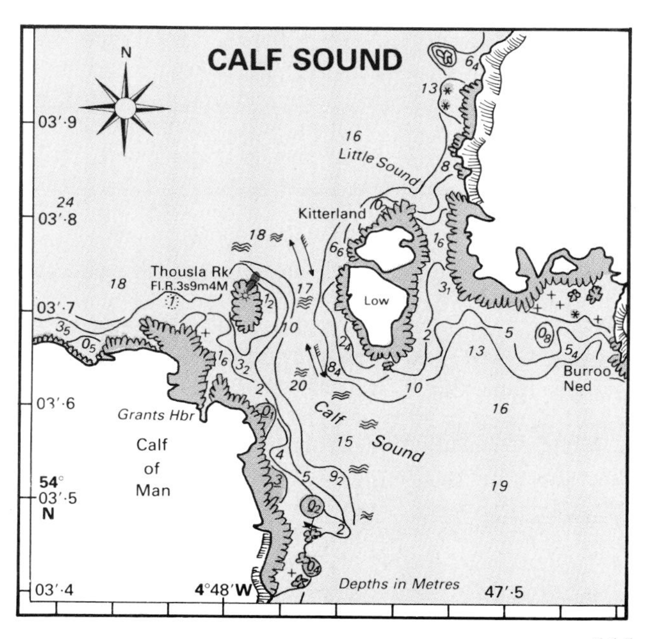

against the stream. From this, it seems wisest to make the passage at slack water, but the timing of this in practice is very difficult, as slack water may only last a few minutes. Therefore the best expedient is to go through with the stream, which brings us to the second anomaly.

The stream in the sound fails to behave in accordance with the general stream of the island. For much of the north-going flood, the stream in the sound runs south, and vice versa. It is for this reason that the sound is best attempted between HW and 2 hours after, heading south to north. This gives a leeway of half an hour either end, when the stream may be unsettled. Conversely, heading north to south, the sound is best attempted between LW and two hours after, again allowing a leeway of half an hour. The sound is not viable at night, being lit only by the Fl.R.3s9m4M of Thousla rocks, with no lights at all on Kitterland; when approaching by day, it is wisest to stand off and see what conditions are like in the sound before making a decision to enter.

Once you are entering the sound with the tide, you are pretty much committed, and the tactics are to go between the octagonal granite tower of Thousla rocks and the two islands of Kitterland. Leave the inner sound, between Kitterland and the mainland, to starboard. Two cables later, the sound is left behind, and one is left wondering what all the fuss was about.

After clearing the sound, a course can be laid on Bradda head, marked by the conspicuous Milner's Tower to NNE. Hold this course until well inside Port Erin Bay, to clear the ruined breakwater guarding the southern entrance to the bay.

SW tip of the Isle of Man via Chicken rock

The chosen route, whether using the sound or going via Chicken rock (see chartlet), will determine the state of tide for leaving Port St Mary. There is a strong tide race around Chicken rock, running at 4·5 knots at springs, leading NW on the ebb for a mile, or NE on the flood for 1½ miles, with large breaking seas over West Bank, a mile to ESE of the Calf.

The best tactic is to arrive at LW slack at Chicken rock, using the weak northerly flood for the passage to Port Erin or Peel.

Port St Mary, 4 to 5 miles from Chicken rock, should be left an hour before LW slack. This timing usually necessitates anchoring off Port St Mary in adequate depth, since it mostly dries.

Heading south, and rounding Kallow Point, the limestone ends; the jagged slate cliffs emerge from underneath it, and then run all the way to Peel on the western side. The Sugarloaf is a large slate mass, detached from the slate beds, standing free at the southern end of Perwick Bay.

From Spanish Head a course can be laid to the south of Chicken rock, between Calf Island and Wart Bank. On the western side of the Calf there is little of interest, since it is very steep and rugged, though there is a small ruin called Bushell's House (invisible from our viewpoint) which, it is said, was the retreat of a follower of the great Lord Bacon, over three centuries ago. He hoped that if he lived in this desolate spot, with great abstinence, he would be blessed with a long life. He probably did not live any longer, but I am sure that it must have felt like it.

Further on, near the southern edge of the Calf, the Buroo, a free-standing rock with an 'eye' through it, is passed, though it cannot be seen from this approach.

It is important when rounding Chicken rock to give it a wide berth, since the sea is very unsettled in this area. A mile or so offing will clear the worst of the overfalls. Chicken rock light, standing 38m, is an excellent landmark, being made of white granite. It is a tribute to perseverance. Work on it commenced in 1869 and, continuing in the summer months only, due to the rock's exposed position, was finally completed in 1874. Characteristics are Fl.5s38m13M Horn 60s.

Chicken rock may derive its name from one of two sources. First, when it is exposed at low water it reveals itself as two masses of rock joined together by a low isthmus, giving it the appearance of two chickens. Second, it is supposedly a favourite perching place for Mother Carey's chickens (stormy petrels), though I would call them rather uncommon birds on the island.

Having rounded Chicken rock, we can take the beginning of the flood round the stack marking the most westerly point of the Calf. This is crested by two old lighthouses, built in 1818 and no longer in use, which gave a transit line on Chicken rock in the days before the advent of the Chicken light. The Calf light (Fl.15s93m28M Horn 45s) is an insignificant little structure between these two towers. A course can be laid off on Milner's Tower on Bradda Head, lying to NE, for entry into Port Erin Bay.

Port Erin Bay

54°05'N 4°46'W

Charts

Admiralty 2696 (1:10,000), 2094 (1:100,000)
Imray C62 (1:280,000), Y70 (85,150)

Tides

HW Dover −0020
Height in metres
MTL 2·9m, harbour dries but has 3·6m at MHWN.

Lights

Ldg Lts 099·1° *Front* F.R.10m5M White tower, red band
Rear 39m from front F.R.19m5M White column, red band, and lantern

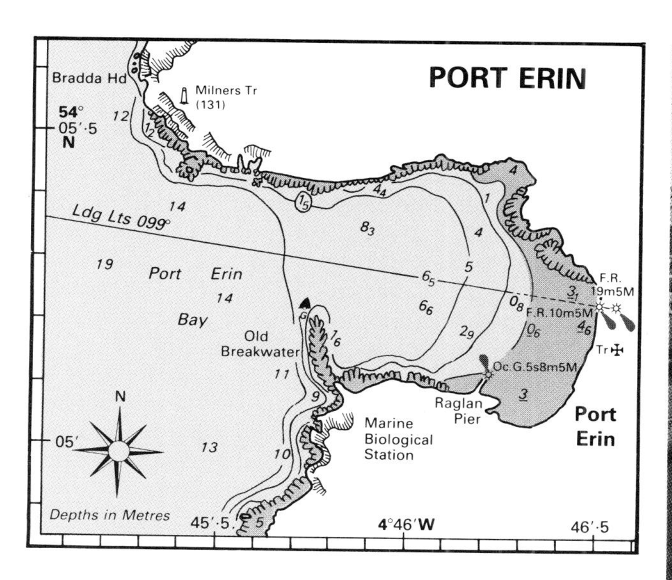

Port Erin Bay is exposed from the westerly arc, but has excellent holding ground.

Raglan pier head Oc.G.5s8m5M White tower, green band
Thousla rock Fl.R.3s9m4M 8-sided concrete tapered pillar
Calf of Man W point Fl.15s93m28M Horn 45s White 8-sided tower on granite building 274°-vis-190°. F.R lights on conspicuous radio mast 3·2M NE
Chicken rock Fl.5s38m13M Horn 60s Granite tower

Radio/telephone

VHF Ch Port St Mary's

On approaching Port Erin Bay, it is important to identify the black conical buoy and leave it to starboard, since this marks the end of the ruined breakwater which uncovers at half ebb, the leading lights marking a course well to the north of this danger.

Port Erin has a sandy bay with excellent holding ground, which is just as well, because it is open to the prevailing westerly arc. However, it is well sheltered from winds north through east to south. It is possible to anchor anywhere in the bay, though the presence of the submarine cable should be kept in mind. There are two visitors' moorings, taking a number of craft Mediterranean style (laying out the hook forward with a stern warp to the buoy, or the other way round, if preferred). Port Erin is an attractive town with much Victorian influence, infrequently visited by yachtsmen, since it is on the unpopular, exposed side of the island.

Full provisions can be obtained here, and there is a lovely cliffy walk up to Milner's Tower, from which one can see the sunset behind the Mourne Mountains in Ireland. The Marine Biological Station is also worthy of a visit, and the sea fishing is excellent.

Peel is 10 miles to the north of Port Erin. The passage follows a very rocky, sheer slate coastline. Devoid of shelter, and a lee shore to the prevailing westerlies, it is not the place to be caught out in by a blow. There are few lights, namely Ayre Point light, Peel light and Calf light (obscured until 3 miles out), which underlines the fact that this is the unpopular side of the island for cruising and fishing traffic. A night passage, therefore, must be undertaken only with extreme care.

Port Erin is an attractive bay on the SW side of the Isle of Man, sheltered from N through E to SW. This picture faces a little E of S with Raglan Pier on the right and, in the background across the peninsula, the south coast of the island. *Peter Cumberlidge*

After rounding Bradda Head, a course can be laid off, keeping half to three quarters of a mile offshore. There are no navigational hazards here until Elby Point, where the Niarbyl (Viking: tail), a tidal reef striking out one third of a mile from the cliffs, must be given a wide berth, unless a landing is to be made on the little shingle beach, featuring an old fisherman's cottage and a café. From here, a road leads to the village of Dalby, a mile away.

On reaching the Niarbyl, you will see Contrary Head, where the tides meet on this western side; it is clearly marked by Corrin's Folly. This monument was built in about 1830 by Mr Corrin, the proprietor of a local estate, who wished to demonstrate that one could be buried without the ceremonies of the established church. He now lies there with his wife and two children, without ceremony, unwittingly affording us seafarers an excellent landmark. Contrary Head is the place to get a good tossing in lively weather, so make sure that you have oilies and harness at the ready. A mile further on, the cliffs start becoming less impressive, until St Patrick's Isle, crowned by Peel Castle, appears.

Peel

54°13'·5N 4°41'·7W

Charts

Admiralty 2696 (1:10,000), 2094 (1:100,000)
Imray C62 (1:280,000), Y70 (85,150)

Tides

HW Dover +0005

Height in metres

MHWS	MHWN	MTL	MLWN	MLWS
5·3	4·2	2·9	1·5	0·5

Lights

Pier head E side of entrance Oc.R.7s8m5M White tower, red band, on office building 156°-vis-249°
Groyne head Iso.R.2s4m
Castle jetty head Oc.G.7s5m4M White tower, 3 green bands
Breakwater head Oc.7s11m6M Bell(4)12s White tower

Radio/telephone

VHF Ch 16, 12 (0830–1630)
☎ Harbourmaster (0624) 842338

After rounding the isle, the approach into the outer harbour at Peel is straightforward. The harbour is enclosed by St Patrick's Isle to the west, the outer pier to the north, and the inner pier to the south, affording good shelter from SE to NW. It is possible to berth alongside the inner arm of the outer pier, if it is not already occupied by fishing craft. This is a good place for fin keelers, since it is dredged to 5m at LW. Alternatively, it is possible to anchor, keeping out of the way of the fairway and the lifeboat slip, and showing a riding light. Because most of the harbour dries, however, fin keelers need to anchor well off.

Although the inner harbour dries completely at LW, it is very large, having originally been built for a vast fishing fleet. Enter by leaving St Patrick's Isle to starboard, and the inner pier, where the harbourmaster's office is situated, to port. The seaward end of Town quay, directly to port, is reserved for the ferry and local trawlers, though further up it may be possible to lie alongside local craft of similar draught. Alternatively, it is usually possible to find a free space on West quay. This is much quieter than Town quay, but it means a half-mile walk into town.

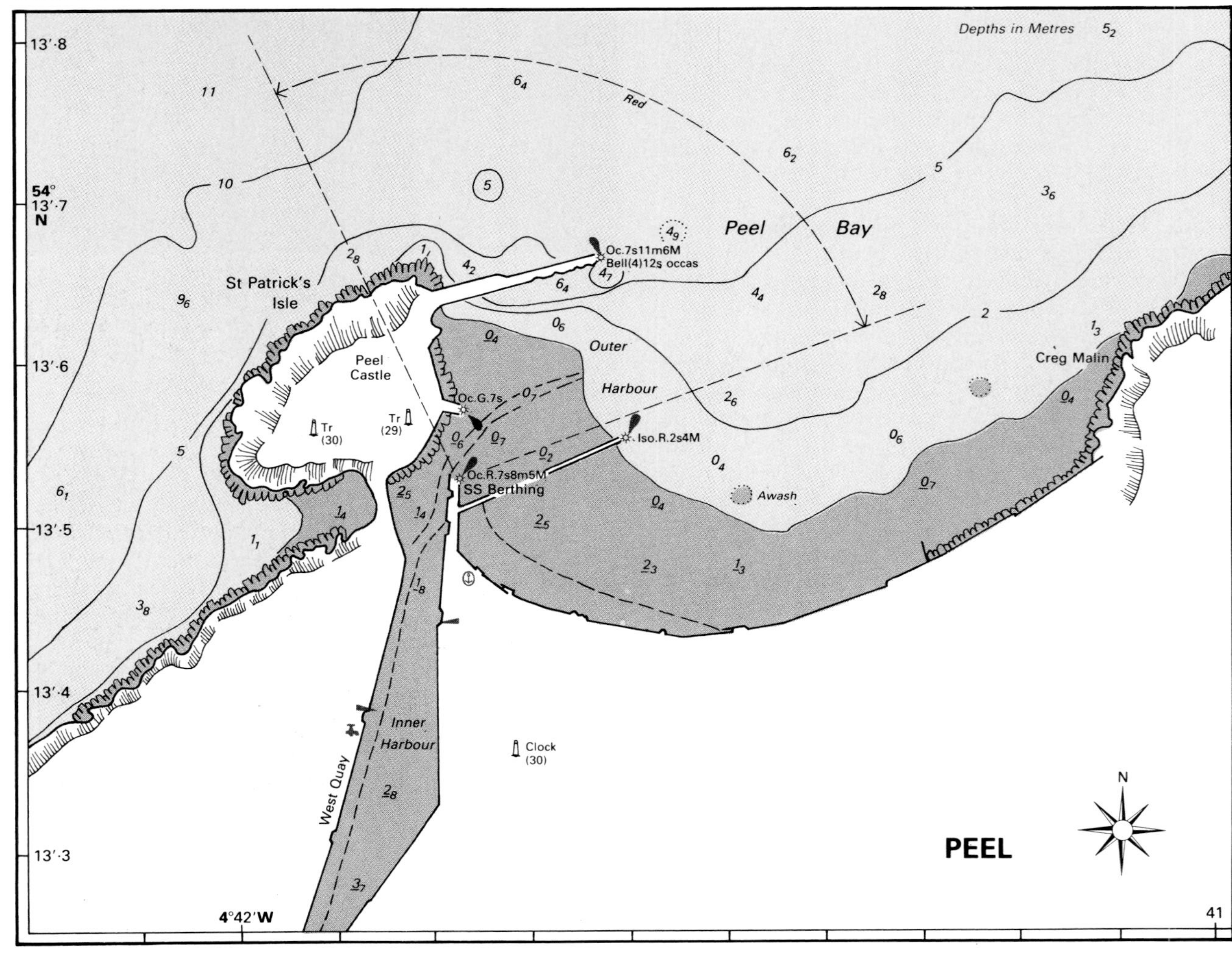

The tidal range inside the harbour is 5m, so it is prudent to watch her down on the first tide, after which she can be left in perfect safety, even in a very strong blow.

Peel is a picturesque place; the houses are mainly built of red sandstone, as are the ruined cathedral and major sections of the castle. The port once had an extensive sea trade, of which smuggling formed the major part, with fishing and coasting coming a close second. The fishing industry is now once again picking up, after years of decline.

Full provisions can be taken aboard here, though there is little in the way of chandlery. There is a small boatyard for local craft. An open-air market is held each Tuesday from May to September.

Since Peel is on the 'wrong' side of the island, life here seems quieter, and it is very easy to blend in with the seafaring atmosphere.

It is now time to contemplate the last leg of our circumnavigation – rounding the NE tip of the island, the Point of Ayre.

Ayre Point

Like the SW tip of the island, the NE tip has its fair share of problems (see page 00). There is a 3-knot stream at springs, and the tip is surrounded by banks which cause the sea to break and foam with any wind over a Force 3. It is important, therefore, to arrive at slack water. Ayre Point is 18 miles from Peel. Allowing a knot of the ebb, and a boat speed of 5 knots, giving a total speed over the ground of 6 knots, Peel should be left 3 hours before LW in order to arrive at Ayre Point at LW slack.

A word of warning about a night passage. There are few lights heading up to the point, and at night the breaking waters over the banks cannot be used as a visual sign; the first indication of their presence is a very wild ride. When rounding the island at night, the SW route is to be preferred, giving a wide berth to Chicken rock.

On leaving Peel, navigation is a matter of keeping a plot while following the coastline northwards, keeping an offing of ½ mile or so for the whole 18 miles. This course takes us inshore of the target

Peel outer harbour, showing the entrance to the inner harbour which is very large, but dries completely.

range off Jurby Head, indicated by large yellow buoys to seaward. (The lights on the target floats are unreliable.)

From the coastguard lookout at Blue Point, the course becomes progressively more easterly, and the high light at Ayre Point can be seen.

Keep half a mile offshore until, on approach to Ayre Point, the foaming waters of Strunakill Bank can be seen. This is left a quarter of a mile to port. Our course is now a quarter of a mile off the coast, taking us around the point in the deep channel which lies up to three quarters of a mile off the point. Once the point has been rounded, steer south, passing the Whitestone buoy (YBY Q(9)15s), marking the Whitestone Bank, with only 0·4m at LW.

Ramsey Bay now opens up, with its sand and gravel foreshore. The town of Ramsey (see page 107), with its large Victorian boarding houses, is to the south.

There is just time to drop the hook and await the flood for entry into Ramsey Harbour, and maybe to open the ship's stores, to celebrate a safe and entertaining circumnavigation of the Isle of Man!

Appendix

I. CHARTS

British Admiralty charts

Chart	*Title*	*Scale*
1121	Irish Sea with Saint George's channel and North channel	500,000
1320	Fleetwood to Douglas	100,000
1344	Kirkcudbright bay	15,000
1346	Solway firth and approaches	100,000
	Ravenglass	15,000
1410	St George's channel	200,000
1411	Irish sea – western part	200,000
1413	Approaches to Holyhead	25,000
1464	Menai strait	25,000
	The Swellies	10,000
1468	Arklow to the Skerries islands	100,000
1484	Plans in Cardigan bay	
	New Quay	12,500
	Fishguard bay	15,000
	Aberystwyth: Aberaeron	18,000
	Aberdovey: Barmouth	25,000
	Aberporth	30,000
	Approaches to Cardigan: Newport bay	37,500
1512	Plans on the Lleyn peninsula	
	Porthmadog harbour	7,500
	Mochras lagoon	10,000
	Pwllheli	12,500
	Porth Dinllaen, Saint Tudwal's roads	18,000
	Approaches to Porthmadog	25,000
1552	Ports in Morecambe bay	
	Fleetwood: Heysham	10,000
	Glasson	12,500
	River Lune and approaches to Heysham; Approaches to Fleetwood	25,000
1826	Irish sea – eastern part	200,000
1951	Approaches to Liverpool	25,000
1953	Approaches to the River Dee	25,000
	Mostyn quay	12,500
1961	Rossall point to St Bee's head	75,000
1970	Caernarvon bay	75,000
1971	Cardigan bay – northern part	75,000
1972	Cardigan bay – central part	75,000
1973	Cardigan bay – southern part	75,000
1977	Holyhead to Great Orme's head	75,000
1981	Approaches to Preston	75,000
	Preston riversway docklands	10,000
2010	Morecambe bay and approaches	50,000
2011	Holyhead harbour	6,250
2013	Saint Bee's head to Silloth	50,000
	Workington harbour	7,500
	Whitehaven harbour: Harrington harbour: Maryport harbour: Silloth docks and approaches	10,000
2093	Southern approach to North channel	100,000
2094	Kirkcudbright to Mull of Galloway and Isle of Man	100,000
2198	North channel – southern part	75,000
	Portpatrick	4,000
2635	Scotland – west coast	500,000
2696	Plans in the Isle of Man	
	Douglas bay	7,500
	Ramsey bay: Calf sound: Peel: Port Erin: Castletown bay: Bay Ny Carrickey	20,000
3164	Barrow harbour and approaches	12,500
	Deep water berth and Ramsden dock entrance	5,000
3478	Manchester ship canal and upper Mersey	25,000
	Manchester docks: Runcorn and Western point docks: Ellesmere port and Stanlow oil docks: Partington basin	10,000
3490	Port of Liverpool	15,000

Imray charts

Chart	*Title*	*Scale*
C16	Western Approaches to the British Isles	612,800
	Plans Brest, Falmouth, Milford Haven, Crosshaven, Crookhaven	
C52	Cardigan Bay to Liverpool	140,700
	Plans Caernarfon, Port Dinorwic, Holyhead, Menai Strait, Porthmadog, Abersoch, Mochras Lagoon, Pwllheli, Conwy, Porth Dinllaen, The Swellies, Barmouth	
C60	Southwest Coasts of Wales	128,000
	Plans Jack Sound, Milford Haven, Ramsey Sound, Tenby and Caldy Islands, Fishguard, Solav	
C61	St George's Channel – Wales to the East Coast of Ireland	270,000
	Plans Portmadoc, Aberystwyth, Tremadoc Bay, Barmouth, Menai Strait, Aberdovey, Cardigan, New Quay, Dublin Bay, Wexford, Arklow, Wicklow, Dunmore East	
C62	Irish Sea	280,000
	Plans Entrance to Carlingford Lough, Portavogie, Skerries Bay, Kilkeel Harbour, Malahide Inlet, Ardglass, Entrance to Strangford Lough	
C63	Firth of Clyde	150,000
	Plans Ayr, Troon, Irvine, East Loch –Tarbert, Campbeltown, Ardrishaig, Crinan, –Gourock, Rothesay, Rhu, Helensburgh, –Largs, Lamlash, Millport	
Y70	Isle of Man	85,150
	Plans Douglas, Port Erin, Peel, Ramsey, Bay Ny Carricky and Castletown Bay	

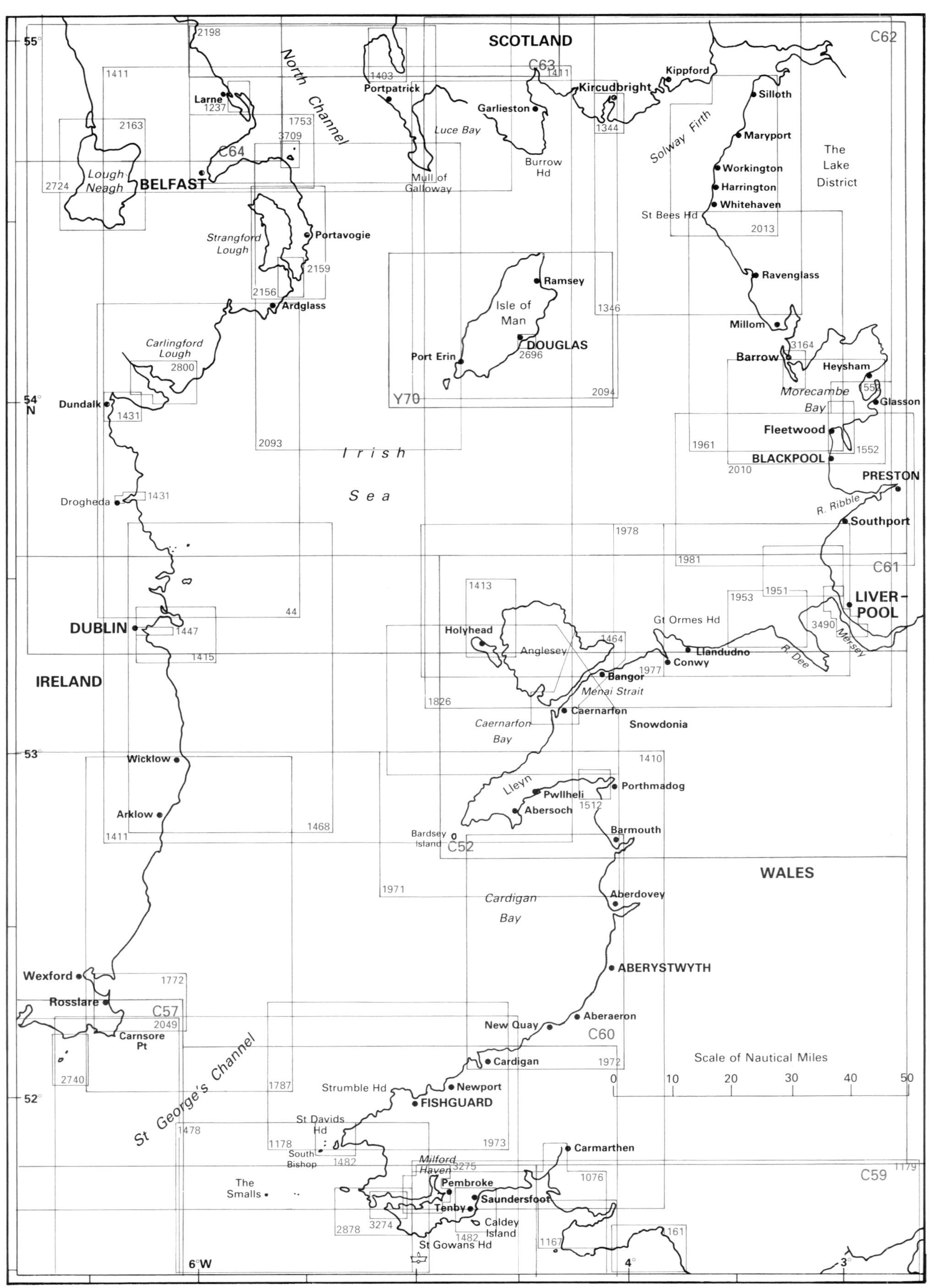

Index of British Admiralty and Imray charts

II. BEAUFORT SCALE

Beaufort No.	*Description of wind*	*Velocity in knots*	*Velocity in mph*	*Velocity in km/h*	*Sea state code*	*Sea state term*	*Sea criterion*	*Wave height in metres*	*Land observations*
0	Calm	<1	<1	<1	0	Calm glassy	Like a mirror.	0	Calm, smoke rises vertically
1	Light air	1–3	1–3	1–5	1	Calm rippled	Ripples.	0–0·1	Direction of wind shown by smoke drift but not by wind vanes.
2	Light breeze	4–6	4–7	6–11	2	Smooth wavelets	Small wavelets.	0·1–0·5	Wind felt on face, leaves rustle, ordinary vanes moved by wind.
3	Gentle breeze	7–10	8–12	12–19	3	Slight	Large wavelets.	0·5–1·25	Leaves and small twigs in constant motion, wind extends light flag.
4	Moderate breeze	11–16	13–18	20–28	4	Moderate	Small waves, breaking.	1·25–2·5	Raises dust and loose paper, small branches are moved.
5	Fresh breeze	17–21	19–24	29–38	5	Rough	Moderate waves, foam.	2·5–4	Small trees in leaf begin to sway, crested wavelets form on inland waters.
6	Strong breeze	22–27	25–31	39–49			Large waves, foam and spray.		Large branches in motion, whistling heard in telegraph wires, umbrellas difficult.
7	Near gale	28–33	32–38	50–61	6	Very rough	Sea heaps up, foam in streaks.	4–6	Whole trees in motion, inconvenience felt walking.
8	Gale	34–40	39–46	62–74			Higher longer waves, foam in streaks.		Breaks twigs off trees, generally impedes progress.
9	Strong gale	41–47	47–54	75–88	7	High	High waves, dense streaks of foam, spray impairs visibility.	6–9	Slight structural damage occurs (chimney pots and slates removed).
10	Storm	48–55	55–63	89–102	8	Very high	Very high tumbling waves, surface white with foam, visibility affected.	9–14	Seldom experienced inland, trees uprooted, considerable structural damage occurs.
11	Violent storm	56–63	64–72	103–117	9	Phenomenal	Exceptionally high waves, sea covered in foam, visibility affected.	>14	Very rarely experienced, accompanied by widespread damage.
12	Hurricane	>63	>72	>118			Air filled with spray and foam, visibility very severely affected.		

Index